PERSPECTIVES 3

Hugh **DELLAR**

Andrew **WALKLEY**

Lewis **LANSFORD**

Daniel **BARBER**

Amanda **JEFFRIES**

**NATIONAL
GEOGRAPHIC**
L E A R N I N G

Australia · Brazil · Mexico · Singapore · United Kingdom · United States

NATIONAL GEOGRAPHIC
L E A R N I N G

Perspectives 3
**Hugh Dellar, Andrew Walkley,
Lewis Lansford, Daniel Barber,
Amanda Jeffries**

Publisher: Sherrise Roehr

Executive Editor: Sarah Kenney

Publishing Consultant: Karen Spiller

Senior Development Editor: Lewis Thompson

Senior Development Editor: Brenden Layte

Editorial Assistant: Gabe Feldstein

Director of Global Marketing: Ian Martin

Product Marketing Manager: Anders Bylund

Director of Content and Media Production:
Michael Burggren

Production Manager: Daisy Sosa

Media Researcher: Leila Hishmeh

Manufacturing Customer Account Manager:
Mary Beth Hennebury

Art Director: Brenda Carmichael

Production Management, and Composition:
3CD

Cover Image: The Hive at Kew Gardens,
London. ©Mark Hadden

> For product information and technology assistance, contact us at
> **Cengage Learning Customer & Sales Support, cengage.com/contact**
>
> For permission to use material from this text or product,
> submit all requests online at **cengage.com/permissions**
> Further permissions questions can be emailed to
> **permissionrequest@cengage.com**

Student Edition: Level 3
ISBN: 978-1-337-27714-3

National Geographic Learning
20 Channel Center Street
Boston, MA 02210
USA

National Geographic Learning, a Cengage Learning Company, has a mission to
bring the world to the classroom and the classroom to life. With our English
language programs, students learn about their world by experiencing it. Through
our partnerships with National Geographic and TED Talks, they develop the
language and skills they need to be successful global citizens and leaders.

Locate your local office at **international.cengage.com/region**

Visit National Geographic Learning online at **NGL.Cengage.com/ELT**
Visit our corporate website at **www.cengage.com**

4 (tl1) Lutz Jaekel/laif/Redux, (tl2) epa european pressphoto agency b.v./Alamy Stock Photo, (cl) Michael Christopher Brown/Magnum Photos, (bl1) Tasso Marcelo Leal/AFP/Getty Images, (bl2) © Bryce Duffy, **5** (tl1) © Marla Aufmuth/TED, (tl2)(cl)(bl1)(bl2) © James Duncan Davidson/TED, **6** (tl1) Christian Ziegler/National Geographic Creative, (tl2) © Hassan Hajjaj/A-WA, (cl) Yva Momatiuk and John Eastcott/National Geographic Creative, (bl1) VCG/Getty Images, (bl2) © Intuitive Surgical, **7** (tl1)(tl2)(cl) © Ryan Lash/TED, (bl1) © James Duncan Davidson/TED, (bl2) © TED, **8-9** Lutz Jaekel/laif/Redux, **10-11** Digital Vision./Getty Images, **13** Paul Darrows/Reuters, **14** Michael Christopher Brown/Magnum Photos, **15** Paul Chesley/Stone/Getty Images, **16-17** © Marla Aufmuth/TED, **18-19** Ed Norton/Lonely Planet Images/Getty Images, **20-21** epa european pressphoto agency b.v./Alamy Stock Photo, **22-23** © Rainforest Connection, www.rfcx.org, **26** (tl) Morten Falch Sortland/Moment Open/Getty Images, (cl) Ellisha Lee/EyeEm/Getty Images, (bl) wundervisuals/E+/Getty Images, **28-29** © James Duncan Davidson/TED, **30-31** © www.fairafric.com, **32-33** Michael Christopher Brown/Magnum Photos, **34-35** Mirco Lazzari gp/Getty Images Sport/Getty Images, **36** Michael Regan/Getty Images Sport/Getty Images, **38** Harry How/Getty Images Sport/Getty Images, **39** Adrian Dennis/AFP/Getty Images, **40-41** © James Duncan Davidson/TED, **42-43** Giovani Cordioli/Moment/Getty Images, **44-45** Tasso Marcelo Leal/AFP/Getty Images, **46-47** Jeroen Koolhaas/Getty Images, **48** Juan Barreto/AFP/Getty Images, **50** Scott R Larsen/Moment/Getty Images, **51** David Pereiras/Shutterstock.com, **52-53** © James Duncan Davidson/TED, **54-55** James Bagshaw/Alamy Stock Photo, **56-57** © Bryce Duffy, **58-59** (spread) © National Geographic Learning, **58** (br) Maxx-Studio/Shutterstock.com, **61** Robert Clark/National Geographic Creative, **62** Puwadol Jaturawutthichai/Alamy Stock Photo, **63** © Hero Images/Getty Images, **64-65** © James Duncan Davidson/TED, **66** Sakura Photography/Moment/Getty Images, **67** © National Geographic Learning, **68-69** Christian Ziegler/National Geographic Creative, **70-71** Dietmar Temps, Cologne/Moment/Getty Images, **73** (bgd) Bryan Mullennix/Stockbyte/Getty Images, (inset) Color4260/Shutterstock.com, (t) Thaiview/Shutterstock.com, **74** Wf Sihardian/EyeEm/Getty Images, **75** Jonathan Blair/National Geographic Creative, **76-77** © Ryan Lash/TED, **78-79** Phil Moore/AFP/Getty Images, **80-81** © Hassan Hajjaj/A-WA, **82-83** © Dave Devries, **85** (bdg) tomograf/E+/Getty Images, © National Geographic Learning, **86** Troy Aossey/The Image Bank/Getty Images, **87** XiXinXing/Shutterstock.com, **88-89** © Ryan Lash/TED, **90-91** Thomas Barwick/Taxi/Getty Images, **92-93** Yva Momatiuk and John Eastcott/National Geographic Creative, **94-95** Jiro Ose/Redux, **97** AP Images/Dario Lopez-Mills, **98** Bettmann/Getty Images, **99** Leila Dougan, **100-101** © Ryan Lash/TED, **102-103** CKN/Getty Images News/Getty Images, **104-105** VCG/Visual China Group/Getty Images, **106-107** © Patrick Meier, **108** Polina Yamshchikov/Redux, **110** Julian Broad/Contour/Getty Images, **111** © Laurie Moy, **112** © James Duncan Davidson/TED, **114** Carrie Vonderhaar/Ocean Futures Society/National Geographic Creative, **116-117** © Intuitive Surgical, **118-119** Reuters/Alamy Stock Photo, **121** Pasieka/Science Source, **122** ZUMA Press, Inc./Alamy Stock Photo, **123** Noor Khamis/Reuters, **124-125** © TED, **126-127** Media Drum World/Alamy Stock Photo.

Printed in China
Print Number: 05   Print Year: 2021

ACKNOWLEDGMENTS

Paulo Rogerio Rodrigues
Escola Móbile, São Paulo, Brazil

Claudia Colla de Amorim
Escola Móbile, São Paulo, Brazil

Antonio Oliveira
Escola Móbile, São Paulo, Brazil

Rory Ruddock
Atlantic International Language Center, Hanoi, Vietnam

Carmen Virginia Pérez Cervantes
La Salle, Mexico City, Mexico

Rossana Patricia Zuleta
CIPRODE, Guatemala City, Guatemala

Gloria Stella Quintero Riveros
Universidad Católica de Colombia, Bogotá, Colombia

Mónica Rodriguez Salvo
MAR English Services, Buenos Aires, Argentina

Itana de Almeida Lins
Grupo Educacional Anchieta, Salvador, Brazil

Alma Loya
Colegio de Chihuahua, Chihuahua, Mexico

María Trapero Dávila
Colegio Teresiano, Ciudad Obregon, Mexico

Silvia Kosaruk
Modern School, Lanús, Argentina

Florencia Adami
Dámaso Centeno, Caba, Argentina

Natan Galed Gomez Cartagena
Global English Teaching, Rionegro, Colombia

James Ubriaco
Colégio Santo Agostinho, Belo Horizonte, Brazil

Ryan Manley
The Chinese University of Hong Kong, Shenzhen, China

Silvia Teles
Colégio Cândido Portinari, Salvador, Brazil

María Camila Azuero Gutiérrez
Fundación Centro Electrónico de Idiomas, Bogotá, Colombia

Martha Ramirez
Colegio San Mateo Apostol, Bogotá, Colombia

Beata Polit
XXIII LO Warszawa, Poland

Beata Tomaszewska
V LO Toruń, Poland

Michał Szkudlarek
I LO Brzeg, Poland

Anna Buchowska
I LO Białystok, Poland

Natalia Maćkowiak
one2one, Kosakowo, Poland

Agnieszka Dończyk
one2one, Kosakowo, Poland

WELCOME TO *PERSPECTIVES!*

Perspectives teaches learners to think critically and to develop the language skills they need to find their own voice in English. The carefully-guided language lessons, real-world stories, and TED Talks motivate learners to think creatively and communicate effectively.

In *Perspectives*, learners develop:

● AN OPEN MIND

Every unit explores one idea from different perspectives, giving learners opportunities for practicing language as they look at the world in new ways.

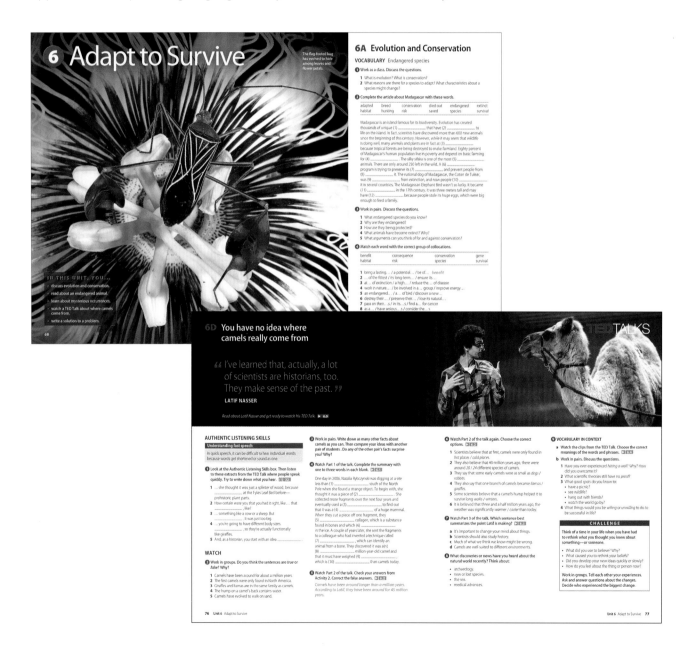

• A CRITICAL EYE

Students learn the critical thinking skills and strategies they need to evaluate new information and develop their own opinions and ideas to share.

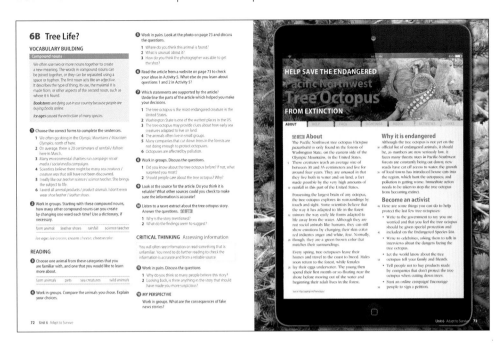

• A CLEAR VOICE

Students respond to the unit theme and express their own ideas confidently in English.

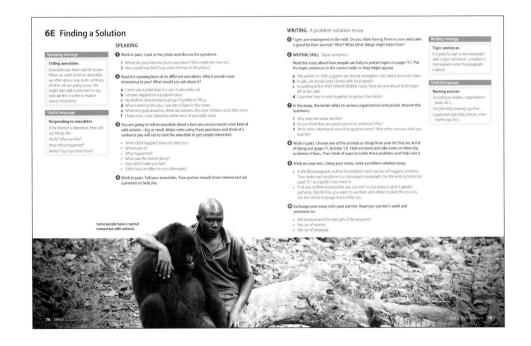

CONTENTS

GRAMMAR	TEDTALKS		SPEAKING	WRITING
Used to and *would* **Pronunciation** *To* in natural speech	**How Airbnb designs for trust**	**JOE GEBBIA** Joe Gebbia's idea worth spreading is that we can design products, services, and experiences that feel more local, authentic, and that strengthen human connections. **Authentic Listening Skills** Reporting	Advice / Making recommendations	A review **Writing Skill** Adding comments
Verb patterns (*-ing* or infinitive with *to*)	**This is what happens when you reply to spam email**	**JAMES VEITCH** James Veitch's idea worth spreading is that spam email can lead us to some surprising, bizarre, and often hilarious exchanges with others. **Authentic Listening Skills** Intonation and pitch	Persuading	A persuasive article **Writing Skill** Getting people's attention **Pronunciation** Intonation for persuasion
Comparatives and superlatives **Pronunciation** Linking words together in fast speech	**Are athletes really getting faster, better, stronger?**	**DAVID EPSTEIN** David Epstein's idea worth spreading is that the amazing achievements of many modern-day athletes are thanks to a complex set of factors, not just natural ability. **Authentic Listening Skills** Slowing down and stressing words	Reporting findings	A survey **Writing Skill** Describing statistics
Future forms 2 **Pronunciation** Contrastive stress	**Building a Park in the Sky**	**ROBERT HAMMOND** Robert Hammond's idea worth spreading is that we can work together to turn abandoned and neglected parts of our cities into vibrant community spaces. **Authentic Listening Skills** Recognizing words you know	Making suggestions	A *for* and *against* essay **Writing Skill** Introducing arguments
Passives 2	**Science is for everyone, kids included**	**BEAU LOTTO AND AMY O'TOOLE** Beau Lotto and Amy O'Toole's idea worth spreading is that all of us can be scientists if we approach the world with the curiosity, interest, innocence, and zeal of children. **Authentic Listening Skills** Fillers	Staging and hypothesizing	A scientific method **Writing Skill** Describing a process

CONTENTS

GRAMMAR	TEDTALKS	SPEAKING	WRITING
Modals and infinitive forms **Pronunciation** Weak form of *have*	**LATIF NASSER** Latif Nasser's idea worth spreading is that in science, and in life, we are making surprising discoveries that force us to reexamine our assumptions. **Authentic Listening Skills** Understanding fast speech *You have no idea where camels really come from*	Telling anecdotes	A problem-solution essay **Writing Skill** Topic sentences
Wish, if only, would rather **Pronunciation** Elision of final consonants *t* and *d*	**ERIN MCKEAN** Erin McKean's idea worth spreading is that making up new words will help us use language to express what we mean and will create new ways for us to understand one another. **Authentic Listening Skills** Speeding up and slowing down speech *Go ahead, make up new words!*	Offering solutions	A report **Writing Skill** Cohesion
Patterns after reporting verbs	**SAFWAT SALEEM** Safwat Saleem's idea worth spreading is that we all benefit when we use our work and our voices to question and enlarge our understanding of what is "normal." **Authentic Listening Skills** *Just* *Why I keep speaking up, even when people mock my accent*	Challenging ideas and assumptions	A complaint **Writing Skill** Using appropriate tone
Participle clauses **Pronunciation** *ing* forms	**BECCI MANSON** Becci Manson's idea worth spreading is that photographs hold our memories and our histories, connecting us to each other and to the past. **Authentic Listening Skills** Intonation and completing a point *(Re)Touching Lives through Photos*	Countering opposition	A letter of application **Writing Skill** Structuring an application
Emphatic structures **Pronunciation** Adding emphasis	**JANINE SHEPHERD** Janine Shepherd's idea worth spreading is that we have inner strength and spirit that is much more powerful than the physical capabilities of even the greatest athletes. **Authentic Listening Skills** Collaborative listening *A Broken Body Isn't a Broken Person*	Developing conversations	A success story **Writing Skill** Using descriptive verbs

1 Travel, Trust, and Tourism

IN THIS UNIT, YOU...

- talk about student exchanges and study-abroad programs.

- read about a disappearing way of traveling for free.

- learn about the Grand Tours that were popular in the past.

- watch a TED Talk about how design can build trust between strangers.

- write a review of a place you have visited.

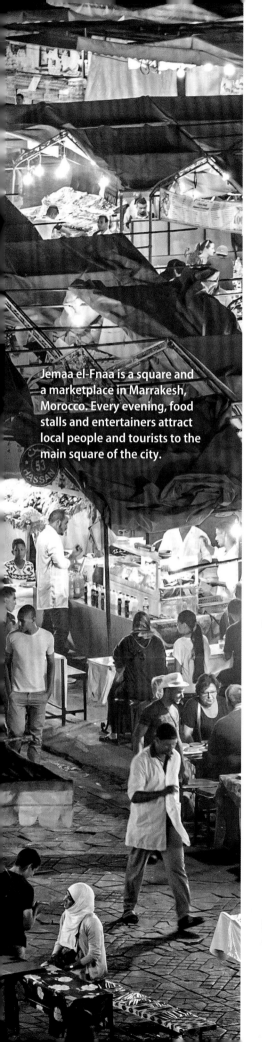

Jemaa el-Fnaa is a square and a marketplace in Marrakesh, Morocco. Every evening, food stalls and entertainers attract local people and tourists to the main square of the city.

1A Cultural Exchange

VOCABULARY Experiences abroad

1 Work in pairs. Discuss the questions.

1 What do you normally do on vacation?
2 Have you been abroad? If yes, where? If no, would you like to? Why?
3 What do you know about student exchanges and study-abroad programs?

2 Check that you understand the words and phrases in bold. Use a dictionary, if necessary. Then tell your partner which experiences you think are good and which are bad. Give your reasons.

1 be **left to your own devices**
2 experience **culture shock**
3 find people very **welcoming**
4 **get a real feel for** the place
5 get **food poisoning**
6 get **robbed**
7 go **hiking** in the mountains
8 **hang out** with local people
9 **lie around** a house all day
10 see all **the sights**
11 stay in **a B&B**
12 stay with **a host family**
13 take a while to **get used to the food**
14 travel **off the beaten path**

3 Work in groups. Look at the words and phrases in Activity 2. Discuss the questions.

1 Which are the most connected to visitors to your country? The least?
2 Which have you done, or which have happened to you? When?
3 Which three do you most want to remember and use? Why?

4 Work in pairs. Look at the photo and discuss the questions.

1 How is the market different from markets near where you live? How would visiting this place make you feel? Why?
2 Which words and phrases from Activity 2 can you use to describe what is happening? Make a list. Then explain your choices to a partner.

5 Complete the description with words or phrases from Activity 2.

In the past, it was very common for teenagers to do student exchanges, where they would go abroad and stay in each other's homes. The idea was not only to learn a new language, but also to (1) _____ with the local teenagers, go to their school, and get a (2) _____ the place and culture. Sometimes the (3) _____ was very welcoming and students got along well with the people in the home; other times the (4) _____ was too much. The students couldn't (5) _____ the food and ended up being left to their (6) _____ . Maybe that's why these days it is more common for teenagers to go on a group trip abroad, where everyone stays in a (7) _____ or hostel together. During the trip, students go and see (8) _____ and only briefly meet up with a group from a local school. This way teenagers don't (9) _____ a foreign house all day, and there is no awkwardness. The worst that could happen might be a case of (10) _____ from a bad clam and some sore feet from walking around the town.

6 Work in pairs. Do you think that the old or new way of doing student exchanges is better? Why?

LISTENING

7 Listen to the first part of a podcast about study-abroad programs. Find out: 🔊 1

1 who can do these programs.
2 how long people can go abroad and study for.
3 when the system started.
4 what the possible benefits are.

8 Listen to Kenji and Catalina. Answer the questions. 🔊 2

1 Where did they do their study-abroad programs?
2 How long did they stay for?
3 Did the trip increase their understanding of other cultures and develop their language skills? If yes, how do you know?

9 Work in pairs. Are the sentences *true* or *false*? Listen again to check your answers. 🔊 2

1 Kenji had visited several countries before studying abroad in Munich.
2 He was really excited about studying abroad.
3 His host family helped him develop a better understanding of the German language.
4 He's still in touch with his host family.
5 Catalina has family roots* in Italy.
6 She felt at home as soon as she arrived.
7 After a few weeks, she spoke enough Italian to do what she needed to do.
8 She's glad she went to Italy, but has no plans to go back.

family roots *original place where a family is from*

10 MY PERSPECTIVE

Work in pairs. Think of two more benefits and three possible issues students might face when doing a study-abroad program. Then discuss the questions.

1 What do you think the biggest benefit is? Why?
2 What do you think the biggest issue is? Why?

GRAMMAR Present and past forms

11 Look at the sentences in the Grammar box. Then answer the questions.

1 Which two are about the present?
2 Which four are about the past?
3 Which two describe actions that happened before something else in the past?
4 Which three use simple forms?
5 Which three use continuous forms?

Present and past forms
a *I was actually thinking about canceling my trip.*
b *I'd been wanting to go there for ages.*
c *We're talking about study-abroad programs.*
d *I'd never left Argentina!*
e *I spent six months in Germany last year.*
f *I miss my host family.*

Check the Grammar Reference for more information and practice.

Some study-abroad programs allow students to visit countries like China, where they can go to places like the Great Wall.

12 Match the rules (1–6) with the examples (a–f) in the Grammar box.

1 We use **the simple present** to talk about habits, permanent states, and things that are generally true.
2 We use **the present continuous** to talk about actions we see as temporary, in progress, and unfinished.
3 We use **the simple past** to describe finished actions in the past, especially when there is one finished action after another.
4 We use **the past continuous** to emphasize an action in progress around a time in the past.
5 We use **the simple past perfect** to emphasize that one thing happened before a particular point in the past.
6 We use **the past perfect continuous** to talk about an action that was in progress over a period of time *up to* or *before* a particular point in the past.

13 Complete the text with the correct form of each verb.

I really (1) _____ (love) traveling. It's probably the most important thing in my life. I'm 17, and I (2) _____ (plan) to spend the summer on a National Geographic Student Expedition! I actually (3) _____ (go) on my first adventure trip a few years ago when I (4) _____ (spend) two months in China. It was the first time I (5) _____ (ever / go) abroad, and I (6) _____ (love) every minute of it! While we (7) _____ (stay) in Beijing, we (8) _____ (visit) the Great Wall of China, which was something I (9) _____ (dream) of doing ever since I was a child. It was amazing! I (10) _____ (hope) to do an expedition to Iceland next year and stay somewhere really off the beaten path.

14 Complete the pairs of sentences with the correct simple form of one of the verbs and the correct continuous form of the other.

1a We usually _____ (spend) the summers with my grandparents at their house on the coast.
1b This summer, though, my brother is in Costa Rica. He _____ (stay) with a host family there.
2a This weekend I _____ (go) hiking in the mountains with some friends.
2b The bus _____ (leave) at six every morning, so we should be at the station 15 minutes before.
3a I _____ (get) really bad food poisoning while I was in Scotland. I have no idea why!
3b Things got worse when somebody stole my suitcase while I _____ (wait) in line to buy train tickets to Glasgow.
4a I spoke good French by the time I left Quebec because I _____ (hang out) with the locals for the last few months of the ski season.
4b It was a great trip, but it was scary, because I _____ never _____ (try) skiing before.

15 Choose one of the situations below. Then plan what you want to say about where you were, when you went, and what happened. Think about how to use all four past forms at least once.

a Something that happened while you were on vacation
b A time you stayed with other people
c A place you have visited

16 Work in pairs. Tell each other your stories.

1B Ask for a Ride

VOCABULARY BUILDING

Phrasal verbs

Phrasal verbs are often used in conversation instead of more formal words. They are very common in English. The meaning of a verb often changes when it is used in a phrasal verb.

1 Rewrite the words in italics using the correct forms of these phrasal verbs.

break down	come down to	line up
pick up	pull over	turn out

1 They offered to give me a ride to the airport and *got me* from the hotel at eight o'clock.
2 The bus *stopped working* on the way there, so we were five hours late.
3 It was New Year's Day, so I had to *wait in line* for hours to get a train ticket.
4 I think the changes *are basically because of* two things: wealth and technology.
5 A car *stopped by the side of the road* and the driver asked us for directions.
6 I was worried because I'd never been abroad before, but everything *was* great in the end.

2 Write sentences using these phrasal verbs.

hang out	lie around	look after	step out

3 Work in pairs. Look at the photo on page 13 and discuss the questions.

1 What is happening?
2 Which of the phrasal verbs from Activity 1 can you connect to the photo? Explain your choices.

READING

4 Read the article about hitchhiking. Match these headings with the numbered paragraphs.

a Fear
b More wealth
c New needs and opportunities
d Legal restrictions
e Low-cost flights
f Greater access to cars

5 Work in pairs. Which of these ideas does the author present? What evidence is given?

1 There used to be far more hitchhikers.
2 There was a high number of robberies involving hitchhikers.
3 It's difficult to find a place to hitchhike these days.
4 More people drive now than in the past.
5 Air travel is safer than driving or hitchhiking.
6 We are wasting a lot of energy by driving alone.
7 People only hitchhike now if they are poor.
8 Hitchhiking brings benefits to communities and individuals.

6 Work in pairs. Imagine you are standing at the side of a road, trying to hitchhike. Tell your story. Before you do, talk and make notes about:

- where you are going.
- why you are hitchhiking.
- how you are feeling.
- what happens next.
- how the story ends.

7 Tell your stories to other people in your class. Vote on the best one. Explain why it is the best story.

CRITICAL THINKING Evaluating ideas

Evaluating ideas and judging them against other perspectives helps to form a basis for developing your own point of view.

8 Work in groups. Discuss the questions.

1 Which is the most important reason the author gives for the decline in hitchhiking? Do you agree? How important are the other reasons?
2 What comparison does the author provide from the website Wand'rly? Is it a fair comparison? Why?
3 How is the example of hitchhiking in Virginia different from other kinds? Does this make it safer? Why?
4 Why do you think the author says he gained a different perspective from other tourists? Do you think that is true? Do you think his perspective was better? Why?

9 MY PERSPECTIVE

Work in pairs. Discuss the questions.

1 Do you think hitchhiking is a good idea? What other reasons could there be for doing it?
2 How could you make hitchhiking safer?

Hitchbot, a hitchhiking robot, waits for a ride at the side of a road. Read more about Hitchbot on page 129.

Hitchhiking

Where did all the hitchhikers go?

🎧 3 I was driving along the other day, and I passed a man sticking his thumb out. He was asking for a ride. When we had gone past, my daughter, who is 15, asked
5 me, "What was that man doing?" The question surprised me, because hitchhiking used to be so common. I used to do it all the time when I was a student going home to visit friends, and I also spent one summer hitchhiking around South America. Often when you went to some
10 hitching spots, you'd have to line up behind several others already waiting for a ride—it was so popular. So what happened? Why is it so rare now? The authors of *Freakonomics*, Stephen Dubner and Steve Levitt, have also asked this question in one of their regular podcasts. They
15 suggest that it probably comes down to five main reasons.

(1) _____
Several horror movies have shown psychotic drivers who kidnap and murder the hitchhiker they pick up (or vice versa). This has been reinforced by certain stories in the
20 media of people getting robbed and being left in the middle of nowhere. Unsurprisingly, this has caused trust to break down. Some people believe that the chances of these things happening are small. The website Wand'rly, for example, suggests that people are far more likely to
25 die by tripping and falling than by hitchhiking.

(2) _____
There are more major roads now than there used to be, and hitching is either banned or drivers are not allowed to pull over on these roads.

30 (3) _____
Alan Piskarsi, a transportation expert, points to the fact that cars last longer, so there are more of them available at a cheaper price. What's more, many more people have driver's licenses than they used to.

35 (4) _____
In the past, young people simply couldn't afford to fly long distances, and traveling by train wasn't necessarily much quicker than traveling by car. Now, however, we have budget airlines, making air travel more accessible.

40 (5) _____
Along the same lines, people's standard of living has increased. Perhaps people opt for higher levels of comfort, privacy, or reliability when they travel.

(6) _____
45 The trouble is that privacy comes at a cost. Levitt and Dubner state that in the United States, 80 percent of passenger space in cars is unused, which makes them more costly to operate and creates unnecessary traffic and pollution. The solution could be more hitchhiking!
50 They give the example of a city in Virginia, where commuters have organized a spot where they meet to hitch a ride so drivers with no passengers can use carpool lanes on the highway that are reserved for cars that contain more than one person.

55 ## Fresh Fears

But what about general travel? I often argued with my parents about the dangers of hitchhiking, and I would tell them about all the amazing experiences I'd had and the generous, interesting people I'd met. I think
60 it genuinely gave me a different perspective on other travelers and tourists. But now, I look at my daughter and think about her going on a trip. Would I want her to go hitchhiking?

Andrew Skurka's longest "Grand Tour" was 7,775 miles.

1C The Grand Tour

GRAMMAR *Used to* and *would*

1 Look at the Grammar box. Match the structures with the uses, based on the examples in bold.

1 simple past
2 *used to*, *would*, simple past
3 *used to* or simple past

a to describe a past state over a period of time
b to describe individual past events and situations
c to describe a habit or regular action in the past

> **Used to and would**
>
> Hitchhiking **used to be** so common. I **used to do it** all the time when I **was** a student going home to visit friends, and I also **spent** one summer hitching around South America. Often when you went to some hitching spots, **you'd have to line up** behind several others already waiting for a ride—it was so popular. **I often argued** with my parents about the dangers of hitching, and **I would tell them about** all the amazing experiences I'd had.

Check the Grammar Reference for more information and practice.

2 Read about Grand Tours. Find out what they were and why people did them.

Humans have always been travelers, moving out of Africa to all parts of the world in search of space, food, and resources. But the idea of guided tourism for leisure and education (1) **didn't really start** until the 17th century, when the Grand Tour (2) **began** to be established. Young aristocrats* from different parts of the world (3) **spent** several months traveling around important sights in Europe after they had finished their schooling. The Tour often (4) **started** in the Netherlands, where the tourists (5) **hired** a horse and carriage, servants, and a tutor to show them the sights and teach them about what they saw.

From the Netherlands, they went to Paris, where they (6) **did** a French language course, before moving on to Switzerland and then crossing the Alps to Italy. After an extensive tour of Italy, they (7) **went** home directly, (8) **traveled** back to the Netherlands via Austria and Germany, or (9) **continued** south to Greece.

The Grand Tour (10) **played** an important part in education and in spreading culture. The tourists would often bring back paintings and books, which influenced artists in their own country. The Venezuelan Francisco de Miranda even (11) **saw** the beginnings of the French Revolution on his Grand Tour, which (12) **led** him to fight for independence for his country.

aristocrat *person belonging to a high class*

3 Change the words in bold in Activity 2 from the simple past to *used to* or *would* + verb, where possible.

4 MY PERSPECTIVE

Work in pairs. Discuss the questions.

1 Do you think anyone does Grand Tours today? Why?
2 Where would you go on a Grand Tour? Why? Think about:

- the sights you would visit.
- the people you would meet.
- the food you would eat.

5 PRONUNCIATION *To* in natural speech

> When unstressed, the word *to* is usually pronounced "tuh."
> *I was a student going home <u>to</u> visit friends.*
>
> It can also be reduced and joined with the previous word.
> *Hitchhiking <u>used to</u> be so common.*
> *You'd <u>have to</u> line up behind several others.*

a Listen to the sentences from the Pronunciation box. Notice the differences between unstressed *to* and the sentences with reductions. 🎧 **4**

b Listen and repeat. 🎧 **4**

6 Read about Andrew Skurka. Decide if *used to*, *would*, and the simple past are used correctly or incorrectly. Change the ones which are incorrect.

Andrew Skurka is an ultra-hiker. Every year, he (1) *used to go* on hikes that are thousands of miles long, walking between 25 and 40 miles a day. One of his most amazing tours was circling the Arctic in 176 days. His boots (2) *got very wet* for 156 of those days and they (3) *used to froze* overnight. He (4) *would then have to* force his feet into the icy boots each morning. Unsurprisingly, he (5) *didn't use to see* many people during his tours and once, he (6) *would spend* 24 days completely on his own. He'd sometimes (7) *get depressed* and (8) *cried,* but one day he came across a herd of caribou and it (9) *used to change* his perspective. He (10) *realized* he was very similar to them—just one more creature on Earth, like them.

7 CHOOSE

Choose one of the following activities.

- What did your parents or grandparents do on vacation when they were growing up? Write any similarities and differences to what you do.
- Work in groups. Share what you know about tourism in your country in the past compared to now. Talk about:
  - resorts.
  - the kinds of people who visit or visited.
  - the kinds of vacations.
  - the number and length of vacations.
  - destinations people from your country visit or visited.
- Work in pairs. Tell your partner about two of the following.
  - Something you used to believe and why you changed your mind.
  - Something you used to like doing and why you don't like it or do it now.
  - Something you do now that you never used to do and why.
  - Someone you used to spend a lot of time with and what you would do.

In the past, only young aristocrats were able to visit classical sites such as the Pantheon in Rome, Italy.

" We were aiming to build Olympic trust between people who had never met. "

JOE GEBBIA

Read about Joe Gebbia and get ready to watch his TED Talk. ▶ 1.0

AUTHENTIC LISTENING SKILLS

Reporting

When people tell stories, they often use present tenses to make events sound more immediate. They also often report what people said or what was going through their mind at the time, as if they were speaking.

1 Look at the Authentic Listening Skills box. Listen and complete the extracts. 🎧 **5**

1 I make the mistake of asking him,
  " _____ ?"

2 And I'm thinking,
  " _____ ?"

3 And the voice in my head goes,
  " _____ ?"

4 I'm staring at the ceiling, I'm thinking,
  " _____ ?"

2 Look at your completed extracts in Activity 1. What do you think happened before? What do you think will happen next?

3 Work in pairs. Read the sentences below. Discuss what may have happened before somebody said each one.

1 So I'm thinking to myself, "What do I do now?"
2 She looks at me and goes, "I've met you somewhere before."
3 The voice in my head says, "Don't do it!"

WATCH

4 Work in groups. Discuss the questions.

1 Have you or your family ever asked for help from a stranger while on vacation? What happened?
2 Have you or someone in your family ever helped a stranger while on vacation? What happened?
3 Why might you trust or not trust a stranger? How do you decide who to trust for help or advice?

5 Watch Part 1 of the talk. Choose the correct options. ▶ 1.1

1 From his meeting with the "Peace Corps guy," Joe learns
  a he should always have an airbed.
  b he should start a hosting business.
  c we should be less fearful of strangers.

2 He decided to start his business because
  a there weren't many hotels in the city.
  b he really needed somewhere to stay.
  c it offered him an opportunity as a designer.

3 The business wasn't immediately successful because
  a people didn't trust Joe and his co-founder.
  b the website wasn't very well designed.
  c it didn't get any additional investment.

6 MY PERSPECTIVE

How can you make people feel that they can trust each other more? Think of three ideas. Then share them with the class. Does anyone have the same ideas as you?

TEDTALKS

7 Watch Part 2 of the talk. Complete these notes. ▶ 1.2

- Experiment—shows how host can feel _____
  but guest can feel _____ = how business
  works. Well-designed reputation (review) system—key
  to _____ .

- _____ must leave reviews before they are
  revealed.

- _____ = people stop worrying about
  differences (reputation beats similarity).

- _____ and prompts = right amount of honesty
  and sharing (disclosure).

8 Watch Part 3 of the talk. Then work in groups and
summarize what Joe said using these ideas. What did
you like about these ideas? ▶ 1.3

- when trust works
- a man having a heart attack
- the sharing economy
- human connection
- Seoul, South Korea
- students and empty-nesters*

empty-nesters *parents whose children have left home*

9 Look back at your ideas in Activity 6. Did Joe mention
any of your ideas? Have any of them changed?

10 **VOCABULARY IN CONTEXT**

a Watch the clips from the TED Talk. Choose the correct
meanings of the words and phrases. ▶ 1.4

b Work in groups. Discuss these questions.

1 What things can increase or reduce *anxiety* when
traveling?
2 Have you ever met someone on vacation you got
along with? Have you *kept in touch*? Why?
3 Would you be *up for* doing any of these things on
vacation? Why?
   - rafting or bungee jumping
   - going to a nightclub
   - doing a guided tour of a museum
   - going camping
4 When did you last *rush* somewhere? Why?
5 Have you ever experienced anything that *tripped you
up*? What?

CHALLENGE

Work in groups. Make a list of things you have which you
could share with others in your area or with people visiting
you on vacation. Think about:

- skills and abilities.
- knowledge.
- possessions that you do not use all the time.

How could you share the things in your list in a way that
people could trust and avoid danger?

1E Trip Advice

Useful language

Making suggestions

If sightseeing is their thing, then the best place to go is…

If they want to experience a genuine local night out, I'd suggest trying…

If they're only staying here for a little while, they should probably…

If you ask me, the one place they really have to go to is…

Reacting to suggestions

If they'd rather try something different, …might be worth a shot.

I wouldn't bother going to…, personally.

They'd be better (off) going to…

Tourists walk across the Perito Moreno Glacier in Santa Cruz Province, Argentina.

SPEAKING

1 Work in pairs. Make a list of three places close to where you live that you would recommend to each of these groups of people. Think about places to stay, eat, shop, and visit.

a couple in their 50s or 60s	a father with a young teenage son
a group of teenage friends	a young married couple with a child

2 Compare your list with another pair. Make suggestions for the best places for each group of people. Use the Useful language box to help you.

3 Put the sentences in the correct order to make a conversation between a local person and a guest. Then listen and check your answers. 🎧 **6**

   a Well, there's a great steak place down by the river.

   b I'm thinking of seeing some sights today. Can you recommend anywhere?

   c In that case, you'd be best off going to Madragora—a nice little vegetarian place near the park.

   d OK. Well, I'll check that out this morning, then. And do you know anywhere good to have lunch?

   e Great. Thanks for the tip.

   f Oh, right. Well, actually, I don't eat meat, so…

   g Well, the Old Town is well worth a visit. There are some amazing buildings there.

4 Roleplay two conversations similar to the one in Activity 3, using places you know. Underline phrases from Activity 3 that you want to use. Then have the conversations. Take turns being the local person and the guest.

WRITING A review

5 Look at page 149 and read the four short online reviews. What kind of place is each review about?

6 Work in pairs. Which reviewer:

1 does not feel that he or she got a good value?
2 managed to negotiate a deal?
3 strongly recommends a place?
4 had to entertain himself or herself quite a lot?
5 complained?
6 had to wait far longer than he or she had been expecting to?
7 felt very comfortable where he or she was?
8 mentions local sights?

7 Look at page 149 again. Underline the sentences in the reviews that helped you answer the questions in Activity 6.

8 **WRITING SKILL** Adding comments

Match the first half of each excerpt (1-4) with the second half (a-d).

1 Our room had a great view of the ocean, but the hotel restaurant closed at nine,
2 We had an amazing time, but terrible weather on the day we left,
3 We complained about the room, so they offered us two full days at the spa,
4 The beach was a five-minute walk from the hotel, but so was the snake market,

a which meant we were delayed for several hours.
b which was rather disappointing.
c which was a bit of a culture shock, to say the least.
d which was kind of them.

9 Choose one of these places and write a review. Use the Useful language box to help you.

- vacation destination
- local tourist attraction
- local cafe or restaurant
- place you have stayed

2 The Business of Technology

A man stands inside a virtual cave at the Gdansk University of Technology in Poland. Virtual caves can be used by architects, doctors, and firefighters to simulate real-world scenarios.

2A Young Business

VOCABULARY Setting up a new business

1 Look at the photo and read the caption. How do you think the virtual cave works? How can it help people? In what other jobs might the virtual cave be useful?

2 Work as a class. Discuss the questions.

1 What is the difference between an **entrepreneur** and a **businessperson**?
2 What qualities and skills do you think you need to be an entrepreneur?
3 How easy is it for young people to become businesspeople or entrepreneurs?
4 Can you think of any young entrepreneurs? Who was the youngest? What was his or her business?

3 Work in pairs. Discuss the questions.

1 How do people **raise money** for a business or a charity?
2 Who might businesspeople **negotiate with**? What about?
3 In what ways do businesses **market products**?
4 What might a business or a person **recover from**?
5 What are good and bad ways of **handling pressure**?

4 What skills do you need to start a new business? Choose the correct option to complete each skill.

1 _____ something new
   a negotiate   **b** invent   **c** redesign

2 _____ money from investors
   a raise   **b** lend   **c** ask

3 _____ with suppliers to get the best deal
   a handle   **b** manage   **c** negotiate

4 find partners to _____ the product in different countries
   a send   **b** distribute   **c** deal

5 have the confidence to _____ from failure
   a recover   **b** repair   **c** accept

6 be good at _____ your product to increase sales
   a meeting   **b** networking   **c** marketing

7 be capable of _____ stress and pressure
   a preparing   **b** holding   **c** handling

8 be able to _____ a diverse range of people
   a deal with   **b** talk   **c** get on

9 _____ a team of people
   a apply for   **b** figure   **c** put together

10 _____ in an impressive office
   a live   **b** be based   **c** show

5 MY PERSPECTIVE

Work in pairs. What are the three most important skills from Activity 4 that make a new business a success? Can you think of any other skills?

6 Explain your choices from Activity 5 to another pair. Do they agree? Why?

LISTENING

7 Listen to a woman talking about entrepreneurs. Think about the questions and take notes. 🎧 **7**

1 How is being an entrepreneur changing?
2 According to the speaker, what is the most important aspect of being an entrepreneur?

8 Work in pairs. Discuss the sentences. Are they *true* or *false*? Listen again to check. 🎧 **7**

1 Nick D'Aloisio became a millionaire when he was eighteen.
2 Amanda Hocking didn't go through a traditional publisher to market her books.
3 The speaker suggests that most investments from banks in the past went to older, wealthy businessmen.
4 D'Aloisio's first investor chose him because he was young and had potential.
5 Kickstarter investors buy a share of the company.
6 Projects advertised on Kickstarter aim to make a profit.
7 The majority of Kickstarter projects get no investments.
8 Hocking is an example of recovering from failure.

9 Work in pairs. Discuss the questions.

1 How has the internet changed entrepreneurship?
2 Do you think Kickstarter is a good idea? What are the benefits and risks of raising money this way?
3 What do you think might be good or bad about being an entrepreneur?

GRAMMAR Present perfect forms and the simple past

10 Look at the Grammar box. Read the sentences. Then answer the questions.

1 Which tense is each of the verb forms in bold?
2 Why do you think the different forms are used?

Present perfect forms and the simple past

a *D'Aloisio's first investor* **contacted** *him by email from Hong Kong.*
b *Kickstarter* **has been running** *for several years now.*
c *Most successful entrepreneurs* **have failed** *at least once.*

Check the Grammar Reference for more information and practice.

11 Based on your ideas from Activity 10, complete the summary. Use each form once.

The number of entrepreneurs (1) _____ (grow) ever since the arrival of new technology and online services. This new technology (2) _____ (reduce) the barriers that previously (3) _____ (discourage) people from setting up a business.

12 Do the underlined verbs use the correct forms? Change the ones you think are incorrect.

Topher White is a young entrepreneur. In college, he (1) <u>trained</u> as a physicist, but since 2012 he (2) <u>ran</u> a non-profit company, Rainforest Connection, to help prevent the illegal practice of logging.* He (3) <u>has invented</u> a system using old cell phones and solar power to hear the sound of saws and vehicles that illegal loggers use. The phones then send a warning to guards so they can stop the activity before it does too much damage. Topher first (4) <u>has tested</u> the system in Borneo, and in 2014, his Kickstarter campaign (5) <u>has raised</u> almost $170,000 to expand the company. Since then he's (6) <u>been working</u> with groups such as the Tembe tribe in South America, as well as with people in Africa and Indonesia to adapt the system to meet local needs. They successfully (7) <u>detected</u> a lot of illegal activity. The work Topher is doing is important because in some parts of the world they (8) <u>have been losing</u> ten percent of forest cover this century, and deforestation is one of the biggest contributors to climate change.

logging *cutting down trees*

Topher White attaches a Rainforest Connection listening device to a tree in the Amazon Rainforest in Brazil to help stop illegal logging.

13 Complete the sentences so they are true for you.
   1 I haven't _____ since _____ .
   2 _____ has been doing a lot better since _____ .
   3 I _____ over the last five years.
   4 I _____ for the first time last year.
   5 The number of _____ has grown a lot over the last few years.

14 MY PERSPECTIVE

Look again at the three most important skills you listed in Activity 5. Give examples of when you have demonstrated these skills. List any other qualities or ideas you have that show that you would be a good entrepreneur.

15 Work in groups. Try to convince other students that you would make the best entrepreneur. Use the present perfect and simple past forms.

I've been running our school debate team for the last two years, so I believe that I can negotiate well with other people.

I took nine exams last year, so I think I'm capable of handling stress and pressure.

2B Risky Business

READING

1 Complete the sentences with these pairs of words.

confirm + scam	deleted + permission
emails + filter	inbox + attached
infected + backups	profile + edit
social media + posting	store + flash drive

1 Some of my posts were _____ without my _____ . I have no idea why!

2 I can't believe how many _____ manage to get through my spam _____ .

3 He's very active on _____ . He's always _____ new updates and adding photos.

4 I keep my _____ very private, and I often go back and _____ things I've written.

5 This strange email just arrived in my _____ with a file _____ to it, so I deleted it.

6 When they asked me to _____ my bank details, I started to think it must be a _____ .

7 I _____ all my documents in the cloud now, rather than using a _____ .

8 My computer got a virus that _____ a lot of my files and I didn't have any _____ .

2 Work in pairs. How do you think the things in Activity 1 can happen? Why would people do them?

3 Look at the infographic and read the stories. Then answer the questions.

1 What mistake did each person make?
2 What was the result of each mistake?

4 Work in pairs. Answer the questions.

1 Who didn't realize they'd made a mistake for a long time?
2 Who received several emails from the same person?
3 Who thought they had found a bargain?
4 Who was scared into responding too quickly?
5 Who accepted the blame for what happened?
6 Who didn't read a product description carefully enough?

5 Read the stories again to check your ideas in Activity 4. Underline the parts that helped you decide.

6 MY PERSPECTIVE

Make a list of the different ways you could protect yourself from the same kinds of online crimes that Laura, Bruno, and Janella encountered.

VOCABULARY BUILDING

Adjective and noun collocations 1

When you learn adjectives, it is a good idea to remember the nouns that they describe. Sometimes the adjective is next to the noun; however, sometimes it appears later in the sentence.
It's a very user-friendly website with lots of functions and it is also very secure.

7 Match the adjectives with the nouns they are used with in the stories on page 25.

1	the normal	**a**	hotels
2	a secondhand	**b**	relative
3	my personal	**c**	PlayStation
4	luxury	**d**	documents
5	common	**e**	fees
6	a distant	**f**	price
7	official	**g**	sense
8	legal	**h**	details

CRITICAL THINKING Interpreting data

You will often see visuals and charts in newspapers, books, and articles online to add information and support the text. You need to check that these statistics are from a reliable source and interpret the data for yourself before you read.

8 Work in groups. Look at the cybercrime graphs on page 25. Discuss the questions.

1 Where does the data come from? Do you think this is a reliable source?
2 What crimes do the graphs focus on? What do you know about them?
3 What's the most common crime? Why do you think that is?
4 Which age groups are the least affected? Which are the most affected? Why do you think that is?
5 Do you think the statistics would be different for your country? Why? Do you know where to find this data?

9 Work in groups. Discuss the questions.

1 Which of the three mistakes do you think is the most serious? Which is the least serious? Why?
2 Why do you think each person acted as they did?
3 What do you think each person did after realizing their mistake?
4 Have you heard any stories about similar mistakes? If so, what happened?

Online Crime

🎧 **8** The world becomes more connected every day. It's now easier than ever to keep in touch with friends and family around the world. Online banking allows people to access their accounts from anywhere that has an internet connection. People don't even have to leave the house to go shopping! However, with greater connectivity comes greater risk. Every year, hundreds of thousands of people become victims of online crime. We asked our readers to share some of their terrible tech tales while we examine where the crimes originate.

Laura One day last year, I got a call from what I thought was my bank. They said someone was trying to take money from my account without my permission, and that they needed to confirm my personal details to stop it. I'll be honest—I didn't really understand what was going on and wanted to stop anything bad from happening, so I gave them my name and address and date of birth. I didn't hear back, but a month later I got my credit card statement and found someone had spent over 11,000 pounds on flights and luxury hotels!

Origin of crime: The United States

Romania

The United States

West Africa

Bruno I was surfing the web one day when I found a site selling Xboxes and PlayStations. I couldn't believe how cheap they were. They had stuff on there for half the normal price! I clicked on one item and bought what was advertised as a "PlayStation 4 original box and receipt." I assumed it was secondhand and, since it was only 150 euros, I bought it without checking the details. You can imagine how I felt a few days later when the postman brought me just the box and the receipt!

Origin of crime: Romania

Janella Looking back, it was my own fault, but when I got an email saying a distant relative had died and left me millions of dollars, common sense went out of the window! It was from someone claiming to be a lawyer in West Africa. I know my dad's side of the family had connections there, so I thought it must be true. They attached documents that looked official and kept writing, so eventually I sent them 8,000 dollars to pay the legal fees. Of course, it was a scam and I never heard from them again… or got my money back!

Origin of crime: West Africa

Cybercrime by age (US)

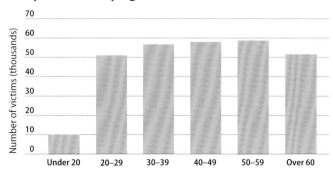

Number of victims (thousands)

Under 20 | 20–29 | 30–39 | 40–49 | 50–59 | Over 60

Cybercrime by type (US)

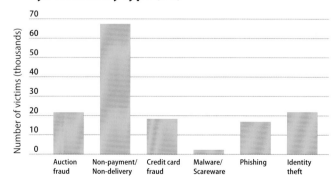

Number of victims (thousands)

Auction fraud | Non-payment/ Non-delivery | Credit card fraud | Malware/ Scareware | Phishing | Identity theft

Source: U.S. Department of Justice / Federal Bureau of Investigation Statistics shown are for 2015.

Do you enjoy posting on social media?

2C What's in a post?

GRAMMAR Verb patterns (*-ing* or infinitive with *to*)

1 Work in pairs. Look at the Grammar box. Which verbs below can be followed by the *-ing* form? Which can be followed by the infinitive with *to*?

admit	agree	arrange	can't stand	consider
decide	delay	enjoy	expect	finish
hope	intend	mind	miss	offer
plan	practice	promise	recommend	refuse

Verb patterns (*-ing* or infinitive with *to*)

When two verbs are used together, the second one often takes the *-ing* form or the infinitive with *to*.

*They attached documents that looked official and **kept writing to me**.*

*Websites such as Kickstarter allow entrepreneurs to **avoid selling** part of their business to an investor.*

*They **needed to confirm** my personal details.*

*Over half of the campaigns on Kickstarter don't receive any funding because they **fail to reach** their set target.*

Check the Grammar Reference for more information and practice.

2 Choose the correct options to complete the blog post.

If you're anything like most people, you probably enjoy (1) *posting / to post* on social media. Maybe you hope (2) *creating / to create* a particular kind of image of yourself, or intend (3) *showing / to show* others what good taste you have. You're probably not planning (4) *providing / to provide* information that could be used against you in the future, but every time you post online or "like" something, you're agreeing (5) *sharing / to share* that personal information with the world!

Most of us avoid (6) *revealing / to reveal* too much about ourselves face-to-face, but for some reason, we don't mind (7) *doing / to do* this online. Everything you decide (8) *making / to make* public on the internet helps to build a very detailed picture of who you are and what you believe—and we're failing (9) *understanding / to understand* that this helps companies guess your age, gender, education, political views… and much more.

Of course, most social media companies refuse (10) *guaranteeing / to guarantee* privacy for users. After all, we are their product. What they sell is the information we give them! Given this, I recommend (11) *using / to use* science to help us gain control over our data! Sites could warn us of the risks we are taking when we post certain kinds of information, for example. Failing that, of course, we could all just consider (12) *posting / to post* less.

3 Work in pairs. Discuss the questions.

1 How much do you think you reveal about yourself on social media? Why?
2 What kinds of things do you post online? Why?
3 Are you concerned about privacy online? Why?
4 What do you think social media sites do with the personal information they gather? How does this make you feel?

4 Complete the comments with the correct form of these verbs.

be	feel	have	hear
post	protect	quit	spend

Eric Wong   Posted 3 hours ago

I can't stand (1) _____ like everything I do online is being used by someone. Really, we should all promise (2) _____ social media! The only reason we don't is because we're too scared we'd miss (3) _____ from friends!

Luisa Hernandez   Posted 2 weeks ago

If you use social media, you should expect (4) _____ these experiences. Why should companies offer (5) _____ our privacy? They already provide us with free services. That should be enough.

Back to the Future   Posted a month ago

The secret of being happy is to practice (6) _____ more patient! Delay (7) _____ until you're sure you really want the world to have access to what you write—and try (8) _____ as much time offline as you can!

5 Work in groups. Do you agree with the comments in Activity 4? Why?

6 Write your own short response to the blog post in Activity 2. Include two or more verbs from Activity 1. Then share your comments in groups.

Objects before -ing and to

Some verbs always have an object before an -ing form or an infinitive with to.

*When they **asked me to confirm** my bank details, I started to think it must be a scam.*

Check the Grammar Reference for more information and practice.

7 Look at the Grammar box. Complete the sentences so that they are true for you. Then explain your ideas to a partner.

1 My parents always expected me _____ .
2 In a few years' time, I can see myself _____ .
3 If I could, I'd hire someone _____ .
4 We should do more to prevent _____ .
5 I can still remember begging my parents _____ .

Verbs with two objects

Some verbs can be followed by two objects.

The indirect object is usually a person and the second, direct object is usually a thing.

*Can you **email me your essays**, please, instead of **handing them to me** in class?*

Check the Grammar Reference for more information and practice.

8 Look at the Grammar box. Complete the sentences with these direct objects. You will also have to add an indirect object. The first one has been done for you.

anything	a loan	a new tablet
a special dinner	permission	~~the remote control~~

1 This show is terrible. Let's see what else is on.
   Pass *me the remote control* .
2 My dad bought _____ for my birthday.
3 If you're under twenty, it's difficult to find a bank that'll give _____ to start a business.
4 By posting on their website, you're basically giving _____ to use your data.
5 If I were you, I wouldn't tell _____ . He can't keep a secret!
6 My sister and I cooked _____ for their wedding anniversary.

9 CHOOSE

Choose one of the following activities.

- Work in pairs. Write a blog post explaining best practices when it comes to using social media. Use as many of the phrases below as you can.

  If I were you, I'd avoid…
  I'd strongly recommend…
  It's best not to agree / try…
  Lots of people fail…
  You may want to prevent people from…
  It's sometimes good to ask friends…
  Don't allow everyone…
  Think carefully before you tell…

- Write a short story about someone who started a new business. Use at least five verbs from pages 21–27.

- Work in groups. Search online for a story about someone who was a victim of cybercrime. Report what happened to another group. Use at least five verbs from pages 21–27.

This is what happens when you reply to spam email

> " Crazy stuff happens when you start replying to scam emails. "

JAMES VEITCH

Read about James Veitch and get ready to watch his TED Talk. ▶ **2.0**

AUTHENTIC LISTENING SKILLS

Intonation and pitch

When we are surprised or shocked by what someone says, we often repeat a key word, phrase, or short sentence with a high pitch and a questioning intonation. We may then add a comment with a falling tone.

1 Look at the Authentic Listening Skills box. Then work in pairs. Practice the exchange.

A We can start with 50 kilograms as a trial shipment.
B Fifty kilograms? There's no point doing this at all unless you're shipping at least a metric ton.

2 Listen to James Veitch. Compare your intonation with his. 🎧 **9**

3 Work in pairs. Take turns responding to the comments using the same intonation pattern as James.

1 I got an email offering to distribute gold.
2 He's sixteen years old.
3 It cost ten dollars.
4 I've never watched *Star Wars*.
5 Her dad is the mayor of our city.
6 My bank called me and asked for my address.

WATCH

4 Work in groups. Guess what this email means and why it was written.

From: Solomon Odonkoh
To: James Veitch
(No Subject)

The business is on. I am trying to raise the balance for the Gummy Bear so he can submit all the needed Fizzy Cola Bottle Jelly Beans to the Creme Egg for the Peanut M&Ms process to start. Send £1,500.00 via a Giant Gummy Lizard.

5 Watch Part 1 of the talk. Answer the questions. ▶ **2.1**

1 How was "Solomon Odonkoh" trying to make money?
2 Do you still have the same answer to Activity 4?

6 Work in pairs. Put the sentences in the correct order.

a I figured I had to knock it on the head.
b On real estate, what about you?
c Dude, you have to use the code!
d I'm a hedge fund executive bank manager.
e I have to go to bed now.
f I could do what I think we've all always wanted to do.
g If we're going to do it, let's go big.
h I didn't hear back. I thought, "I've gone too far."

7 Watch Part 1 of the talk again to check your ideas in Activity 6.
▶ 2.1

8 Work in groups. Discuss why you think James Veitch replies to spam. Which of these points is he trying to make?

1 He replies to spam email when he is bored.
2 He suggests it is a good way to spend any spare time.
3 He replies to spam email to take up the time of the spammer. He suggests that this stops them from contacting other people.
4 He replies to spam email because he is interested in the financial benefits. He suggests that people can make money by doing business online.

9 Watch Part 2 of the talk. Check your ideas in Activity 8. How effective do you think James's approach is? Why?
▶ 2.2

10 Watch Part 3 of the talk. How are the emails James receives from "Solomon Odonkoh" and the emails he receives this time similar? ▶ 2.3

⓫ VOCABULARY IN CONTEXT

a Watch the clips from the TED Talk. Choose the correct meanings of the words and phrases. ▶ 2.4

b Work in pairs. Tell your partner about:
• something or someone who *turned up* unexpectedly.
• a situation that *got out of hand* / *went too far*.
• something or someone that / who *intrigues* you.

⓬ MY PERSPECTIVE

Work in pairs. Come up with five different ways to deal with internet scams. Then discuss which ones are most relevant to these groups of people. Explain your reasons.

• elderly people
• people who enjoy playing video games
• people who do a lot of online shopping

CHALLENGE
Work in groups. Design a questionnaire to find out about people's experiences with internet scams. You should find out how much is already known and what, if anything, people are doing to reduce the risks. You will need at least ten questions.

2E Investment Opportunity

Speaking strategy

Persuading

When we are persuading people, we sometimes turn our own experiences and opinions into a negative question to challenge the other person's ideas.

I think it will lose money.
Don't you think it'll lose money?
I'd find it really useful.
Wouldn't you find it really useful?
I have sometimes had that problem.
Haven't you ever had that problem?

SPEAKING

1 Work in groups. Discuss the questions.

   1 Are there any TV shows about business or selling products in your country? Do you watch them? Why?
   2 Would you be good at selling a product? Why?
   3 Have you ever had to present something in front of people? What did you present? Was the presentation successful? Why?

2 Work in pairs. Read about the Kickstarter project. One person should think of reasons to invest and one person should think of reasons not to invest. Then discuss your reasons and try to persuade each other.

mXers was set up by high school student Bharat Pulgam. He has invented a new kind of earbuds that allow you to easily replace the different parts that can break, so you don't have to buy a whole new set. They also allow you to customize your earbuds for an individual look. mXers needs money to develop the product and start production.

3 Make negative questions from these sentences. Which negative questions could you use to support your reasons from Activity 2? Why?

   1 It'd be good to have something like that.
   2 I think it's a bad idea to give money to strangers online.
   3 There's something similar to that already.
   4 Sometimes I've wished that I could do that.
   5 I would be happy to pay a little more to help.

4 **PRONUNCIATION** Intonation for persuasion

   a Listen to the negative questions and notice the intonation. 🎧 10
   b Practice saying the negative questions.
      1 Wouldn't it be good to have something like that?
      2 Don't you think it's a bad idea to give money to strangers online?
      3 Isn't there something similar to that already?
      4 Haven't you ever wished that you could do that?
      5 Wouldn't you be happy to pay a little more to help?

An woman harvests cocoa in Ghana for Fairafric.

5 Work in pairs. Read about two other Kickstarter projects. Choose one each and try to persuade each other to invest.

The Possible Project is an after-school program that teaches teenagers, mainly from low-income families, the skills to be entrepreneurs. The project has been running for several years and has trained over 250 students. The team wants to raise money for a laser cutter so that students can make a variety of products quickly.

Hendrik Reimers is a German chocolate maker. He has set up a chocolate-making company, Fairafric, in Ghana. By producing the chocolate bars in their own country, rather than only exporting cocoa beans, people in Ghana can earn over 25 percent more—even compared to fair-trade chocolate. The money raised will help fund production, packaging, shipping, and distribution.

WRITING A persuasive article

6 Read the short article on page 149 and find out:

1 what the aim of the article is.
2 what the nightmare is.
3 what the business is.

7 WRITING SKILL Getting people's attention

Work in pairs. Look at the article again and answer the questions.

1 How does the article grab your attention?
2 How does the article try to persuade you to continue reading?
3 Where does the factual information come from?
4 What is the purpose of the final paragraph?

8 Would you invest in the *i-save*? Why? Discuss with a partner.

9 Using the product you chose in Activity 5, a product you have heard about recently, or something you invented yourself, write an article to explain the product and encourage people to invest or find out more about it.

10 Work in groups. Share your article. People in your group should ask you questions or share comments about your article.

3 Faster, Higher, Stronger

Sports fans experience a range of emotions as they watch an event.

3A Incredible Achievements

VOCABULARY Describing athletes

1 Work in groups. Look at the photo and discuss the questions.

   1 Would you like to be in a crowd like this? Why?
   2 Which sport do you think they are watching? Is it popular in your country?
   3 Which are the most popular sports in your country? Do you like them? Why? Do you know any famous people who take part in them?

2 Work in pairs. Choose the option which cannot complete the sentence.

   1 He has… *incredible awareness / very energetic / great technique / a real passion for the game.*
   2 She's… *a very skillful player / a really great attitude / a forward / a positive role model.*
   3 She won… *a great goal / silver at the Olympics / the world championship / a gold medal.*
   4 He scored… *an average of 20 points a game / 300 goals in his career / the most last season / the race.*
   5 *He set a new / He won the / He holds the / He smashed the old…* world record.
   6 *She captained / She was the star of / She competed / She played a key role on…* the team.

3 Complete the sentences with words from Activity 2.

   1 Everyone on the team has a really great _____ . They always fight right to the end of the game.
   2 She still _____ the world record she set 30 years ago.
   3 When I was younger, I won a gold _____ in the 400 meters.
   4 He has incredible _____ . He can anticipate the other players' moves and create opportunities for scoring.
   5 He was a key player in their success, but he never _____ the team.
   6 I've always had a real passion _____ wrestling.
   7 She's _____ in four Olympics and won two golds, one _____ , and one bronze.
   8 He scored the winning _____ in the last World Cup final.

4 Choose five phrases from Activity 2 to describe an athlete, a friend, and a family member. Then tell your partner about the people you thought of.

My favorite soccer player is Pierre-Emerick Aubameyang. He has incredible awareness and scores some amazing goals.

I think my big sister is a positive role model for me. She has a great attitude and never gives up.

5 MY PERSPECTIVE

How do you think sports and athletes have changed in your lifetime? With a partner, discuss changes in these categories.

   • fame / celebrity status
   • equipment
   • achievements

LISTENING

6 Listen to four people explain why they admire certain athletes. As you listen: 🎧 11

1 find out where each athlete is or was from.
2 find an example of something each athlete won.

7 Listen to the four people again. What does each person say about the following? 🎧 11

1	275 times	
	over 150	
	eight or nine out of ten	

2	popular	
	Italian	
	celebrations	

3	videos	
	personal problems	
	a great lesson	

4	her future husband	
	introduced	
	fought	

8 Work in groups. Discuss which of the four athletes you think achieved the most. Explain your ideas.

GRAMMAR Determiners

9 Complete the information about the functions of determiners using these words.

articles	demonstratives	possessives	quantifiers

Determiners are words used before nouns. They have two main functions:

- They show which noun we mean, using
  (1) ＿＿＿＿＿＿ (*the, a[n]*), (2) ＿＿＿＿＿＿
  (*this, that, these, those*), and (3) ＿＿＿＿＿＿
  (*my, your, his, her, its, our, their*).
- They show how much or how many of something there is, using (4) ＿＿＿＿＿＿ .

10 Look at the Grammar box. Underline the determiners in the sentences.

Determiners

a *That year, Susi won the women's singles.*
b *Ask any Indonesian of his generation.*
c *He won many medals, including one gold.*
d *Without him, fewer people would watch motorcycle road racing.*
e *We'd never won any gold medals.*

Check the Grammar Reference for more information and practice.

Valentino Rossi (left) attempts to overtake Maverick Vinales during a race at the Motorland Aragón Circuit in Alcañiz, Spain.

11 Work in pairs. Complete the sentences with determiners. Then discuss.

1 She used to be _____ forward on _____ US women's soccer team and she's one of the most successful soccer players ever.
2 She played for _____ country 275 times and scored 150 goals. _____ man has ever managed that!
3 Not _____ people can claim to have made a sport popular more or less on _____ own.
4 He has _____ ego problems and _____ great personality.
5 _____ coach has shown me some videos of Joaquín when he was at _____ best.
6 She always fought right to _____ end, even when it seemed there was _____ hope.

12 Work in pairs. Look at the corrected sentences. Discuss why you think the original sentences were wrong.

1 I don't like ~~no~~ *any* sports.
2 Hardly any ~~athlete~~ *athletes* from my country ~~has~~ *have* ever won an Olympic medal.
3 I think I'm pretty healthy. I eat very ~~few~~ *little* junk food.
4 There aren't ~~much~~ *many* places near here where you can exercise outside.
5 A ~~little~~ *few* people I know are crazy about sports.
6 I don't think it's right that some athletes earn so ~~many~~ *much* money.
7 Most ~~of~~ people I know have no interest in soccer.
8 I try to exercise every ~~weekends~~ *weekend* if I can.

13 Decide which sentences you agree with in Activity 12. Change the sentences that you do not agree with. Share your ideas in groups.

Number 1 isn't true for me. I like some sports. I'm really into basketball and baseball.
Number 2 isn't true. Lots of athletes from my country have won medals!

14 Complete the biography with one word in each blank.

Yao Ming is (1) _____ retired professional basketball player. He stopped playing a (2) _____ years ago, but he's still one of (3) _____ most famous athletes in China. I have a (4) _____ of great memories of watching him play. He spent (5) _____ years playing in the NBA in North America, which was amazing because (6) _____ Chinese player had ever done that before—and (7) hardly _____ have done it since. (8) _____ , if not all, Chinese people know him and are very proud of what he achieved. He's instantly recognizable because he's 7 feet 6 inches tall. He made (9) _____ other player in the NBA look small in comparison! In the end, though, he had a (10) _____ of injuries that ended his career.

15 Think again about the people you chose in Activity 4. Make notes about their lives, achievements, and why you admire them.

16 Work in groups. Tell each other about the people you wrote about in Activity 15. Ask each other more questions.

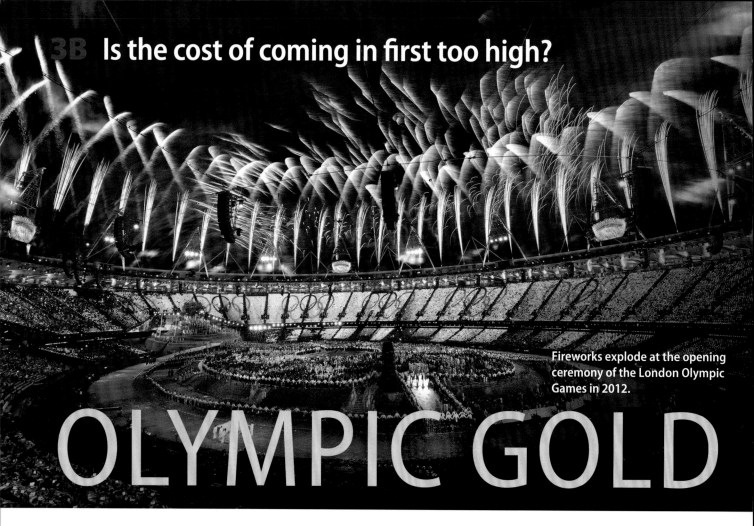

3B Is the cost of coming in first too high?

Fireworks explode at the opening ceremony of the London Olympic Games in 2012.

OLYMPIC GOLD

VOCABULARY BUILDING

Synonyms in texts

Writers often use words or phrases with similar meanings to make their work more interesting and to avoid repetition.

*Countries competing to **host the Olympics** will often spend huge amounts to **hold the 16-day event**.*

1 Complete the sentences with these synonyms. Use a dictionary, if necessary.

establish	funding	hold
selected	sums	top

1 Countries compete to **host** the Olympics.
Countries spend huge amounts to _____
the 16-day event.
2 Hosts spend huge **amounts**.
Hosts invest large _____ of money.
3 They have programs for **elite** athletes.
They support _____ competitors.
4 There is **money** to help develop successful athletes.
This _____ is directly linked to success.

5 They helped to **set up** a program that promotes excellence in sports.
They helped to _____ a system that promotes excellence in sports.
6 Children are **chosen** as potential stars.
Children hope to be _____ as potential stars.

2 Work in pairs. Rewrite the phrases using synonyms.

prove to have talent—*prove to have a natural ability*

1 achieve their targets
2 core principle
3 got its highest ranking
4 linked to success
5 tackle the challenges you face

READING

3 Work in groups. Which of these statements do you agree with?

1 The most important thing is not winning, but taking part.
2 Hosting the Olympics is a waste of money.
3 In sports and in life, you get what you pay for.
4 Increasing participation in sports at low levels could help tackle health and social challenges.

🎧 **12** When Baron Pierre de Coubertin set up the first modern Olympics in Athens in 1896, he declared that "The most important thing in the Olympic Games is not winning, but taking part; the essential thing in life is not conquering, but fighting well." These days, it can seem that this core principle has been forgotten, (1) _____.

The hosting countries spend huge amounts of money to hold the 16-day event. Many of the countries taking part invest huge sums in programs for elite athletes. And that money is not spent to come in fourth; the only thing that matters is having "the best Games" and winning medals—preferably gold.

The figures are enormous! Depending on who you ask, China spent 40 billion dollars on the Beijing Olympics and Russia invested 50 billion in Sochi; the Rio and London Games each cost between 14 and 18 billion dollars. In terms of money for athletes, the UK spent over 400 million dollars supporting 1,300 top competitors. This funding is directly linked to success: those who fail to achieve their targets will have their funding cut and, in some cases, completely removed. (2) _____!

Similarly, several years ago, China established a system known as *Juguo Tizhi* ("whole country support for the elite sport system") for developing athletes. Children are identified as potential sports stars between the ages of six and nine, and are sent to special sports schools run by the local government, (3) _____ . Those who prove to have talent move on to a semi-professional schedule of four to six hours a day, five or six days a week. Later, the top performers move on to provincial training centers. Students there live and breathe their sport and hope to be selected for their provincial team (4) _____ . There are around 400,000 young people in this system, whose main purpose is to win glory for their nation. In the years before Beijing, it accounted for a very large percentage of all sports funding.

In both sports and life, you tend to get what you pay for; (5) _____ . China came in first in Beijing, and Great Britain got its highest ranking in over 100 years in 2016. The question is whether this search for success at all costs comes at the expense of investing in something which is arguably more valuable: (6) _____ . Seeing your team win can obviously lift your spirits. However, this feeling is only temporary, while taking part in regular exercise and sports has been shown to have long-term physical and psychological benefits. Given this, surely spending more money on increasing sports participation from the lowest levels up would be a better way of tackling some of the health and social challenges that many countries face.

4 Read about what some countries will do to host the Olympics and do well. Complete the text with the phrases (a–f).

a the more money you spend, the better the results

b overtaken by the other motto de Coubertin is known for: "faster, higher, stronger"

c local clubs and competitions; facilities for people to stay healthy and play for fun

d and then to be full-time professional athletes representing their country

e where they train for up to 15 hours a week

f So much for the value of just "taking part"

5 MY PERSPECTIVE

Work in pairs. Discuss the questions.

1 Would you like to participate in a system like *Juguo Tizhi*? Why?

2 Do you know any schools that specialize in sports? Do you think they are a good idea? Why?

3 Do you have to play sports at school? How much importance is given to winning?

4 Have you seen any great sporting events? How did they make you feel? Why?

CRITICAL THINKING Supporting arguments

Sometimes writers select information to support their point of view.

6 Work in pairs. Read the facts below. Do they support an argument for spending money on the Olympics? Why?

1 Six million dollars of the Beijing Olympics' costs went toward sports. The rest included new subway lines, an airport terminal, a light railway, and roads.

2 The majority of *Juguo Tizhi* athletes retire from their sport without a formal education.

3 According to the Chinese National Audit Office, the Beijing Olympics made a profit of 146 million dollars.

4 Montreal took over 30 years to pay off its debts from holding the Olympics.

7 A city in your country wants to host the Olympics. Divide into two teams—one for and one against. In your teams, discuss the arguments you would give. Then debate the issue as a class. Think about:

- the impact on the local community.
- what would happen after the Olympics.
- alternatives to hosting the Olympics.

Swimmers wear caps and body suits to help them move through the water faster than other competitors.

3C Getting Better All the Time

GRAMMAR Comparatives and superlatives

1 How much do you agree with this quote? Give examples to show how things are better or worse now than they were in the past.

"This is the best time to be alive—ever." —TED Speaker Gareth Cliff

Comparatives and superlatives

a Bicycles have improved and become **far** _more aerodynamic_.
b There are **many** _more people_ training today.
c Athletes are training _harder and more intelligently_ than before.
d The running tracks used in the 1930s were _not as fast as_ the ones today.
e The soft surface of old running tracks stole **much** _more energy_ from athletes' legs compared to modern tracks.
f Usain Bolt is _the fastest man_ in history.
g On average, elite shot-putters now are **two and a half inches** _taller_ and **130 pounds** _heavier_ than they were in the 1920s.
h The current hour record in cycling is **only slightly** _better_ than it was over 40 years ago.
i _The more money_ governments spend on athletes, _the better_ the results.

Check the Grammar Reference for more information and practice.

2 Look at the Grammar box. Read the sentences about how sports and athletes have changed. Answer the questions.

1 Which sentences use a comparative form with:
   - an adjective?
   - an adverb?
   - a noun?

2 Which sentence uses a superlative adjective?
3 Which sentence emphasizes that something is "less than"?
4 Which of the words in bold show a small difference and which show a big difference?
5 Why do we say _many more people_, but _much more energy_? What is the opposite of each of them?
6 Which sentence shows how one change causes another change to happen at the same time?

3 **PRONUNCIATION** Linking words together in fast speech

When one word ends in a consonant sound and the next begins with a vowel sound, we often link the two words together when speaking.
I don't do it as much… may sound like: _I don't do it as_ (tas) _much…_

If one word ends with a consonant sound and the next word starts with the same consonant sound, we often leave out the first consonant sound.
…than it did last season may sound like: _…than it did last season_

a Read about linking words together in fast speech. Then listen to the sentences. Underline where you hear the links. 🔊 **13**

1 I'm better at it than I used to be.
2 It's the best thing I've experienced in my life.
3 I don't do it as much as I used to.
4 It's a lot more popular than it used to be.
5 It's a bit more difficult than it was in the past.
6 It's far easier than it was in the past.
7 I'm not as good at it as I'd like to be.
8 They're doing worse than they did last season.

b Work in groups. Replace *it* in each sentence to make sentences that are true for you.

I'm better at speaking English than I used to be!

4 Read about how small changes made a big difference for the British cycling team. How can small changes make big differences in your life?

Between the Olympics in 1908 and 2004, the British cycling team won just three gold medals. No British cyclist had even come close to winning (1) _____ world's greatest cycle race, the Tour de France. Yet over the next twelve years, the British team won more than 25 gold medals and had two winners of the Tour. How could the team perform so (2) _____ better?

The first thing was that cycling received a (3) _____ more funding (4) _____ it had before and, thanks also to a new Olympic track in Manchester, the team could train (5) _____ intensively. The coaches also began to focus on making small improvements in lots of areas. This was not just about training better and eating (6) _____ healthily, but also included things like teaching the cyclists to wash their hands properly and finding the (7) _____ comfortable pillow for them to use at night! (8) _____ cleaner their hands, the (9) _____ colds and viruses the cyclists pick up, and the more training they can do. If they do not get as much sleep (10) _____ they need, they may ride one percent (11) _____ the next day. The more of these small improvements you can make, the (12) _____ the difference compared (13) _____ your competitors.

With the recent successes in British cycling, there are (14) _____ more people cycling in the country than there used to be. Having a much bigger pool of riders improves the chances of finding talented cyclists to continue that success.

There is a lesson here for all of us. We often set big goals which aren't so easy to achieve when perhaps we should focus on all the things we can do (15) _____ better. Small changes can add up to a big difference.

5 Complete the summary in Activity 4 with one word in each blank. Compare your ideas with a partner.

6 CHOOSE

Choose one of the following activities.

- Write a short essay on the question in Activity 1. Use comparatives in your response.

- What is better now than in the past? What is worse? Make lists of five things that are better and five things that are worse. Use comparatives to explain the differences.

- Work in pairs. How many small changes can you think of which would contribute to these big improvements? Explain how the changes will affect the final result.
  - Improving the performance of a school's sports team
  - Getting better grades at school
  - Increasing people's life expectancy in your country
  - Stopping global warming

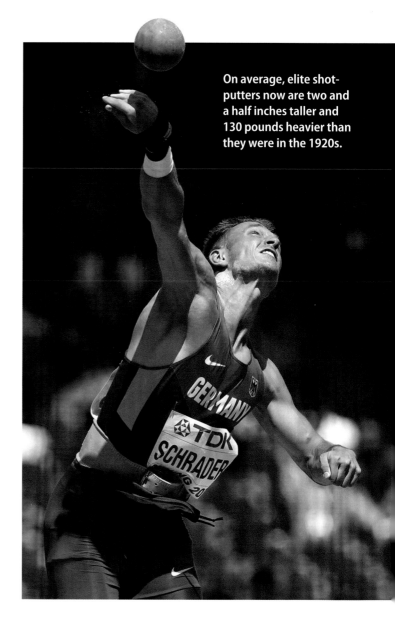

On average, elite shot-putters now are two and a half inches taller and 130 pounds heavier than they were in the 1920s.

Are athletes really getting faster, better, stronger?

" We all have this feeling that we're somehow just getting better as a human race… but it's not like we've evolved into a new species in a century. "

DAVID EPSTEIN

Read about David Epstein and get ready to watch his talk. ▶ **3.0**

AUTHENTIC LISTENING SKILLS

Slowing down and stressing words

Speakers will often slow down and stress words when they are contrasting two ideas. The surrounding language can sound very fast.

1 Look at the Authentic Listening Skills box. Listen to an extract from the TED Talk. Underline where David slows down and stresses words. 🎧 **14**

The winner of the 2012 Olympic marathon ran two hours and eight minutes. Had he been racing against the winner of the 1904 Olympic marathon, he would have won by nearly an hour and a half.

2 Work in pairs. Underline the contrasts in the extracts. Then practice saying them aloud.

1 Usain Bolt started by propelling himself out of blocks down a specially fabricated carpet designed to allow him to travel as fast as humanly possible. Jesse Owens, on the other hand, ran on cinders.

2 Rather than blocks, Jesse Owens had a gardening trowel that he had to use to dig holes in the cinders to start from.

3 …had he been running on the same surface as Bolt, he wouldn't have been fourteen feet behind—he would have been within one stride.

4 Rather than the last beep, Owens would have been the second beep. Listen to it again.

5 Rather than the average body type, you want highly-specialized bodies that fit into certain athletic niches.

WATCH

3 Work in pairs. Which of these sports do you do or watch? What equipment, skills, and physical attributes do you need for each one?

basketball	cycling	gymnastics	soccer
swimming	tennis	track and field	water polo

4 Watch Part 1 of the talk. Guess what David is going to argue. ▷ **3.1**

a The human body has evolved to be better at sports.
b New records in sports are largely due to technology and professionalism.
c Sport is a natural part of human development.

5 Watch Part 2 of the talk. Complete the summary with a number, year, or measurement in each blank. ▷ **3.2**

In (1) _____ , Jesse Owens held the world record in the (2) _____ meters. If he had run more recently against Usain Bolt, he would've finished (3) _____ feet behind him. However, Owens was competing in very different times, and modern runners are greatly helped by technological advances. Given the same conditions, Owens would have been within (4) _____ stride of Bolt!

Technology also helped to improve the hour record that cyclist Eddy Merckx set in (5) _____ by almost (6) _____ miles, but after the rules were changed in (7) _____ , cyclists had to use the same equipment. Subsequently, they were only able to go (8) _____ feet farther than Merckx.

6 Watch Part 3 of the talk. Match what David mentions (1–6) with the points he is making (a–f). ▶ 3.3

1 high-jumpers and shot-putters
2 digital technology
3 financial incentives, fame and glory
4 Michael Phelps and Hicham El Guerrouj
5 the Kalenjin tribe
6 a radiator

a The move towards specialized types of bodies for particular sports accelerated.
b Kenyans are the best marathon runners.
c It made elite sports more available to a wider group of people.
d Some people might have long, thin legs because of evolution.
e Swimmers have long torsos, and runners require proportionately longer legs.
f Specific groups of people have advantages for some sports.

7 Watch Part 4 of the talk. Are the statements *true*, *false*, or *not stated*? ▶ 3.4

1 When a person gets an electric shock, it activates their muscles.
2 We only use a small percentage of our brain power at any one time.
3 We can train our brains to accept more pain.
4 Primates are more suited to endurance than humans.
5 Kílian Jornet was the first person to ever run up the Matterhorn.
6 David does not expect Kílian's record to be broken.

8 VOCABULARY IN CONTEXT

a Watch the clips from the TED Talk. Choose the correct meanings of the words and phrases. ▶ 3.5

b Work in pairs and think of at least one example of:
1 a recent change or event that has affected people *throughout* the world.
2 someone or something that *changed the face of* your country.
3 two brands which are *essentially* the same.
4 an activity that has *shrunk* in popularity.

9 Work in pairs. Discuss the questions.
1 How much of David's talk was new to you? Was there anything he said you already knew?
2 What were the three most interesting facts for you?
3 What do you think is the most important factor in improving results that David mentions? Why?
4 Do you think all sports are better than they were in the past? Why?

CHALLENGE

Choose a sport you are interested in. Find out:

- if it has changed in the ways David Epstein describes.
- if there have been any other changes.
- how the records today compare to 50 years ago.
- why any changes have occurred.

3E Surveys

Introducing main findings

The most surprising / interesting thing we found was that…

You won't be surprised to hear that… but one thing that was interesting was…

The main thing we discovered was…

(By far) the most popular… was…

Introducing other points

Another thing that was interesting was…

Apart from that, we found that…

Some other things worth mentioning are…

What sports have you participated in during the last month?

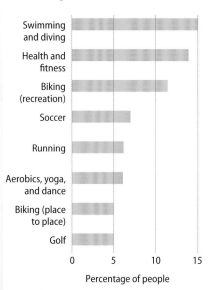

Percentage of people

Source: UK Department for Culture, Media and Sport

Beach soccer is popular on Ipanema Beach in Rio de Janeiro.

SPEAKING

1 Work in groups. The bar graph on this page shows the results of a survey into which sports people had done during the previous month. Discuss:

- whether anything shown surprises you. If so, why?
- why you think certain activities were more or less popular.
- which results you would expect to be similar and different where you live.

2 Work in pairs. Discuss which claims are supported (S) and not supported (NS) by the data in the graph.

1 One fifth of those surveyed used a gym in the month before the survey.
2 Swimming and diving are the most popular sports.
3 One in twenty of those surveyed played golf in the month before the survey.
4 Just under five percent of those surveyed bike to and from work.
5 The popularity of certain sports may change depending on the season.

3 Work in pairs. You are going to conduct a survey. Choose a question from below or think of one that interests you. Your survey should have at least six options.

1 What activities have you done in your free time in the past two weeks?
2 What is your favorite type of movie to watch?
3 What subjects do you want to study in college?

4 Interview as many students as you can and take notes. Discuss your notes with your partner. Then present the findings to the whole class.

WRITING A survey

5 Work in pairs. Read the description on page 150 of the bar graph on this page. Answer the questions.

1 What extra information is included which was not shown in the bar graph?
2 Which part of the description expresses opinion rather than fact?

6 Passive forms are often used in reports. Complete the sentences using the past participles of the verbs in parentheses. You will learn more about passives in Unit 5.

1 The graph shows the result of a survey _____ (conduct) at our school last month.

2 Fifty students _____ (age) thirteen to fifteen were _____ (interview) about their reading habits.

3 As can be _____ (see), only 20 percent of those _____ (survey) said they had read a novel in the previous six months.

4 The most popular author was J.R.R. Tolkien, _____ (follow) by Anthony Horowitz.

5 We might expect a higher response if the survey were _____ (repeat) with a younger age group.

7 **WRITING SKILL** Describing statistics

Replace the percentages in italics with these phrases.

Almost half	A significant majority	A tiny percentage
Just under three quarters	Roughly a third	The vast majority

1 *2%* of those surveyed spend more than an hour a day exercising.

2 *35%* of those who responded play a team sport at least once a month.

3 *48%* of those who responded prefer exercising alone.

4 *65%* of those surveyed would do more sports if they had more free time.

5 *74%* of respondents play fewer sports now than they did five years ago.

6 *96%* of the people I spoke to recognize the importance of exercise.

8 Work in pairs. Refer to the Writing strategy and use the passive forms in Activity 6 to describe the statistics in this bar graph.

Writing strategy

Describing statistics

When we describe statistics, we sometimes use phrases or estimates instead of specific percentages. Instead of *10.3 percent cycled*, we might say **one in ten** *biked*. We do this for variety or to emphasize a point. For example, **over half** may sound bigger than *52 percent*.

Sports Participation by Gender   ▢ Male ▢ Female

Sport	Male	Female
Soccer	90.8	9.2
Golf	86	14
Biking (place to place)	68.9	31.1
Biking (recreation)	68.3	31.7
Hiking	62.7	37.3
Running	60.2	39.8
Health and fitness	51	49
Swimming / diving	42.7	57.3
Aerobics / dance	24.1	75.9
Yoga	17.5	82.5

Source: UK Department for Culture, Media and Sport

4 Cultural Transformation

4A Putting the Town on the Map

VOCABULARY Cultural events

❶ Work in groups. Look at these cultural attractions and discuss the questions.

art gallery / museum	art / music festival
comedy club	food festival
movie theater	music venue
public art	theater

1 Which of these cultural attractions do you have near where you live?
2 Do you go to any of them? Why?
3 Would you like to have any of them near where you live? Why?

❷ Complete the summary by putting the words in bold in the correct order.

The Rio Carnival, one of the world's leading festivals, (1) **every held is February** in Rio de Janeiro, Brazil. During the festival, organizers (2) **huge put on a of parades number** and parties all over the city, which (3) **million tourists almost a attract**. The festival (4) **on impact has a the city big** and on people's cultural lives. The carnival involves around 200 Samba schools which compete to have the best costumes, dance routines, and musical bands. It (5) **million over income $750 in generates** locally in Rio, which comes from tourists who (6) **four-day attend event the** and the Samba schools, which can sometimes spend over 3 million dollars on costumes and preparations. The festival also (7) **Brazil's economy boosts broader**. But it's not just about money. There's (8) **wide for support festival the** because (9) **it together people brings** and helps (10) **create a of pride sense** in the country. Many of the Samba schools are from the poorest neighborhoods in the city, and the festival (11) **opportunities to offers young people part take** in cultural activities and learn new skills. In many ways, the festival has (12) **put map on the Rio** as a world city and cultural hotspot.

❸ Listen to the summary. Check your answers in Activity 2. 🎧 **15**

❹ Complete the sentences with six different cultural attractions you know of. Then work in pairs and share your ideas.

1 _____ is held every year.
2 _____ attracts a lot of tourists to our area.
3 _____ has had a big impact on our country.
4 _____ brings people together.
5 _____ has very wide support.
6 I'd like to get involved in _____ .

❺ Work as a class. Use the words and phrases in bold from Activity 2 to talk about the places and events you thought of in Activity 1.

We have a music venue near where we live. The promoters put on a lot of small concerts and parties.

❻ MY PERSPECTIVE

Work in pairs. Discuss the question.

What other benefits can you think of that are related to cultural attractions and events? Think about the benefits to you, your town, and your country.

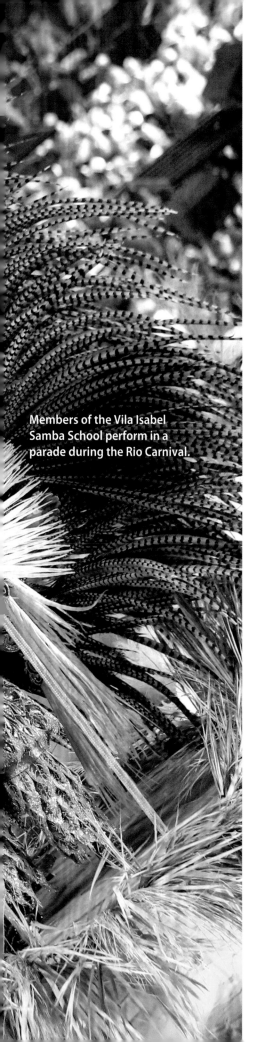

Members of the Vila Isabel Samba School perform in a parade during the Rio Carnival.

LISTENING

7 Work in groups. Look at the photo and discuss the questions.

1 Where do you think the photo was taken?
2 What has been done to the building? Why?
3 Do you like it? Why?
4 Have you ever seen anything similar? Where?

8 Listen to a podcast about two big art projects aiming to make a difference. What are the plans for these places? 🎧 16

1 Port-au-Prince, Haiti   2 Birmingham, UK

9 Work in pairs. Do the speakers mention these points in reference to *Port-au-Prince*, *Birmingham*, or *both*. Listen again and check your answers. 🎧 16

1 The project is based on previous work.
2 The project aims to improve the local economy.
3 The project is initially expensive.
4 Local people are involved in creating the work of art.
5 Other things are being built as well.
6 It will bring people together.
7 It may be difficult to keep the art in good condition.
8 There might be an alternative that costs less.

10 MY PERSPECTIVE

Think about your community. What would you choose if you had to decide between the two public art projects and Mark's suggestion of putting on a local festival? Why?

GRAMMAR Future forms 1

11 Look at the Grammar box. Why do you think the forms in bold are used in each sentence?

Future forms

a *And in Haiti, the project **is certainly going to create** jobs, and it'll be employing local artists.*

b *I guess that work **won't last**, but I think the locals are hoping the project **will attract** interest in the area.*

c *The piece should be low maintenance, so they **won't be spending** thousands of pounds every year to keep it in good condition.*

d *What about once it**'s been completed**?*

e *What'll happen when the paint **fades**?*

f *We**'re about to put on** a community arts festival.*

g *We**'re holding** various shows and events over a week.*

h *You can continue the discussion on the Arts Spot website and get information on Mark's festival, which **starts** soon.*

Check the Grammar Reference for more information and practice.

12 Match each explanation of how to create future forms with an extract in the Grammar box. There are two extracts for one of the explanations.

1 The simple present is used to refer to a scheduled or regular event.
2 The simple present or present perfect is used because it follows a time word.
3 The present continuous is used because they are talking about an arrangement they have made with other people.

With the help of Haas and Hahn, members of a Caribbean community came together to transform a part of their community.

4 *Will* + infinitive is used because they are making predictions about the future they are certain about.

5 The future continuous is used because they are talking about an ongoing or unfinished future action.

6 *Be about to* + verb is used to talk about something which is going to happen in the very near future but has not started yet.

7 *Be going to* + verb is used because they are making a prediction. *Going to* can also be used to talk about arrangements and scheduled events.

13 Choose the correct options.

Our town (1) *holds / is going to hold* a festival next year for the total solar eclipse. There (2) *will be being / are going to be* some small events in the week before the eclipse (3) *takes / is taking* place, like talks and music. On the actual day, the eclipse is expected early in the morning, so we (4) *are about to put on / are putting on* a concert with some local bands as the sun (5) *rises / will rise*. After the concert (6) *has ended / will end*, we're going to have a huge breakfast barbecue to prepare for the big event. It should be great! A lot of people (7) *will be coming to / come to* the area next year to catch the eclipse, so we (8) *will hopefully get / are hopefully getting* a few visitors here, although that's not the main reason for putting on the event. We're really doing it because we want to bring people together, and it's not like we (9) *will be spending / spend* thousands of dollars on it. If (10) *it's going to be / it will be* a success, we'll need lots of volunteers.

14 How many times can you complete the sentences so that they are correct and true? Compare with a partner and see who got the most.

1 I'm _____ next weekend.
2 I'm going to _____ after _____ .
3 There's about to be _____ in our town.

4 I will be _____ , so I can _____ .
5 Next semester, _____ .
6 In five years' time, _____ .

15 Work in pairs. Make a list of at least four ideas for pieces of art, cultural events, or festivals for your community.

16 Work with another pair of students. Compare the ideas you came up with in Activity 15. Discuss which you think would:

- be the most fun.
- be best at bringing the whole community together.
- do most to boost the local economy.
- have the longest lasting impact.
- be the most difficult to organize.

17 Work in the same groups. Choose one of your ideas. Discuss more about the details of the project. Use future forms. Think about:

- the venue.
- how long it will take to set up and how long it will last.
- who will take part.
- who will organize it (professionals / volunteers).
- how much it will cost.
- how you will raise the money.
- any permission you will need.
- how to get people to support the project.
- anything else you think might be important.

18 Present your ideas to the class. Vote for your favorite.

4B Music to Their Ears

A SYSTEM THAT'S LEADING THE WAY

Gustavo Dudamel is the musical director of the Venezuelan Youth Orchestra.

VOCABULARY BUILDING

Adjective and noun collocations 2

It is a good idea to notice and learn adjective-noun collocations. When you learn them, consider how they might be used. Think about:

- what verbs or phrases go with the collocation.

*give an **individual performance** / get a mark for your **individual performance***

- examples from real life.

*We have to work in groups, but we get a mark for our **individual performance**.*

1 Work in pairs. Look at these adjective-noun collocations. Take turns explaining what each one means. Use a dictionary, if necessary.

diverse social backgrounds	fierce ambition
hard work	innovative program
leading orchestra	low income
mixed results	private companies
straightforward process	strict set of rules

2 Work in pairs. Put the collocations in Activity 1 in pairs and say how they might be linked together.

fierce ambition / private companies

To get to the top of a private company, you need fierce ambition.

READING

3 Read about *El Sistema*, a program for teaching music. Put the sentences in the correct places in the article. There is one extra sentence that you do not need to use.

- **a** It has also been credited with improving relations between different communities and saving many children from getting involved in gangs and violence.
- **b** Obviously, the resources that the Venezuelan government puts into *El Sistema* are important.
- **c** Central to *El Sistema* is a focus on discipline and commitment.
- **d** Abreu was also a politician and a minister in the government.
- **e** However, it seems that there are always individuals whose lives are changed.

🎧 17 JOSE ANTONIO ABREU trained and worked as an economist for many years, but his dream was to have a life in music. He fulfilled that dream, first through individual performance, but later, and more importantly, by founding *El Sistema*. *El Sistema* is an innovative program for teaching music to children from diverse social backgrounds. It has been so successful that an orchestra that is part of the program, the Venezuelan National Youth Orchestra, has been named among the five leading orchestras in the world. (1) _____ .

When he first started the orchestra, Abreu had managed to get 50 music stands for the 100 children he was expecting to come and rehearse. In the end, only 11 showed up. What was he going to do? Give up? Try to get more children involved? In fact, he went several steps further, and promised those 11 students that he would turn the orchestra into a world leader! So apart from this fierce ambition, how did it happen?

(2) _____ . It pays for instruments and teaching for over 500,000 young musicians who are involved in the program and also provides monthly grants to older students as a reward for their hard work. It also pays for performances and teaching younger children in the program. Private companies often sponsor local groups and parents also raise funds for tours.

However, money is not the only factor in its success. (3) _____ . New students can start from as young as three, but students and their parents must agree to a strict set of rules and attend classes and rehearsals for between one and four hours a day, up to six days a week. Teachers may visit parents to help them understand the hours required to improve and how to support their children.

While discipline is important, the musical training also emphasizes fun, team spirit, physical expression, and the value of performance. Students start in a choir and work on rhythm and percussion, before moving on to playing the recorder, and then finally choosing their instrument at the age of seven. (4) _____ .

El Sistema is seen by many people from low-income families as a way to stay in education and escape poverty. It can present opportunities to travel via tours within Venezuela and abroad. (5) _____ . No wonder many other countries have looked to copy the program.

Setting up a "sistema" is not a straightforward process, and there have been mixed results. (6) _____ . As one parent from the Scottish Sistema put it, "My son was struggling, and I was worried he was going to drop out of school and end up hanging out with the wrong kids. *El Sistema* has made a huge difference. He's gained confidence, learned discipline, and he's definitely back on track."

f Yet, 40 years ago, such an idea seemed a long way off.

g Lessons are mainly conducted as a group, with all the class working towards performing a piece in front of an audience.

4 Read about *El Sistema* again. Answer the questions.

1 How many children went to Abreu's first rehearsal? How many participate now?

2 How old are children when they choose a musical instrument?

3 How much do they practice?

4 Why do other countries like *El Sistema*?

5 Work in pairs. Discuss the questions.

1 Have you ever learned how to play a musical instrument? How good were / are you?

2 If you gave up playing a musical instrument, why?

3 If you still play a musical instrument, how much do you practice? Do you ever perform?

4 What kind of music do you listen to? What do you like about it?

6 Work in pairs. Look at the adjective-noun collocations in Activity 1 again. Tell each other what was said about them in the article. Check your answers.

CRITICAL THINKING Understanding and evaluating ideas

If you want to copy a successful idea or make use of what you have learned in a new context, you need to understand all the factors that made the idea a success and evaluate how far they can be applied in a new context.

7 Work in groups. Discuss the different factors you read about that help make *El Sistema* a success.

8 Work as a class. Discuss:

1 Are all the factors you discussed in Activity 7 possible in your country? Why?

2 Are there any factors that you think are not necessary? Why?

3 Would *El Sistema* work in your country? Why?

9 MY PERSPECTIVE

Would you like to participate in a program like *El Sistema*? Why?

The Guggenheim Museum contributed to the "Bilbao Effect."

4C High Hopes

GRAMMAR Future forms 2

❶ Look at the Grammar box. Then look at the sentences in each set. Which sentence in each set does not show the future in the past?

a *was / were going to*
   1 Before the election, the mayor said he **was going to** make changes.
   2 I **was going to** enter a painting competition but didn't finish in time.
   3 I fell asleep in the car when we **were going to** the gallery.

b *would*
   1 I **would** really like to go to the Edinburgh Festival next year.
   2 They thought it **would** bring a lot of investments into the city.
   3 If we did more cultural activities here, I'm sure we **would** attract more tourists.

c *was / were* + **present participle**
   1 The show **was starting** in a matter of minutes, so we had to rush.
   2 I couldn't hear the movie because the people behind me **were talking**.
   3 I only bought two tickets because I thought your brother **wasn't coming**.

> ### The future in the past
>
> **a** *My son was struggling, and I was worried he **was going to** drop out of school and end up hanging out with the wrong kids.*
>
> **b** *He went several steps further and promised those 11 students that he **would** turn the orchestra into a world leader!*
>
> **c** *Abreu had managed to get 50 music stands for the 100 children he thought **were coming** to rehearse.*

Check the Grammar Reference for more information and practice.

❷ Complete the first parts of the sentences using *was / were going to* and these verbs. Then match them with the second parts of the sentences.

be	cost	get	hold	play	rain

   1 They said the building _____ something like $35 million,
   2 The forecast did say it _____ a bit,
   3 We _____ tickets for the concert next month,
   4 They told us the band _____ on stage around nine,
   5 I thought they _____ all their hits,
   6 When they announced they _____ the World Cup here,

   a but they just played loads of new stuff. They were absolutely terrible.
   b but it literally sold out in seconds. I couldn't believe it.
   c loads of people were actually against it.
   d but it cost way more than that.
   e but we had to wait for hours. It must've been midnight before they came on.
   f but it just poured all day.

❸ **PRONUNCIATION** Contrastive stress

   a Listen to how the quantity words in the second part of the sentences are stressed to emphasize the contrast with previous plans or predictions. 🎧 18
   b Practice saying the complete sentences from Activity 2.

4 Read about the Bilbao Effect. What is it? Which of the italicized parts are grammatically incorrect? Correct them.

By the 1990s, the city of Bilbao in northern Spain was no longer the industrial center it once was and the future (1) *was looking* bleak. It was hard to see how new jobs (2) *was going to be* created or what could be done to ensure things (3) *improve*. Local authorities decided to invest over $1 billion in the hope that a new focus on culture (4) *would attract* visitors. The money (5) *was going to be spent* on transportation, bridges, parks, libraries, and the remarkable Guggenheim Museum, designed by Frank Gehry. Once people saw what the building (6) *was looking like*, excitement grew. When it opened, the authorities (7) *were expecting* around 300,000 visitors in the first year, but by the end of that year it had attracted a million! The impact on the city has been even more dramatic than people hoped it (8) *was*, so it's no wonder other cities are now desperate to copy what has become known as the "Bilbao Effect"!

5 MY PERSPECTIVE

Think of three possible reasons why the "Bilbao Effect" might not work in another city.

6 Listen to three people describing cultural events they went to. Answer the questions. 🎧 **19**

1 What event did each person go to?
2 How did they feel about it? Why?

7 Think of places or cultural events you have been to. Plan what you want to say, using the language below. Then share your experiences in groups.

It was much / way… than I thought it would be.

I wasn't expecting it to be very…, but it was actually…

It was nowhere near as good as I was expecting.

I was expecting it to be pretty… but it was actually very…

8 Work in pairs. Look at the Grammar box. Answer the questions.

1 What is the form of the future perfect? What is the form of the future perfect continuous?
2 Which form do we use to emphasize the duration of an activity before a certain point in the future?
3 Which form do we use to emphasize completed actions by a certain point?
4 Which word shows a point in the future?

The future perfect

Use the future perfect to show the time in the future by which something will be complete.

*It **will** soon **have been running** for 70 years, and over 10 million people **will have seen** it.*

Check the Grammar Reference for more information and practice.

9 Complete the sentences with the future perfect or future perfect continuous form of the verb.

1 By the end of next year, the band _____ (play) together for 30 years!
2 By the end of this course, I _____ (study) English for ten whole years!
3 I can't talk now. I'll call you after five. I _____ (finish) school by then.
4 He's originally from Peru, but by June he _____ (live) in Canada for ten years.
5 This museum _____ soon _____ (be) open for a whole century.

10 CHOOSE Choose one of the following activities.

- Find out about a new development in your town or country. Why was it built? Has it been a success?
- List ten things that will have happened in your life by the time you are 30. Then work in pairs. Which are the most or least likely to happen?

The Zubizuri (Basque for "white bridge") stretches across the Nervion River in Bilbao.

can have to transform how people experience their city and interact with each other. "

ROBERT HAMMOND

Read about Robert Hammond and get ready to watch his TED Talk. ▶ **4.0**

AUTHENTIC LISTENING SKILLS

Recognizing words you know

Sometimes you may not recognize words in fast speech because you expect to hear the full form. For example, in a dictionary *with* is shown as /wɪθ/, but in fast speech it may sound more like /wɪ/.

1 Look at the Authentic Listening Skills box. Then listen and complete the extracts from the TED Talk. 🎧 **20**

1 And by 1980, the last train rode. It was a train
_____ .

2 I first read about it in the *New York Times*, in an article
_____ demolished.

3 And _____ we were the only two people that were sort of interested in the project.

4 And that's really where we started… the idea coalesced around… let's make this a park, and
_____ this wildscape.

2 Listen to the extracts again. Which of the words were the most difficult to hear? 🎧 **20**

3 Say each sentence twice, slowly the first time—with a gap between each word—then faster, linking the words in each part of the sentences together.

WATCH

4 Work in pairs. Discuss the questions.

1 Where you live, are there any old buildings, industrial places, or pieces of land that are no longer used? Do you know when or why they stopped being used?

2 Do you know of any old buildings or places that used to be used for one purpose, but are now used for a different purpose? Do you like the change?

3 What's your favorite public space? Why? How often do you go there?

5 Watch Part 1 of the talk. Choose the correct options. ▶ **4.1**

1 In the old days, the freight line trains:
a used cowboys to protect the goods they were carrying.
b were pulled by horses.
c caused several fatal accidents.

2 As time went by:
a more freight started being transported by road.
b the line was mainly used to transport meat.
c people in the neighborhood wanted it demolished.

3 At the community board meeting, Robert:
a offered to volunteer to help preserve the High Line.
b realized he was in a small minority.
c knew a writer from the *New York Times*.

4 The main inspiration for the project came from:
a the spectacular views of Manhattan.
b the industrial architecture of the line.
c the way nature had started reclaiming the abandoned space.

6 Watch Part 2 of the talk. Why were the following mentioned? ▶ **4.2**

1 9/11
2 100 million
3 20 years and 250 million
4 half a billion
5 three

7 Work in groups. Robert Hammond explains that a special study was designed to show whether the High Line would add value to the city. Discuss:

- how the creation of a park on the High Line might add value to the local area.
- how demolishing the High Line might add value to the area.
- who you think would benefit most in each case—and which plan of action is better.

8 Watch Part 3. Are the sentences *true* or *false*? ▶ 4.3

1 Twice as many people as expected used the High Line last year.
2 Architects have taken inspiration from the High Line.
3 Some parts of the High Line have been elevated to a higher level.
4 Robert Hammond doesn't really like the design.
5 He believes the space encourages people to behave in ways they wouldn't normally.

9 **VOCABULARY IN CONTEXT**

a Watch the clips from the TED Talk. Choose the correct meanings of the words and phrases. ▶ 4.4

b Work in pairs. Discuss the questions.
1 What different ways of reducing the number of people who get *run over* can you think of?
2 What problems might arise if ancient *relics* are found in a construction area?
3 Who do you usually talk to if you need to *figure out* what to do about a problem? Why?

4 Which ideas do you think your town or city would really *get behind*? Why?
- Free art gallery and museum entrance for everyone
- Spending more money on public art
- Official areas for young people to put up street art
- Free art materials for all schoolchildren
- Displaying work by local poets on public transportation

CHALLENGE

Work in pairs. Make a list of all the activities you think Friends of the High Line had to do at each stage to transform the abandoned rail line into a park.
Think about:

- events and meetings.   • money.
- people.   • the law.

Work with another pair of students. Then use some of the phrases below to discuss:

- what personal qualities are needed to help change a neighborhood in this way.
- which of these qualities you think you have.
- how you could develop these kinds of qualities and skills.

I think you'd need to be very … if you were going to …

You'd have to be a very … kind of person if you wanted to …

I'd like to think I'm fairly …

I'd be lying if I said I was …

The best way to get better at … would be to …

4E What's the plan?

Making suggestions

Do you feel like going to…?

I was wondering if you'd like to go to…?

Rejecting suggestions

To be honest, it's not really my kind of thing.

Doesn't really sound like my kind of thing, I'm afraid.

Suggesting alternatives

OK. Well, in that case, how about going to…?

OK. Well, if you'd rather, we could always go to…

SPEAKING

1 Choose the options that are true for you. Then work in pairs and explain your choices.

1 I usually go out to meet friends *four or five times a week / two or three times a week / maybe once a week*.

2 I *hardly ever / sometimes / often* go out with my parents.

3 I prefer going out *alone / with one or two close friends / with a big group*.

4 When it comes to deciding where and when to meet, *I let other people decide / we generally try to reach a group decision / I basically like to take charge*.

5 I mostly like going to *the same place / different kinds of places*.

6 When I go out with friends, *I like to plan everything in advance / I'm happy to just go with the flow and see what happens*.

7 I *often / rarely / never* go to cultural events like concerts, exhibits, and plays.

2 Listen to two friends making plans. Answer the questions. 🎧 21

1 What different cultural events do they mention?

2 What do they decide to do in the end?

3 Why are the other ideas rejected?

4 Where and when do they arrange to meet? Why?

3 Listen to the two friends again. Complete the sentences by adding two or three words in each blank. 🎧 21

1 I was wondering. Do you _____ somewhere with me tomorrow?

2 Where did you have _____ ? Anywhere in particular?

3 OK. What _____ is it? I'm not really into art, so…

4 How about _____ this band that are playing in the park tomorrow night?

5 What about just going to see a film? Would you be _____ that?

6 Let's _____ the later one—but meet a little bit earlier.

7 I'll book tickets _____—just to _____ .

4 Work in pairs. Make plans to go to a cultural event. Make sure you:

- use real places or events that are local to you.
- reject at least one suggestion and explain why.
- arrange where and when to meet.
- use language from Activity 3 and the Useful language box.

Some festivals and events that attract a lot of people like this color run sometimes require a large cleanup operation.

WRITING A *for* and *against* essay

5 Work in pairs. Look at this essay title. Think of two reasons why you might agree with the statement in the title, and two reasons why you might disagree.

Building a new museum would boost tourism in the area and benefit the whole community

6 Read the essay on page 150. Does the writer agree with the statement in the essay title? Why?

7 WRITING SKILL Introducing arguments

Work in pairs. Look at the essay on page 150 again. Use the Writing strategy box to identify each of the three stages of the introduction. Answer the questions.

1 How does the writer stress the importance of the subject?
2 What phrase is used to introduce an opposing point of view?
3 How does the writer signal a disagreement?

8 Complete the sentences, which give a weak argument, with these words.

believed	claimed	common	seen	sometimes	supposedly

1 It is _____ said that art is a mirror of society. In fact,...
2 Creativity _____ belongs to the world of the arts. In reality, though,...
3 It is widely _____ that music can help to connect young people from different backgrounds. However,...
4 It is often _____ that comedy works best when it's cruel. However,...
5 Museums are sometimes _____ as being of no interest to young people. However,...
6 One _____ argument against more focus on the arts in schools is that they do not make students more employable. In reality,...

9 Work in pairs. Complete the second sentences in Activity 8 to show how each of the arguments could be seen as weak.

10 Choose one of the options and write a *for* and *against* essay of 250 words.

a Argue the opposite point of view to the student essay you read on page 150.
b Write an essay on one of these titles:
What our city needs is a big new concert hall
We should not host a festival because the cleanup is too expensive
New technologies have had a very negative effect on our cultural lives

Writing strategy

Opening paragraph

When writing the opening paragraph of a *for* and *against* essay:

- show the reader you know why the subject is relevant.
- give what you feel is a weak argument or point of view.
- say why you disagree and give your own opinion.

Useful language

Showing relevance

Over recent years,... has become increasingly important.

...is getting better and better / worse and worse at the moment.

Over the last few years, there has been a dramatic increase / drop in...

Introduce an opposing view

It is sometimes said that...
It is often claimed that...

Say why we disagree

...but, in fact,...
In reality, though,...
However,...

5 It's Not Rocket Science

Taylor Wilson is the youngest person ever to produce a type of energy called *nuclear fusion*. He did it by building a reactor in his parents' garage.

5A Life Hacks

VOCABULARY Science in action

1 Work in groups. Discuss the questions.

1 In what ways has science made life easier or better in your lifetime?
2 Can you think of two mysteries science has yet to solve?
3 Which scientists have you heard of? Why are they famous?
4 What personal qualities are most important if you want to be a scientist? Why?

2 Work in pairs. Do you understand the words in bold? Use a dictionary, if necessary.

1 **design** an experiment
2 **conduct** research
3 **form** a hypothesis and **prove** it
4 **put** a substance in water and **heat** it **up** to help it **dissolve**
5 **create** a chemical reaction that **releases** a gas
6 **track** students' progress
7 **record** the results of an experiment and **analyze** them
8 **write** a report and **add** references at the end
9 **place** something under a microscope
10 **reward** hard work
11 **get rid of** a chemical
12 **submit** an assignment

3 Work in pairs. Do the actions in Activity 2 happen in your science classes at school? Who does each activity? Give examples.

We don't really design experiments at school. We just follow the ones in the textbook or do what the teacher tells us to do.

4 Complete the phrases. Add verbs from Activity 2 that are commonly used with each set of words.

1 …a theory / …an opinion
2 …samples / …the results
3 …an operation / …a survey
4 …chemicals into the atmosphere / …an animal
5 …an essay / …it before the deadline
6 …their effort / …her for her work
7 …the movement of birds / …your progress

5 Work in pairs. Compare your answers in Activity 4. Then think of one more word or phrase to go with each verb. Use a dictionary, if necessary.

6 Look again at your completed phrases in Activity 4. Who might perform each action? Why?

7 MY PERSPECTIVE

Work in groups. Discuss the questions.

1 What science experiments have you done at school that you enjoyed?
2 Have you ever designed an experiment yourself? If yes, what for? If no, why not? What experiment would you like to design?

LISTENING

8 Work in pairs. Read the definition. Then tell each other any life hacks you know for:

1 smartphones.
2 computers / computer games.
3 the home.
4 food and drink.

Life hack /laɪf hæk/ *noun* [countable]
A simple solution or a piece of advice that helps you solve a problem, save time, or improve how something works.

9 Listen to an extract from a radio show called *Life Hacks*. Answer the questions. 🎧 22

1 What four life hacks are mentioned?
2 What problems do the life hacks help solve?

10 Correct the false information in each sentence. Then listen again to check your ideas. 🎧 22

1 Marie bought herself a phone for her birthday.
2 Marie's a morning person.
3 It's best to put the paper cup right next to your bed.
4 The cup throws the sound around the room.
5 The app alters your sleep patterns.
6 Phones can be charged faster on airplanes.
7 Spicy food increases the temperature in your mouth.
8 The chemical in chilies is easily dissolved with water.

11 Complete the extracts with three words in each blank. Then listen again to check. 🎧 22

1 Well, I _____ this lovely new smartphone.

2 And of course it works better as an alarm if the cup _____ far away from your bed, as then _____ to get up to turn it off.
3 The cup channels the sound in one direction, whereas normally _____ around all over the place.
4 _____ to track your sleep patterns and wake you up during light sleep rather than deep.
5 If your _____ and you need it done ASAP, then what you need to do is put it in airplane mode.
6 An email has _____ to me by Maxine, who's suggested a hack for anyone out there who likes a spicy curry from time to time.

12 MY PERSPECTIVE

Which of the four life hacks do you think is:

• the most useful? the least? Why?
• the easiest to understand from a scientific point of view? the hardest? Why?

GRAMMAR Passives 1

13 Work in groups. Look at the Grammar box. Then answer the questions.

1 What tense are each of the passive forms in Activity 11?
2 Why is the passive used in each case?
3 Identify the object(s) in the sentences in the Grammar box. Are the objects direct or indirect? What do they refer to?

The passive

The passive is made by using a form of the verb *be* + past participle.

a *I was recently given this lovely new smartphone.*
b *An email has just been sent to me by Maxine.*

Check the Grammar Reference for more information and practice.

14 Complete the blog entry with the correct passive forms.

If you're making a list of the most important inventions ever, the internet should (1) _____ (place) right at the top! Our lives (2) _____ completely _____ (transform) since the first web page (3) _____ (create) in 1990. It could even (4) _____ (say) that the internet is the ultimate life hack! Of course, various linked systems of computers (5) _____ (use) for some time before the birth of the world wide web, and early versions of what was to become the web (6) _____ regularly _____ (test) throughout the 1970s and 80s. Today, though, it's rare to meet someone who has no interest in (7) _____ (connect). For many young people, that means more than 20 hours a week online! Indeed, the internet has become so essential to our lives that some argue it is like air, and that everyone should (8) _____ (give) free access to it.

15 PRONUNCIATION Stress in passives

When using the passive, greater stress is placed on the main verb and less stress is placed on the auxiliary verb.

a Look at the completed blog entry in Activity 14. Which word is stressed in each passive construction?
b Work in pairs. Practice reading the blog entry in Activity 14 with the correct stress.

16 Work in pairs. Discuss the questions.

1 Do you agree that the internet is the most important invention ever? Why?
2 What other inventions would you put near the top of the list? Why?

17 Underline the passives in the descriptions. Can you name the things described?

1 The name is taken from Tagalog, a language that's spoken in the Philippines, where it was used as a weapon for hundreds of years. It was first produced as a toy in California in the 1920s.
2 It is thought that it was first produced in Mocha, Yemen, over a thousand years ago. It's now consumed all over the world—particularly in the morning.
3 It was first invented in Ancient China over 2,000 years ago for use in government, but wasn't introduced into Europe until the 11th century.
4 You've probably been asked to type letters into one of these when using the web. They're used to prevent spam and were invented by TED speaker Luis Von Ahn from Guatemala.

18 Work in pairs. Write a description of something like in Activity 17. Use the passive. Then work with another pair of students. Can they correctly guess what is being described?

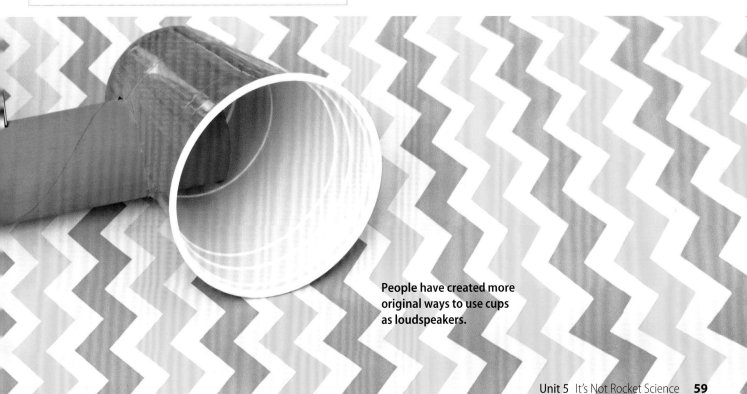

People have created more original ways to use cups as loudspeakers.

5B Curiosity, Cats, and Kids

VOCABULARY BUILDING

Adjective endings

Adjectives can sometimes be recognized by their endings. Common adjective endings include:

-ous: curious, tremendous, previous

-able: reliable, treatable, adaptable

-ive: effective, innovative, imaginative

-ful: beautiful, hopeful, helpful

-al: practical, electrical, social

1 Work in pairs. Think of a noun that each adjective in the Vocabulary Building box often goes with. Use a dictionary, if necessary.

2 Choose four pairs of words from Activity 1. Write a sentence for each pair.

*Research needs to have **practical applications**.*

3 Choose the correct options.

It is often thought that (1) *innovation / innovative* in science comes from the labor of (2) *curiosity / curious* geniuses: the kinds of individuals who work in isolation, find (3) *pleasure / pleasurable* in exploration, and who don't worry too much about the (4) *practicality / practical* applications of their findings. While it is true that the (5) *use / useful* of many new discoveries is not always immediately clear, you only have to look at the results of scientific work conducted by teams to see that it is a (6) *social / society* process and involves far more (7) *cooperation / cooperative* than is often imagined. (8) *Collaborative / Collaboration* can not only help to speed up scientific work; it can also enhance the quality of the work and help share knowledge amongst a wider group of individuals.

4 MY PERSPECTIVE

Work in pairs. Answer the questions.

1 What are the advantages and disadvantages for scientists or researchers working on their own, as part of a small team, and in a much bigger team?

2 How do you prefer to work? Why?

READING

5 Read the article about curiosity. Which sentence is the best summary of the main point?

a Technology can help us become more curious, but it can also kill our curiosity.

b It's more important than ever to make sure kids learn to be curious.

c Social media doesn't help us know people better.

d We run the risk of becoming less curious if we're not careful.

6 Work in pairs. Which statements do you think the writer would likely agree and disagree with? Refer to the article to explain why.

1 Parents should make sure kids don't experiment too much.

2 You can't create anything new unless you recognize the limits of your understanding.

3 The people funding scientific research should demand clear outcomes.

4 Humans are basically programmed to ask why.

5 You don't get a full picture of people from the way they present themselves online.

6 We need to share ideas with like-minded people if we are to develop our curiosity.

7 Work in groups. Do you agree with the statements in Activity 6? Why?

CRITICAL THINKING Asking critical questions

To check ideas and deepen understanding, ask questions about statements or research. For example:

Research has shown that curiosity is just as important as intelligence in determining how well students do at school.

The starting points for thinking critically about this statement might be:

How is student success measured? In what subjects?

How are curiosity and intelligence measured? How different are they?

Can you be intelligent without being curious, and vice versa?

Can you be successful at school without one of these characteristics?

Is curiosity important for doing well in a job? What kind of jobs?

8 Work in pairs. What are two questions you would ask if you wanted to think critically about each statement?

1 Hard work is more important for success than either curiosity or intelligence.

2 There is some evidence that bees can think like humans.

3 It has been shown that you can only learn seven words in a language lesson.

9 Compare your ideas in Activity 8. How many of the questions can you already answer? What is the best question to explore each statement?

Back to the future?

Curiosity allows us to embrace unfamiliar circumstances, brings excitement into our lives, and opens up new possibilities. But how curious are we in the 21st century?

🎧 **23** Perhaps you've heard the old saying "curiosity killed the cat." It's a phrase that's often used to warn people—especially children—not to ask too many questions. Yet it's widely agreed that curiosity actually makes learning more
5 enjoyable and effective. In fact, research has shown that curiosity is just as important as intelligence in determining how well students do in school.

Curiosity also allows us to embrace unfamiliar circumstances, brings excitement into our lives, and opens up new
10 possibilities. Being curious requires us to be both humble enough to know we don't have all the answers, and confident enough to admit it. Asking the questions that help us bridge the gap between what we already know and what we'd like to know can lead us to make unexpected discoveries.

15 In science, basic curiosity-driven research—conducted without pressure to produce immediate practical results—can have unexpected and incredibly important benefits. For example, one day in 1831, Michael Faraday was playing around with a coil and a magnet when he suddenly saw
20 how he could generate an electrical current. At first, it wasn't clear what use this would have, but it actually made electricity available for use in technology, and so changed the world.

Unsurprisingly, there are chemical and evolutionary theories
25 to explain why humans are such curious creatures. When we become curious, our brains release a chemical called dopamine, which makes the process of learning more pleasurable and improves memory. It is still not known why learning gives us such pleasure, but one theory is that we
30 may have developed a basic need to fight uncertainty—the more we understand about the world around us, the more likely we are to survive its many dangers!

However, curiosity is currently under threat like never before—and perhaps the biggest threat comes from
35 technology. On one level, this is because technology has become so sophisticated that many of us are unable to think too deeply about how exactly things work anymore. While it may be possible for a curious teenager to take a toaster apart and get some sense of how it works, how much do
40 you understand about what happens when you type a website address into a browser? Where does your grasp of technology end and the magic begin for you?

In addition to this, there's the fact that we all now connect so deeply with technology, particularly with our phones.
45 The more we stare at our screens, the less we talk to other people directly. To make matters worse, all too often we accept the images of people that social media provides us with, and then feel we know enough about a person not to need to engage further with them.

50 The final—and perhaps most worrying—way in which technology stops us from asking more has to do with algorithms, the processes followed by computers. As we increasingly get our news via social media, algorithms find out what we like and push more of the same back to us,
55 meaning that we end up inside our own little bubbles, no longer coming across ideas that challenge our pre-existing beliefs. Perhaps the real key to developing curiosity in the 21st century, then, is to rely less on the tech tools of our age.

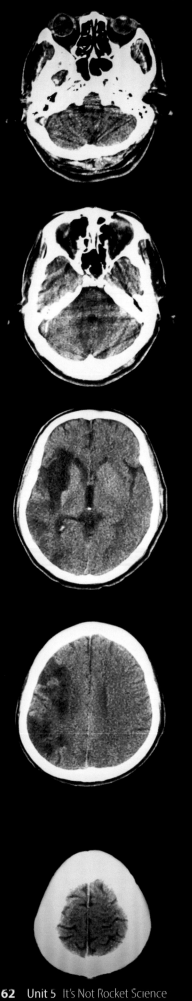

5C Mind-blowing!

GRAMMAR Passives 2

1 Work in groups. Look at the Grammar box. Do you believe the sentences are true? Explain why using these phrases.

I'm absolutely sure.
I'm not sure but, if I had to guess, I'd say…
I read about it recently. / We did it in class.
I remember hearing about it.
I've got a feeling it's a myth / it's a trick question.

Passive reporting verbs

a *The heart was believed to be the center of intelligence until the Middle Ages.*
b *It is claimed that computer training programs can limit the effects of aging on the brain.*
c *Einstein's brain was said to be bigger than average, which explains his intelligence.*
d *It is estimated that the human brain is about 75 percent water.*
e *It is well known that most of the time we only use ten percent of our brain capacity.*
f *Exercising is thought to create chemicals that reduce your ability to think.*
g *The part of the brain called the hippocampus is known to be connected with our sense of direction.*
h *It has been generally accepted that creative people have a dominant right brain.*

Check the Grammar Reference for more information and practice.

2 Listen and find out which sentences in the Grammar box are true. How many did you get right? 🎧 **24**

3 Work in pairs. Look at the Grammar box again and:

1 identify the whole passive reporting pattern in the sentences that begin with *It*.
2 identify the form of the verb that follows the passive forms in sentences that do not begin with *It*.
3 discuss what you notice about the different patterns.

4 Write sentences about the brain using these notes and the passive.

1 The brain / estimate / contain…around 12 percent fat.

The brain is estimated to contain around 12 percent fat.

2 It / once / think / the brain / become…fully mature by the time children were six.
3 The brain / now / know / develop…most during the teenage years.
4 It / once / believe / the brain's networks / become…fixed as we aged.
5 Brain training activities / claim / improve…listening skills and memory.
6 It / sometimes / say / brain size / affect…intelligence.
7 It / still / not really know…why we dream while we sleep.
8 Brain transplants / generally accept / be…impossible.

5 Work as a class. Discuss how you think research into the brain is carried out.

6 Choose the correct options to complete the article about brain research. Does the article cover the ideas you thought of in Activity 5?

Our understanding of the brain has changed with developments in science, surgery, and medical technology. For example, as new technologies were invented, the brain was thought (1) *to be / that it is* like a mechanical watch or telephone communication. More recently, it (2) *has been described / describes* as a computer.

After Galen proved that the brain was the center of intelligence, it was generally assumed that different parts of the brain (3) *to control / controlled* certain senses and functions of the body. However, the brain could only really (4) *understand / be understood* from the outside by studying animal brains and dissecting human bodies. Knowledge increased as a result of surgery where a patient had a tumor removed from their brain and the resulting physical change meant that functions could be mapped to the part of the brain that had been operated on. This mapping came about as much through failed operations as successful ones. Now, operations (5) *sometimes conduct / are sometimes conducted* while the patient is awake and talking. If a part of the brain (6) *touched / is touched* and it affects one of the patient's senses, he or she can tell the surgeon!

Since the late 1970s, medical technology, such as MRI scanning, (7) *has allowed / has been allowed* safe research into the brain without the need for surgery or X-rays. MRI uses powerful magnets and computer imaging to see high blood flows in different parts of the brain that (8) *believe / are believed* to show brain activity. If people (9) *have / is* their brains scanned while doing various thinking activities, researchers think they can (10) *identify / be identified* more accurately how the brain works. One result of this research is to show the limits of the brain-computer comparison. For example, it is now understood that memories are not stored in one place, but are the result of activity in many parts of the brain.

Causative *have* and *get*

a *Scientists can do research into the brain by using scanners.*

b *Research into the brain can be done (by scientists) by using scanners.*

c *To get the research done, scientists used a brain scan.*

Check the Grammar Reference for more information and practice.

Since the late 1970s, medical technology, such as MRI scanning, has allowed safe research into the brain without the need for surgery or X-rays.

7 Look at the Grammar box. Then complete the explanation.

- In the first sentence, _____ is the object of the verb *do*.
- In the second sentence, *research* becomes the _____ of the passive structure *can be done*.
- In the third sentence, we use the structure *get* + something + _____ so we can make the person affected by an action (scientists) the subject of the sentence.

8 Write normal sentences in the passive, based on these sentences.

1 They had their brains scanned while they were singing.
2 The hospital is having a new MRI scanner installed.
3 The scientists had their research evaluated.
4 I'm going to have my examination later.
5 My dad had his head examined when we were in the hospital.

9 Work in pairs. Complete the sentences in as many different ways as you can. Use a dictionary, if necessary.

1 The patient had _____ scanned.
2 I had _____ examined.
3 They should have _____ tested.
4 The scientists are having the laboratory _____ .
5 I'm going to have my injury _____ .
6 The research center is going to have _____ .

10 CHOOSE

Choose one of the following activities.

- Write a set of sentences like the ones in the first Grammar box. Share your facts.

- Discuss ways in which the brain could be compared to:
  – a city.   – a computer.
  – an orchestra.   – a spider's web.

- Write about one of these experiences.
  – a time you had to have something scanned or tested
  – a time something in the news proved to be wrong

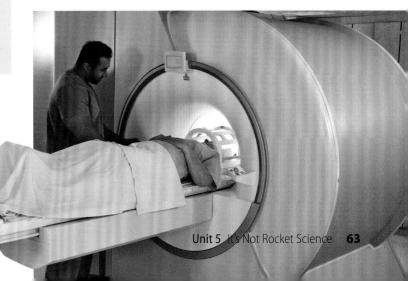

" Play is one of the only human endeavors where uncertainty is actually celebrated. Uncertainty is what makes play fun. *"*

BEAU LOTTO

Read about Beau Lotto and Amy O'Toole and get ready to watch their TED Talk. ▶ **5.0**

AUTHENTIC LISTENING SKILLS

Fillers

You can use words and phrases like *right, all right,* and *you know* to ask for agreement, to check that people are understanding, or as a filler while we pause or move on to the next point.

So, this game is very simple. All you have to do is read what you see. **Right?**

1 Look at the Authentic Listening Skills box. Listen to the extract. Identify where Beau adds *right* or *all right*. 🎧 **25**

What are you reading? There are no words there. I said, read what you're seeing. It literally says, "Wat ar ou rea in?" That's what you should have said. Why is this? It's because perception is grounded in our experience. The brain takes meaningless information and makes meaning out of it, which means we never see what's there, we never see information, we only ever see what was useful to see in the past. Which means, when it comes to perception, we're all like this frog. It's getting information. It's generating behavior that's useful.

2 Practice reading aloud the extract in Activity 1 in a similar style to Beau.

WATCH

3 Work in groups. Discuss the questions.

1 Are you good at science? Why?
2 In what ways do you think science is similar to play?
3 Have you ever asked someone a question about science that they could not answer? What was it?

4 Put the sentences (a–h) in order. The first and last are given.

1 Perception is grounded in our experience.
  a These are the exact same ways of being you need in order to be a good scientist.
  b If perception is grounded in our history, it means we're only ever responding according to what we've done before.
  c Uncertainty is what makes play fun. It opens possibility and it's cooperative.
  d The question "why?" is one of the most dangerous things you can ask, because it takes you into uncertainty.
  e But actually, it's a tremendous problem, because how can we ever see differently?
  f So what is evolution's answer to the problem of uncertainty? It's play.
  g So if you add rules to play, you have a game. That's actually what an experiment is.
  h Now… all new perceptions begin in the same way. They begin with a question.
10 So armed with these two ideas—that science is a way of being and experiments are play—we asked, can anyone become a scientist?

5 Watch Part 1 of the talk. Check your order of the sentences in Activity 4. ▶ **5.1**

6 What does Beau not mention when he talks about uncertainty making play fun?

a Play is adaptable to change.
b Play is cooperative.
c Play opens up possibility.
d Play is unrewarding.

TEDTALKS

7 Watch Part 2 of the talk. Are the sentences *true, false,* or *not stated*? ▶ 5.2

1 None of the questions the children thought of had ever been studied before.
2 The children wanted to research if bees adapt their behavior to solve problems like humans do.
3 Bees are one of the most intelligent insects.
4 The experiment required bees to recognize the correct color to get a reward.
5 There were several ways for the bees to solve the puzzle the children set up.
6 The results of the experiment were surprising.
7 Beau wrote the journal article.
8 The paper was rejected by the publisher because it was written in the wrong style.

8 Watch Part 3 of the talk. Answer the questions. ▶ 5.3

1 How did the research finally get published?
2 What was the reaction to the research?
3 What were two lessons that Amy learned?

9 Amy says that changing the way a person thinks about something can be easy or hard. Explain why you think it would be easy or hard to change the way people think about:

• what they eat.
• what they watch on TV.
• where they shop.

10 MY PERSPECTIVE

Did the TED Talk change your views about science and scientists at all? In what way?

11 VOCABULARY IN CONTEXT

a Watch the clips from the TED Talk. Choose the correct meanings of the words and phrases. ▶ 5.4

b Work in pairs. Talk about:
• a time you received a *reward* for doing something.
• a time you regret *not bothering* to do something.
• an interesting or possible *link* that scientists have discovered in recent times.
• a time you had to *adapt* to a new situation.
• people you think should be given more of *a voice*.

CHALLENGE

Beau and Amy do not explain much about how the experiment worked, apart from showing the one pattern of flowers. Work in groups. Discuss how you would:

• give rewards to bees for going to "good flowers."
• identify which bees are going to which flowers.
• train the bees to learn the pattern of one color surrounded by another.
• check that the bees aren't just "smelling" the good flowers.
• check that the bees aren't just choosing the good flowers by color.
• check that the bees aren't just choosing the flowers in the middle.

Read the paper about Blackawton Bees and see exactly how the children set up the experiment and what they discovered. It's available on the TED website.

5E Conducting Experiments

Useful language

Staging

The first thing we'd need to do is…

We'd also need to make sure that we (didn't)…

I suppose then we should…

Preparing research questions

I wonder if / how / why…

It'd be good to know what / whether…

We'd need to try to figure out…

Hypothesizing

I'd expect the results to show…

I'd imagine that the data would probably reveal…

I would / wouldn't have thought it would be possible to prove that…

SPEAKING

1 Work in pairs. Look at the questions. Discuss why it might be useful to know the answer to each of them. What do you think the answers are?

1 How much does homework improve exam results?
2 Do goldfish only have a ten-second memory?
3 How many words can you learn in an hour?
4 Does going out with wet hair cause colds or the flu?
5 Do boys get more attention in class? If so, why?
6 Are people who listen to pop music happier?
7 What is the quickest way to have people board a plane?

2 Work in groups. If you were going to design an experiment for a question like one of those in Activity 1, what steps would you need to complete?

3 Listen to a short lecture on how to design experiments. Note the six main steps. Then compare your answers with a partner. Use the light bulb experiment to explain each stage. 🎧 26

4 As a class, discuss why you think:

1 certain kinds of hypotheses are easier to prove than others.
2 proving a hypothesis wrong can be an important step towards learning.
3 it's important to record in detail how experiments are set up and conducted.
4 proving a hypothesis right in the way described could be seen as insufficiently scientific.

5 Work in pairs. Design an experiment to:

a find the answer to a question in Activity 1.
b see if one of the life hacks you learned about earlier actually works.
c test another life hack you have heard about.

Use some of the language in the Useful language box. Decide:
• how you would set the experiment up.
• what kind of data you would record.
• what points of comparison you would need.
• what you would expect the results to prove.

6 Work with another pair. Explain the design of your experiment. Can your partners see any way in which it could be improved?

How can you find out if goldfish really have a ten-second memory?

WRITING A scientific method

7 **WRITING SKILL** Describing a process

Work in pairs. How do you think writing about a process is different from telling a story? Is the guidance typical of stories or scientific reports?

1 You avoid using personal pronouns, such as *I*, *he*, or *she*.
2 You use a wide variety of words and descriptive language.
3 You use a lot of passive sentences.
4 You write steps in the order they happened.
5 You define words you think your reader may not know.
6 You use idioms and colloquial language.
7 You summarize what you are going to tell people at the beginning.
8 You explain the reason for doing something.
9 You may add a diagram of what you are describing.
10 You have a final sentence or comment that summarizes the point of the text.

8 Read about the process that was completed in preparation for the Blackawton Bee experiment on page 151. Which of the features in Activity 7 can you identify?

9 Look at the Useful language box. Use the language and these verbs to retell the process in the diagram on this page. Then look at the process on page 151 and check how well you did.

let into	paint	pick up	place	put into
release	remove	return	turn off	warm up

10 Write a method like the one on page 151, describing:

- one of the experiments you designed in Activity 5.
- an experiment you have conducted at school.
- a famous historical experiment that you are interested in.

Useful language

Introducing the process

The experiment aimed to show that…

The purpose of the experiment was to find out if…

The diagram illustrates the process used to…

Figure one shows how…

Linking steps

First of all,…

Before starting the experiment,…

The bees were then released…

Once the bees had been released…

After being released, the bees…

Finally,…

Explaining the steps

*They were marked **to** identify them.*

*They were marked **in order to** identify them.*

*They were marked **so that** they **could** be identified.*

In order to do this,…

6 Adapt to Survive

The flag-footed bug has evolved to hide among leaves and flower petals.

6A Evolution and Conservation

VOCABULARY Endangered species

1 Work as a class. Discuss the questions.

1 What is evolution? What is conservation?
2 What reasons are there for a species to adapt? What characteristics about a species might change?

2 Complete the article about Madagascar with these words.

adapted	breed	conservation	died out	endangered	extinct
habitat	hunting	risk	saved	species	survival

Madagascar is an island famous for its biodiversity. Evolution has created thousands of unique (1) _____ that have (2) _____ to life on the island. In fact, scientists have discovered more than 600 new animals since the beginning of this century. However, while it may seem that wildlife is doing well, many animals and plants are in fact at (3) _____ because tropical forests are being destroyed to make farmland. Eighty percent of Madagascar's human population live in poverty and depend on basic farming for (4) _____ . The silky sifaka is one of the most (5) _____ animals. There are only around 250 left in the wild. A (6) _____ program is trying to preserve its (7) _____ and prevent people from (8) _____ it. The national dog of Madagascar, the Coton de Tulear, was (9) _____ from extinction, and now people (10) _____ it in several countries. The Madagascan Elephant Bird wasn't so lucky. It became (11) _____ in the 17th century. It was three meters tall and may have (12) _____ because people stole its huge eggs, which were big enough to feed a family.

3 Work in pairs. Discuss the questions.

1 What endangered species do you know?
2 Why are they endangered?
3 How are they being protected?
4 What animals have become extinct? Why?
5 What arguments can you think of for and against conservation?

4 Match each word with the correct group of collocations.

benefit	consequence	conservation	gene
habitat	risk	species	survival

1 bring a lasting… / a potential… / be of… *benefit*
2 …of the fittest / its long-term… / ensure its…
3 at… of extinction / a high… / reduce the… of disease
4 work in nature… / be involved in a… group / improve energy…
5 an endangered… / a… of bird / discover a new…
6 destroy their… / preserve their… / lose its natural…
7 pass on their…s / in its…s / find a… for cancer
8 as a… / have serious…s / consider the…s

5 Look through the collocations in Activity 4. Underline any phrases that are new to you. Write an example sentence for each of the new phrases.

LISTENING

6 Listen to the interview with a conservationist. Who mentions these points—the interviewer (I), the conservationist (C), or both (B)? 🎧 27

1 Most animals have died out.
2 Conservation goes against evolution.
3 Genetic changes through evolution do not make a species more perfect.
4 Animals can't choose to adapt to a new environment.
5 Human activity is increasing the number of extinctions.
6 We must protect endangered species because we can.
7 Conservation is expensive.
8 Humans may become extinct sooner rather than later.

7 What reasons for possible human extinction did you hear in the interview? Listen again and check. 🎧 27

8 Work in pairs. Discuss the questions.

1 Do you like television shows about the natural world? What was the last one you saw? What was it about?
2 Have you studied anything about conservation at school? What other things did you learn?
3 Would you like to be a conservationist? What might be good or bad about the job?
4 Have you ever taken action to protect something? What did you do?

GRAMMAR Modals and meaning

9 Look at the Grammar box. Then compare the first and second sentence in each item below. Notice the changes in the use of modals. What is the difference in meaning?

1 You might stop weak species from going extinct.
  You will stop weak species from going extinct.
2 Maybe we shouldn't interfere.
  We must not interfere.
3 "The survival of the fittest" can suggest evolution is a kind of competition.
  "The survival of the fittest" suggests evolution is a kind of competition.
4 If that habitat disappeared for whatever reason, they'd easily die out.
  When the habitat disappears, the animals die out.
5 Will you leave it there?
  Could you leave it there?

Modals and meaning

A modal (*would, will, may, might, could, can, should, shall, must*) adds a general meaning to another verb to show a speaker's attitude or intention.

*The first thing that **will strike** people is…*
= I am certain it strikes people.

*The first thing that **should strike** people is…*
= I believe it strikes people, but I'm not certain.

Other meanings are: certainty, uncertainty, obligation, permission, suggestion, possibility, and frequency (habit).

Check the Grammar Reference for more information and practice.

Baobab trees in Madagascar have adapted to survive in places where there is little rainfall. Their wide trunks can store large amounts of water.

10 Read about National Geographic explorer Cagan Sekercioglu. What similarities can you find with what you heard in the interview? Think about:

1 the rate of extinction.
2 the importance of conservation.
3 what happens to animals that adapt and then face a sudden change.

Growing up in Turkey, Cagan Sekercioglu was once taken to a child psychologist because he (1) <u>constantly brought</u> small animals and insects <u>back</u> to his house. Fortunately, it didn't end his interest in wildlife, and now he's a professor of biology working to protect birds in countries such as Costa Rica, Australia, Ethiopia, the United States, and Turkey. He says (2) <u>losing 25 percent of all bird species this century is a possibility</u>, and that whatever happens to birds (3) <u>is certain to happen</u> to other animals and even people. The question is not if (4) <u>it's better for us to do something</u> about it, but when (5) <u>are we going to decide to do something</u> and (6) <u>what are we going to decide to do</u>?

In Costa Rica, he's found that species (7) <u>sometimes become</u> endangered because the area of forest they live in shrinks as it becomes surrounded by agriculture. The birds are so well adapted to a certain part of the forest that they (8) <u>refuse to</u> move, even when bigger areas of forest (9) <u>are possibly</u> close by. Cagan says (10) <u>it's essential that conservationists work</u> with local people to improve the situation by explaining to farmers why (11) <u>they're better off encouraging</u> bird diversity. For example, if farmers encourage birds to live on their land, (12) <u>the birds will eat</u> insects that destroy their crops, which could possibly increase farmers' profits.

11 Rewrite the underlined parts in Activity 10 using modals. Use each modal in the Grammar box at least once.

12 Write nine sentences about yourself, using a different modal in each sentence. Your teacher will read the sentences to the class. Guess who the person is.

13 MY PERSPECTIVE

Make a list of animals, habitats, jobs, languages, customs, activities, or skills that are at risk of dying out. Would you try to preserve any of them? Why?

6B Tree Life?

VOCABULARY BUILDING

Compound nouns

We often use two or more nouns together to create a new meaning. The words in compound nouns can be joined together, or they can be separated using a space or hyphen. The first noun acts like an adjective. It describes the type of thing, its use, the material it is made from, or other aspects of the second noun, such as where it is found.

Bookstores are dying out in our country because people are buying books online.

Ice ages caused the extinction of many species.

1 Choose the correct forms to complete the sentences.

   1 We often go skiing in the *Olympic Mountains / Mountain Olympics,* north of here.
   2 On average, there is 20 centimeters of *rainfall / fallrain* here in March.
   3 Many environmental charities run *campaign social media / social media campaigns.*
   4 Scientists believe there might be many *sea creatures / creature seas* that still have not been discovered.
   5 I really like our *teacher science / science teacher.* She brings the subject to life.
   6 I avoid all *animal products / product animals.* I don't even wear *shoe leather / leather shoes.*

2 Work in groups. Starting with these compound nouns, how many other compound nouns can you create by changing one word each time? Use a dictionary, if necessary.

farm animal	leather shoes	rainfall	science teacher

ice age: ice cream; cream cheese; cheesecake

READING

3 Choose one animal from these categories that you are familiar with, and one that you would like to learn more about.

farm animals	pets	sea creatures	wild animals

4 Work in groups. Compare the animals you chose. Explain your choices.

5 Work in pairs. Look at the photo on page 73 and discuss the questions.

   1 Where do you think this animal is found?
   2 What is unusual about it?
   3 How do you think the photographer was able to get the shot?

6 Read the article from a website on page 73 to check your ideas in Activity 5. What else do you learn about questions 1 and 2 in Activity 5?

7 Which statements are supported by the article? Underline the parts of the article which helped you make your decisions.

   1 The tree octopus is the most endangered creature in the United States.
   2 Washington State is one of the wettest places in the US.
   3 The tree octopus may provide clues about how early sea creatures adapted to live on land.
   4 The animals often live in small groups.
   5 Many companies that cut down trees in the forests are not doing enough to protect octopuses.
   6 Octopuses are affected by pollution.

8 Work in groups. Discuss the questions.

   1 Did you know about the tree octopus before? If not, what surprised you most?
   2 Should people care about the tree octopus? Why?

9 Look at the source for the article. Do you think it is reliable? What other sources could you check to make sure the information is accurate?

10 Listen to a news extract about the tree octopus story. Answer the questions. 🎧 29

   1 Why is the story mentioned?
   2 What do the findings seem to suggest?

CRITICAL THINKING Assessing information

You will often see information or read something that is unfamiliar. You need to do further reading to check the information is accurate and from a reliable source.

11 Work in pairs. Discuss the questions

   1 Why do you think so many people believe this story?
   2 Looking back, is there anything in the story that should have made you more suspicious?

12 MY PERSPECTIVE

Work in groups. What are the consequences of fake news stories?

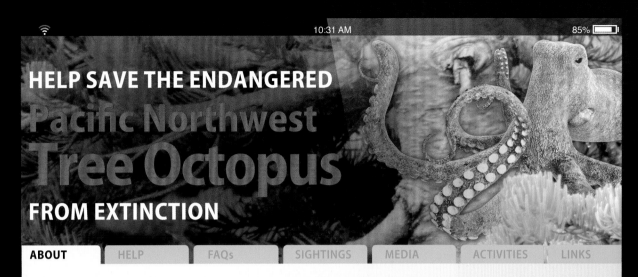

HELP SAVE THE ENDANGERED
Pacific Northwest Tree Octopus
FROM EXTINCTION

ABOUT | HELP | FAQs | SIGHTINGS | MEDIA | ACTIVITIES | LINKS

🔊 28 About

The Pacific Northwest tree octopus (*Octopus paxarbolis*) is only found in the forests of Washington State, on the eastern side of the Olympic Mountains, in the United States.
5 These creatures reach an average size of between 30 and 35 centimeters and live for around four years. They are unusual in that they live both in water and on land, a fact made possible by the very high amounts of
10 rainfall in this part of the United States.

Possessing the largest brain of any octopus, the tree octopus explores its surroundings by touch and sight. Some scientists believe that the way it has adapted to life in the forest
15 mirrors the way early life forms adapted to life away from the water. Although they are not social animals like humans, they can still show emotions by changing their skin color: red indicates anger and white, fear. Normally,
20 though, they are a green-brown color that matches their surroundings.

Every spring, tree octopuses leave their homes and travel to the coast to breed. Males soon return to the forest, while females
25 lay their eggs underwater. The young then spend their first month or so floating near the shore before moving out of the water and beginning their adult lives in the forest.

Source: http://zapatopi.net/treeoctopus/

Why it is endangered

Although the tree octopus is not yet on the
30 official list of endangered animals, it should be, as numbers are now seriously low. It faces many threats: trees in Pacific-Northwest forests are constantly being cut down; new roads have cut off access to water; the growth
35 of local towns has introduced house cats into the region, which hunt the octopuses; and pollution is getting worse. Immediate action needs to be taken to stop the tree octopus from becoming extinct.

Become an activist

40 Here are some things you can do to help protect the last few tree octopuses:

- Write to the government to say you are worried and that you feel the tree octopus should be given special protection and
45 included on the Endangered Species List.

- Write to celebrities, asking them to talk in interviews about the dangers facing the tree octopus.

- Let the world know about the tree
50 octopus: tell your family and friends.

- Tell people not to buy products made by companies that don't protect the tree octopus when cutting down trees.

- Start an online campaign! Encourage
55 people to sign a petition.

Mount Merapi erupts in Indonesia. Volcanic gases are made up of many different gases, including methane.

6C Mysterious Changes

GRAMMAR Modals and infinitive forms

1 Listen to three people. What did they change their minds about? Why? 🎧 30

2 Listen to the people again. Complete the sentences. 🎧 30

    1a I _____ attention when I read about it.

    1b All the links about the different kinds of tree octopuses go to the same page. I really _____ that.

    1c Even my little brother _____ me that the photos were fake.

    2a I mean, you _____ me how cruel it was, and I honestly _____ .

    2b I don't know, but if it was that, it _____ an impact because I've been vegan for quite some time now.

    3a I _____ touch one or pick one up if the chance had arisen.

    3b I _____ certainly _____ about owning one, that's for sure.

    3c Our favorite is a python called Monty. We _____ him for three years this November.

3 Look at the sentences in Activity 2. Answer the questions.

    1 Which sentence describes a period leading up to a future point?

    2 Are the other sentences about the past, the present, or the future?

    3 Which modal emphasizes that an action was in progress at the same time as another?

Modals and infinitive forms

Modals can be followed by different kinds of infinitive forms.

I **can't see** it.
We **should be doing** more to help.
It **wouldn't have made** any difference.
You **can't have been listening** properly.
More attention **must be paid** to this issue.
The eggs **must have been moved** from the nest.

Check the Grammar Reference for more information and practice.

4 Work in groups. Look at the Grammar box. Does each pair of sentences have the same meaning? Discuss any differences.

    1a They must not have been serious.

    1b They must have been joking.

    2a I should have helped him.

    2b I would have helped him.

    3a It must have been really interesting.

    3b It was really interesting.

    4a I guess that might have been the reason.

    4b I guess that could have been the reason.

    5a You shouldn't have texted me.

    5b You shouldn't have been texting me.

    6a It should have arrived by now.

    6b It will have arrived by now.

5 PRONUNCIATION Weak form of *have*

When the sentences in Activity 4 are said slowly and carefully, *have* is often pronounced differently than how it is pronounced in fast speech.

a Listen to each sentence from Activity 4. Notice how *have* changes its sound in fast speech. Repeat what you hear. 🎧 31

b Work in pairs. Practice reading the sentences in Activity 4 slowly and quickly.

6 Complete the summary using the modals and the correct form of the verbs in parentheses. Make one modal negative.

Reported sightings of the Loch Ness Monster
(1) _____ soon _____ (will / go on) for a century! In 1933, a man named George Spicer reported seeing something that looked like a plesiosaur, a kind of long-necked marine dinosaur. Some people think such a creature (2) _____ very easily (could / survive) in the quiet Scottish waters, away from people, while others are convinced that Spicer (3) _____ (must / lie) or that he (4) _____ (might / see) a piece of wood covered in green water plants. Most scientists question the whole story and claim that a creature like this (5) _____ (can / live) in the loch* for so long without any real human contact. If it was real, they say, it (6) _____ (would / capture) by now—or at least caught on film. Others, though, suspect that the monster (7) _____ (might / develop) special skills that help it to hide from those hunting it. Even today, true believers can be found on the shores of the loch trying to spot a beast that (8) _____ (should / die out) 65 million years ago.

loch *a Scottish word for a lake.*

7 Work in pairs. Read the two paragraphs about mysteries of the natural world. Then discuss what you think happened. Use modals where necessary.

The Great Dying
Around 250 million years ago, long before dinosaurs roamed the Earth, about 95 percent of all species were suddenly wiped out. This was by far the biggest mass extinction the world has ever seen. The event—widely known as the Great Dying—came close to ending all life on the planet. Everything alive today comes from the five percent of species that survived back then.

The Bloop
The Bloop was an extremely low and very powerful underwater sound first detected at points across the vast Pacific Ocean by NOAA, the National Oceanic and

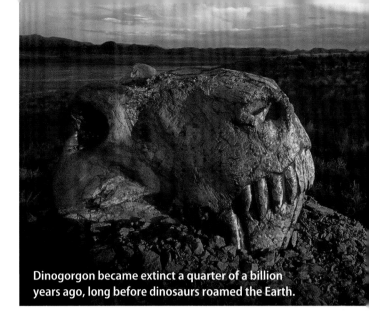

Dinogorgon became extinct a quarter of a billion years ago, long before dinosaurs roamed the Earth.

Atmospheric Administration. The Bloop was significantly different from other previously recorded sounds and many theories emerged to explain the mysterious noise.

8 Read about what really happened. Student A: read about the Great Dying; Student B: read about the Bloop. See if you guessed correctly. Then report back to your partner.

Student A: The Great Dying
Many theories to explain the Great Dying have been put forward—everything from asteroids from space hitting Earth to huge volcanic eruptions. Volcanoes did in fact play a part in the event. At the time, Siberian volcanoes were erupting almost constantly, sending out huge quantities of a gas called methane. This resulted in the oceans and the atmosphere being poisoned and so many species dying out.

Student B: The Bloop
Theories put forward to explain the Bloop ranged from the sensible to the strange. Some people thought the noise must be from an unknown deep-sea creature while others thought it could be mermaids or voices from a lost city. In the end, it turned out that the sound was actually made by an icequake. A large mass of ice in Antarctica was slowly breaking up and was picked up by NOAA.

9 CHOOSE

Choose one of the following activities.

- Work in groups. Prepare a short presentation about a mystery you have read about or know. Include at least four different modals.

- Write a story about something you regret doing—or not doing. Include at least four different modals.

- Work in pairs. Write a conversation between two people about an influential or inspiring person. Include at least four different modals.

AUTHENTIC LISTENING SKILLS

Understanding fast speech

In quick speech, it can be difficult to hear individual words because words get shortened or sound as one.

1 Look at the Authentic Listening Skills box. Then listen to these extracts from the TED Talk where people speak quickly. Try to write down what you hear. 🔊 **32**

1 … she thought it was just a splinter of wood, because _____ at the Fyles Leaf Bed before— prehistoric plant parts.
2 How certain were you that you had it right, like… that _____ , like?
3 … something like a cow or a sheep. But _____ . It was just too big.
4 … you're going to have different body sizes. _____ , so they're actually functionally like giraffes.
5 And, as a historian, you start with an idea _____ .

WATCH

2 Work in groups. Do you think the sentences are *true* or *false*? Why?

1 Camels have been around for about a million years.
2 The first camels were only found in North America.
3 Giraffes and llamas are in the same family as camels.
4 The hump on a camel's back contains water.
5 Camels have evolved to walk on sand.

3 Work in pairs. Write down as many other facts about camels as you can. Then compare your ideas with another pair of students . Do any of the other pair's facts surprise you? Why?

4 Watch Part 1 of the talk. Complete the summary with one to three words in each blank. ▶ **6.1**

One day in 2006, Natalia Rybczynski was digging at a site less than (1) _____ south of the North Pole when she found a strange object. To begin with, she thought it was a piece of (2) _____ . She collected more fragments over the next four years and eventually used a (3) _____ to find out that it was a (4) _____ of a huge mammal. When they cut a piece off one fragment, they (5) _____ collagen, which is a substance found in bones and which (6) _____ in the ice. A couple of years later, she sent the fragments to a colleague who had invented a technique called (7) _____ , which can identify an animal from a bone. They discovered it was a(n) (8) _____ million-year-old camel and that it must have weighed (9) _____ , which is (10) _____ than camels today.

5 Watch Part 2 of the talk. Check your answers from Activity 2. Correct the false answers. ▶ **6.2**

Camels have been around longer than a million years. According to Latif, they have been around for 45 million years.

6 Watch Part 2 of the talk again. Choose the correct options. ▶ 6.2

1 Scientists believe that at first, camels were only found in *hot places / cold places*.
2 They also believe that 40 million years ago, there were around *20 / 24* different species of camels.
3 They say that some early camels were as small as *dogs / rabbits*.
4 They also say that one branch of camels became *llamas / giraffes*.
5 Some scientists believe that a camel's hump helped it to survive long *walks / winters*.
6 It is believed that three and a half million years ago, the weather was significantly *warmer / cooler* than today.

7 Watch Part 3 of the talk. Which sentence best summarizes the point Latif is making? ▶ 6.3

a It's important to change your mind about things.
b Scientists should also study history.
c Much of what we think we know might be wrong.
d Camels are well suited to different environments.

8 What discoveries or news have you heard about the natural world recently? Think about:

• archaeology.
• new or lost species.
• the sea.
• medical advances.

9 VOCABULARY IN CONTEXT

a Watch the clips from the TED Talk. Choose the correct meanings of the words and phrases. ▶ 6.4

b Work in pairs. Discuss the questions.

1 Have you ever experienced *hitting a wall*? Why? How did you overcome it?
2 What scientific theories still have no *proof*?
3 What good *spots* do you know to:
  • have a picnic?
  • see wildlife?
  • hang out with friends?
  • watch the world go by?
4 What things would you be *willing* or *unwilling* to do to be successful in life?

CHALLENGE

Think of a time in your life when you have had to rethink what you thought you knew about something—or someone.

• What did you use to believe? Why?
• What caused you to rethink your beliefs?
• Did you develop your new ideas quickly or slowly?
• How do you feel about the thing or person now?

Work in groups. Tell each other your experiences. Ask and answer questions about the changes. Decide who experienced the biggest change.

6E Finding a Solution

Telling anecdotes

Anecdotes are short real-life stories. When we want to tell an anecdote, we often give a very short summary of what we are going to say. We might also add a comment or say how we felt in order to make it sound interesting.

Useful language

Responding to anecdotes

If the listener is interested, they will say things like:

Really? Why was that?

Wow! What happened?

Really? They have foxes there?

SPEAKING

1 Work in pairs. Look at the photo and discuss the questions.

  1 Where do you think the photo was taken? Who might the man be?
  2 How would you feel if you were the man in the photo?

2 Read the opening lines of six different anecdotes. Which sounds most interesting to you? What would you ask about it?

  a I once saw a polar bear in a zoo. It was really sad.
  b I almost stepped on a scorpion once.
  c My brother once tracked a group of gorillas in Africa.
  d When I went to the city, I saw lots of foxes in the street.
  e Where my grandma lives, there are vultures. We once climbed up to their nests.
  f I hate cows. I was chased by some once. It was really scary!

3 You are going to tell an anecdote about a time you encountered some kind of wild animal—big or small. Make notes using these questions and think of a sentence you will say to start the anecdote to get people interested.

  • When did it happen? How old were you?
  • Where was it?
  • What happened?
  • What was the animal doing?
  • How did it make you feel?
  • Did it have an effect on you afterwards?

4 Work in pairs. Tell your anecdotes. Your partner should show interest and ask questions to help you.

Some people have a special connection with animals.

WRITING A problem-solution essay

5 Tigers are endangered in the wild. Do you think having them in zoos and parks is good for their survival? Why? What other things might help them?

6 **WRITING SKILL** Topic sentences

Read the essay about how people can help to protect tigers on page 151. Put the topic sentences in the correct order as they might appear.

a The author J.A. Mills suggests we should strengthen rules about domestic tigers.
b Finally, we should work closely with local people.
c According to the WWF (World Wildlife Fund), there are only about 4,000 tigers left in the wild.
d Countries have to work together to protect the habitat.

7 In the essay, the writer refers to various organizations and people. Answer the questions.

1 Why does the writer do this?
2 Do you think they are good sources to reference? Why?
3 What other information would be good to know? What other sources could you look for?

8 Work in pairs. Choose one of the animals or things from your list that are at risk of dying out (page 71, Activity 13). Find out more and take notes on three big problems it faces. Then think of ways to tackle these problems and help save it.

9 Work on your own. Using your notes, write a problem-solution essay.

- In the first paragraph, outline the problems and say you will suggest solutions. Then tackle each problem in a subsequent paragraph. Use the writing model on page 151 as a guide if you need to.
- Find two or three sources that you can add to your essay to give it greater authority. Decide how you want to use them and where to place the sources. Use the Useful language box to help you.

10 Exchange your essay with your partner. Read your partner's work and comment on:

- the structure and the strength of the argument.
- the use of sources.
- the use of language.

7 Outside the Box

7A Rules of Creativity

The members of the band A-WA are three Israeli sisters who mix traditional Yemenite music with modern electronic dance music.

VOCABULARY Breaking the mold

1 Work in pairs. How many different words based on the root word *create* can you think of? Think of at least two collocations for each.

create   *create a group, create excitement*

2 Complete the sentences with words based on the root word *create*. You can use the same word more than once.

1 Everyone should learn a musical instrument in their spare time to encourage _____ .

2 Students have not needed to learn facts since the _____ of the internet.

3 You need to study a lot and copy other people before you can be _____ yourself.

4 There aren't many people who actually _____ something completely new.

5 Watching a lot of television kills people's _____ .

6 People who can think _____ do better in school.

3 Identify the collocations with the different forms of *create* from Activity 2. Were they the same as the ones you thought of in Activity 1?

4 Work in pairs. Do you agree with the sentences from Activity 2? Why?

5 Complete the phrases with these pairs of words. Use a dictionary, if necessary.

approaches + solution	comes up with + adapts
invents + follows	makes up + writes
obeys + breaks	writes + scores

1 someone who does what he is told and _____ the rules or someone who _____ them

2 someone who _____ a test or someone who _____ highly on a test

3 someone who _____ a new word or someone who _____ word definitions

4 someone who comes up with a wide variety of _____ to a problem or someone who analyzes things and comes up with a simple _____

5 someone who _____ something or someone who _____ a set of rules to make something

6 someone who _____ new ways of doing things or someone who _____ existing ways of doing things

6 MY PERSPECTIVE

Work in pairs. Which person in each phrase in Activity 5 do you think is more creative? Explain your ideas.

LISTENING

7 Listen to an extract from a podcast. Which sentence best summarizes the main point? 🎧 **33**

   a You can only be truly creative if you think like a child.
   b The best monsters are usually created by children.
   c Schools could do more to encourage creativity.
   d In the future, there will be lots of new kinds of jobs.

8 Listen again. Choose the correct options. 🎧 **33**

   1 *The Monster Engine*:
     a exists across a range of different formats.
     b has only been around for a few years.
     c was created by Dave Devries and his children.

   2 Dave Devries started working on *The Monster Engine*:
     a to make one of his relatives happy.
     b because he illustrates comic books.
     c after being inspired by a young child.

   3 Sir Ken Robinson claimed that:
     a drawing cartoons makes you more creative.
     b if you're creative, you're more likely to do well in the future.
     c people will need to work harder in the next 20 or 30 years.

   4 The speaker thinks that, at its heart, creativity is about:
     a playing games.
     b listening to young people more.
     c not giving up and learning from mistakes.

9 Work in groups. Discuss whether you agree with the statements.

   1 It's sometimes useful to see the world like a child.
   2 Jobs will be very different in the future.
   3 Skills are more important than knowledge.
   4 Trying and failing are important parts of the creative process.

GRAMMAR First, second, third, and mixed conditionals

10 Work in pairs. Look at the Grammar box. Discuss which forms you see in the *if* clauses and result clauses in each of the four sentences.

> ### First, second, third, and mixed conditionals
>
> **First conditionals**
> **a** *If you're in school today, you'll probably start working sometime in the 2020s.*
>
> **Second conditionals**
> **b** *If these drawings were painted more realistically, they would look amazing.*
>
> **Third conditionals**
> **c** *If Dave Devries hadn't spent a day with his niece back in 1998,* The Monster Engine *would never have happened.*
>
> **Mixed conditionals**
> **d** *If their schools had encouraged unusual ways of seeing the world, lots of adults would be more creative.*

Check the Grammar Reference for more information and practice.

11 Which kind of conditional sentences do we use to talk about:

   1 an imaginary past situation and an imaginary present result?
   2 an imaginary situation and result now or in the future?
   3 an imaginary situation and result in the past?
   4 a possible situation and result now or in the future?

Dave Devries applies color and shading to children's artwork (right) to bring their pictures to life.

12 Complete the conditional sentences by using the correct forms of the verbs in parentheses.

Many people think of creativity as chance Eureka moments.* The mathematician and inventor who coined the term *Eureka*, Archimedes, discovered that the weight of an object floating on water is the same as the amount of water it displaces. He made this discovery by chance. If he (1) _____ (pay) more attention to the amount of water in his bathtub, he (2) _____ (not step) into it and spilled water over the side. Apparently, we (3) _____ (not have) penicillin today if Alexander Fleming (4) _____ (be) a bit neater and washed his petri dishes before he went on vacation. On his return, he discovered the penicillin mold had killed bacteria on the dishes. What (5) _____ (our world / be) like now without these discoveries?

The book *Inside the Box* by Drew Boyd and Jacob Goldenberg suggests that such moments are rare and if we (6) _____ (rely) on these "methods," we would not get very far. In fact, the authors say, most inventions come from following a limited set of rules. The rules can help failing schools and companies; if they (7) _____ (integrate) the rules into their teaching and product development, they (8) _____ (become) more successful. The implication of their argument is that it's not all up to luck.

Eureka moment *sudden understanding of a previously unknown solution to something*

13 Work in pairs. Read the situations. How many conditional sentences can you come up with to talk about:

- the different outcomes and how the situations could have been avoided?
- what could be done next?

Situation 1

Some schoolchildren were waiting outside before lunch. There was snow on the ground. The teacher who usually supervises the children arrived late because of a meeting. The students were pushing each other and playing around. Two students slipped on the ice and one ended up in the hospital. The treatment cost a lot of money. The parents complained, but the school says that students have to wait outside because a health and safety report explained that there was not enough space inside. Therefore, it was dangerous to line up inside.

Situation 2

Last year, the teacher who usually helps students with study skills lost her job because the school was trying to save money. Since then, one of the best students in the school has gotten into trouble because she copied an essay from the internet. She is worried this will ruin her chances of going to a good college. She says she did it because she was under a lot of pressure from her parents and did not have anyone to go to for advice.

14 Work with another pair of students. Compare your ideas from Activity 13. Who thought of the most conditional sentences? Who has the main responsibility for the outcomes in both situations?

7B Testing Times

VOCABULARY BUILDING Noun forms

1 Look at these pairs of words. How are the nouns formed from verbs and adjectives?

Verb	Noun	Adjective	Noun
analyze	analysis	concerned	concern
assess	assessment	intelligent	intelligence
conclude	conclusion	flexible	flexibility
know	knowledge	fluent	fluency
publish	publication	logical	logic
vary	variety	useful	usefulness

2 Choose the correct words from Activity 1 to complete the sentences.

1 I know a lot of words in English, but I need to become more _____ in using them!
2 My main _____ when I do anything in English is not to make any mistakes.
3 I got a good grade in the last _____ I did for English.
4 I'd like to write a novel and _____ it myself.
5 I like to do things in a(n) _____ order, from A to B to C.
6 The _____ in my study schedule allows me to study when I feel most productive.
7 I don't think exams are a(n) _____ demonstration of how much people know.

3 Work in pairs. Which sentences in Activity 2 are true for you? What do you think they say about you? Which sentences do you think are signs of creativity? Why?

4 Work in groups. Think of other *verb / noun* and *adjective / noun* combinations that follow the patterns in Activity 1.

READING

5 Work in groups. Discuss the questions.

1 What do you think it means to be creative?
2 Do you think creativity is only connected to the arts?
3 How important is creativity these days? Why?
4 Do you think it is possible to assess levels of creativity?
5 Who is the most creative person you know? Why?

6 Read about a set of tests commonly used to assess creativity. Think about the questions as you read.

1 What do the tests involve?
2 Does the author think they are good tests of creativity?

7 Work in pairs. Answer the questions and discuss your ideas. Then read about the tests again to check.

1 When were the tests first published?
2 How are the tests scored?
3 How are divergent and convergent thinking different?
4 Why were people worried about children's test scores in the United States?
5 What are the possible causes for the drop in test scores?
6 How does problem-based learning encourage creativity?

8 Look at the four examples of divergent thinking tasks in lines 11–22. Work in groups to complete one.

9 Compare your results from Activity 8 with a partner. Use the questions to evaluate their creativity. What do you think the questions tell you about a person's creativity?

1 How many logical solutions are there to the task?
2 How original are the solutions?
3 How well can the solutions be explained?

CRITICAL THINKING Fact and opinion

Facts are statements that are true. **Opinions** are statements showing what people believe.

10 Read the statements about Torrance's *Tests of Creative Thinking*. Do they present *facts* or *opinions*? Does each fact or opinion support the value of the tests as a test of creativity? Why?

1 Torrance found that people often scored very differently on the different parts of the tests.
2 Torrance believed you could teach creativity. The tests were originally teaching tools.
3 The tests give the idea that creativity is all one thing. Fail the tests and you are not creative.
4 Torrance collected information about adults' creative success by asking them to fill out a form to report what they had achieved creatively.
5 Learning to solve one problem rarely helps to solve another kind of problem.
6 It's difficult to see how the tests measure creativity in science or mathematics.

11 MY PERSPECTIVE

Work in pairs. Discuss the questions.

1 Would you like to use the problem-based way of learning? Why?
2 How is creativity encouraged in your school?

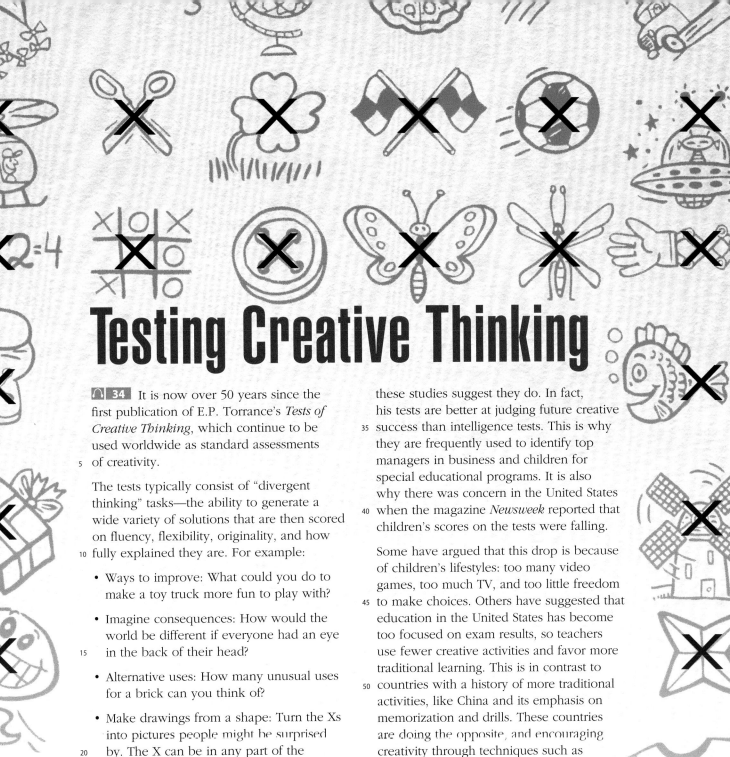

Testing Creative Thinking

🎧 **34** It is now over 50 years since the first publication of E.P. Torrance's *Tests of Creative Thinking*, which continue to be used worldwide as standard assessments
5 of creativity.

The tests typically consist of "divergent thinking" tasks—the ability to generate a wide variety of solutions that are then scored on fluency, flexibility, originality, and how
10 fully explained they are. For example:

- Ways to improve: What could you do to make a toy truck more fun to play with?

- Imagine consequences: How would the world be different if everyone had an eye
15 in the back of their head?

- Alternative uses: How many unusual uses for a brick can you think of?

- Make drawings from a shape: Turn the Xs into pictures people might be surprised
20 by. The X can be in any part of the picture. Add details to tell complete stories and give each picture a title.

Some question if the tests fully assess creativity because they say creativity is about
25 originality and usefulness. Creativity not only requires divergent thinking but also "convergent thinking," where you find one single solution that you feel is the best for the problem you are trying to solve.

30 Torrance followed the lives of children who first took his tests to see if they predicted creative achievements as adults. Analyses of these studies suggest they do. In fact, his tests are better at judging future creative
35 success than intelligence tests. This is why they are frequently used to identify top managers in business and children for special educational programs. It is also why there was concern in the United States
40 when the magazine *Newsweek* reported that children's scores on the tests were falling.

Some have argued that this drop is because of children's lifestyles: too many video games, too much TV, and too little freedom
45 to make choices. Others have suggested that education in the United States has become too focused on exam results, so teachers use fewer creative activities and favor more traditional learning. This is in contrast to
50 countries with a history of more traditional activities, like China and its emphasis on memorization and drills. These countries are doing the opposite, and encouraging creativity through techniques such as
55 problem-based learning.

Problem-based learning involves setting a genuine problem, such as reducing noise in a school library or deciding on a week of meals for an athlete. In reaching
60 a conclusion, students have to do research across several subjects and be creative in the fullest sense. No doubt Torrance would have approved if he was still alive.

One of the tests for creative thinking involves making drawings from a shape.

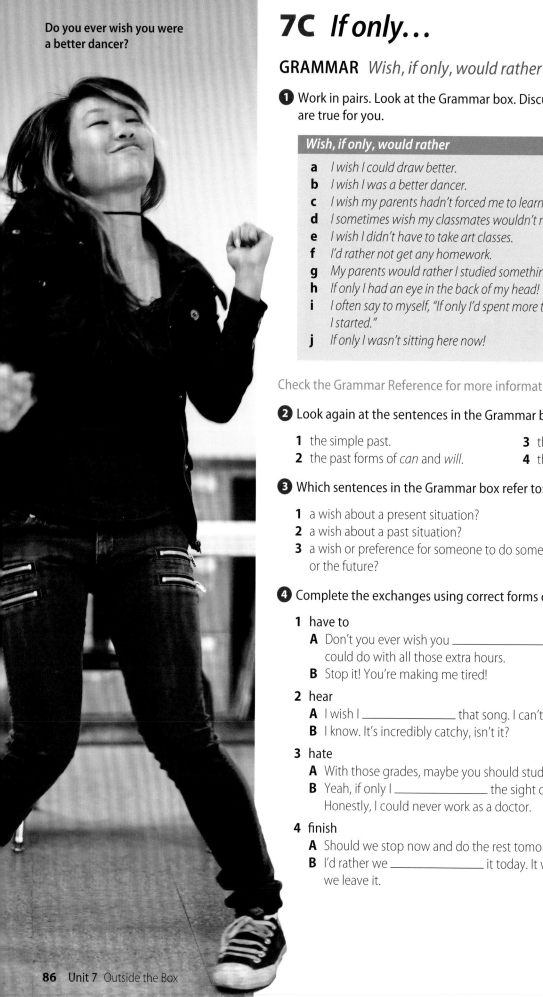

Do you ever wish you were a better dancer?

7C *If only…*

GRAMMAR *Wish, if only, would rather*

① Work in pairs. Look at the Grammar box. Discuss which of the statements are true for you.

> ### Wish, if only, would rather
>
> **a** *I wish I could draw better.*
> **b** *I wish I was a better dancer.*
> **c** *I wish my parents hadn't forced me to learn Latin.*
> **d** *I sometimes wish my classmates wouldn't make so much noise.*
> **e** *I wish I didn't have to take art classes.*
> **f** *I'd rather not get any homework.*
> **g** *My parents would rather I studied something else in college.*
> **h** *If only I had an eye in the back of my head!*
> **i** *I often say to myself, "If only I'd spent more time thinking about this before I started."*
> **j** *If only I wasn't sitting here now!*

Check the Grammar Reference for more information and practice.

② Look again at the sentences in the Grammar box and find examples of:

1 the simple past.
2 the past forms of *can* and *will*.
3 the past continuous.
4 the past perfect.

③ Which sentences in the Grammar box refer to:

1 a wish about a present situation?
2 a wish about a past situation?
3 a wish or preference for someone to do something differently in the present or the future?

④ Complete the exchanges using correct forms of the verbs in bold.

1 have to
  A Don't you ever wish you _____ sleep? Imagine what you could do with all those extra hours.
  B Stop it! You're making me tired!

2 hear
  A I wish I _____ that song. I can't get it out of my head now.
  B I know. It's incredibly catchy, isn't it?

3 hate
  A With those grades, maybe you should study medicine.
  B Yeah, if only I _____ the sight of blood or needles! Honestly, I could never work as a doctor.

4 finish
  A Should we stop now and do the rest tomorrow?
  B I'd rather we _____ it today. It will bother me all night if we leave it.

5 have + be

  A You four should start a band. You could be really big!

  B Yeah, if only we _____ the money to buy equipment—and could come up with ideas!

  A You have lots of good ideas! I wish I _____ as creative as you!

6 be + relax

  A I wish you _____ there. You would've loved it.

  B Yeah, I know. I wish my parents _____ and let me go out more.

  A Well, maybe next time.

5 PRONUNCIATION Elision of consonants *t* and *d*

> When people talk fast, they often leave out the final consonant when the next word starts with a consonant.
>
> *I'd get bored* will often sound like *I-ge-bored.*

a Look at the phrases with *wish*, *if only*, and *I'd rather* in Activity 4. Which final consonants do you think might disappear?

b Listen to the phrases and repeat them. 🎧 **35**

6 We often add comments to statements with *wish*, *if only*, and *would rather*. Match the statements (1–5) with the pairs of follow-up comments (a–e). Does each comment refer to an imagined consequence (IC) or the actual situation (AS)?

1 I wish you'd told me earlier. *c*
2 If only he was taller.
3 I'd rather we didn't talk now.
4 I wish they would do more to help.
5 I wish I didn't have to go.

a People might hear.
   I need to think more carefully about it.
b The place is a mess.
   We could get things done a lot faster.
c It would've saved me a lot of effort. *IC*
   I don't have time to do it now. *AS*
d I don't really like meetings.
   Unfortunately, he's expecting me to be there.
e He could have become a model.
   He probably would make the basketball team.

7 Work in pairs. Look again at the sentences that are true for you in Activity 1. Add comments, like in Activity 6.

8 Read the poem. What do you think happened?

Regrets

I wish I could tell you how I really feel
And say what's on my mind.
I wish I hadn't done what I did
Or had thought before I acted.
I wish I was spending my time with you
Instead of sitting here all alone.

9 CHOOSE Choose one of the following activities.

- Write a poem similar to the one in Activity 8 about regrets. Write it from the perspective of another person, such as a student, a teacher, or an athlete.

- Write a list of eight sentences like those in the Grammar box for your classmates to discuss.

- Write five things you would wish for if anything was possible. Discuss your ideas with a partner.

  I wish money grew on trees.

Do you ever wish you were taller?

> " Everybody who speaks English decides together what's a word and what's not a word. "

ERIN MCKEAN

Read about Erin McKean and get ready to watch her TED Talk. ▶ **7.0**

AUTHENTIC LISTENING SKILLS

Speeding up and slowing down speech

Speakers often vary the speed of their speech in order to maintain people's interest, as well as for other specific reasons. For example, they may speak more quickly when they are saying very common phrases, making jokes, or making comments that are not important. They may speak more slowly when they are starting their speech, emphasizing something important, or thinking of what to say next.

1 Look at the Authentic Listening Skills box. Then listen to the opening of Erin's talk. Identify where her speech slows down and speeds up. 🎧 **36**

I'm a lexicographer. I make dictionaries. And my job as a lexicographer is to try to put all the words possible into the dictionary. My job is not to decide what a word is; that is your job. Everybody who speaks English decides together what's a word and what's not a word. Every language is just a group of people who agree to understand each other. Now, sometimes when people are trying to decide whether a word is good or bad, they don't really have a good reason. So they say something like, "Because grammar!" I don't actually really care about grammar too much—don't tell anybody.

2 Work in pairs. Compare your answers from Activity 1. Practice reading the paragraph using the same kind of speech patterns as Erin.

WATCH

3 Work in pairs. Discuss the questions.

1 Which dictionaries do you use? Why?
2 Do you know how dictionaries are made? How?
3 Do you like learning new words in English? in your own language? Why?
4 Have you seen or heard any new words recently? Where? What do they mean?
5 Have you ever made up a new word? What was it? What does it mean?

4 Watch Part 1 of the talk. Match the excerpts from the talk (a–e) with these notes (1–3). ▶ **7.1**

1 New words
2 The unconscious natural grammar rules that live inside our brains
3 The grammar of "manners," known as usage

a "Because grammar!"
b "This is a wug, right? It's a wug. Now… there are two…"
c "…take a hoodie, don't forget to obey the law of gravity."
d "Can you wear hats inside?"
e "No! No. Creativity stops right here, whippersnappers."

5 Work in pairs. Compare your ideas from Activity 4 and explain the point Erin was making in each excerpt.

6 Look at these notes about six ways to make new words. Watch Part 2 of the talk. Complete the notes. ▷ **7.2**

Erin gives six ways to create new words in English:

1 _____ : using words from another language, e.g. *kumquat* and *caramel*.
2 Compounding: putting two words together, e.g. _____ .
3 _____ : putting parts of two words together, e.g. _____ .
4 Functional _____ : e.g. using a noun as a verb, e.g. _____ .
5 Back formation: _____ a part of the word to create a new one, e.g. _____ .
6 Acronym: taking the first letter of several words, e.g. _____ .

7 Watch Part 3 of the talk. The purpose of her talk is to: ▷ **7.3**

a explain her job and what is important about it.
b argue that words are more important than grammar.
c encourage people to create words and contribute to her online dictionary.
d argue that it is important to break rules to be more creative.
e explain different ways new words are formed and disappear from use.

8 VOCABULARY IN CONTEXT

a Watch the clips from the TED Talk. Choose the correct meanings of the words. ▷ **7.4**

b Work in pairs. Discuss the questions.
1 What did your parents teach you about *manners*? Do you think good *manners* are important?
2 Why might someone be *heartbroken*? What would you do or say for him or her?
3 What do you do to *edit* your essays before you hand them in? Do you get anyone else to help?
4 Give an example of a time when it was difficult to *get your meaning across*. Did you succeed?
5 What movies or books *grabbed* your attention right at the beginning? How? Did they keep your attention?

9 MY PERSPECTIVE

Work in groups. Discuss the questions.

1 Why do you think these groups of people might invent new words? Is it always to aid in communication?

poets	politicians	scientists	teenagers

2 Why do you think some words disappear from use?
3 If you are learning English, do you think it's OK to create new words? Why?
4 How might knowing how to make new words help you to develop your English?

CHALLENGE

Work in groups. How many examples of the six different ways of forming words can you think of?

- borrowing
- blending
- back formation
- compounding
- functional shift
- acronyms

7E Creative Solutions

Useful language

Raising concerns

I don't see how that would work.

The issue with that is…

If we did that, wouldn't… ?

Suggesting a better approach

If you ask me, I think we should…

Giving reasons

That way you could…

That allows / enables…

If we do that,…

SPEAKING

1 Work in groups. Look at the photo and discuss the questions.

   1 In what ways is this class similar to and different from yours?

   2 How many ways of improving your learning environment can you think of? Which two ways would make the biggest difference to the teacher and the learners? Why?

2 Read the situations (a–c). As a class, choose the situation you want to resolve. Then work in groups and:

   discuss what additional facts you would like to find out about the situation.

   2 use divergent thinking to make a list of as many different ways of approaching the situation as you can.

    a Your town or city wants to attract more tourists. It is planning to spend a lot of money on advertising, but no decisions have yet been made about how best to sell the town or city—or what kind of advertisements might work best.

    b This year, a lot less money is going to be available for your school. The school will need to continue offering a great education to students while spending up to 50 percent less. No decisions have yet been made on what changes will need to be made.

    c Your English class has been given some money to make an app or a website to help current and future students deal with their biggest problems. No decisions have yet been made about what should go on the app or website.

3 Exchange the list you made in Activity 2 with another group of students. Then use convergent thinking and the expressions in the Useful language box to:

   • discuss the difficulties there might be with each of the ideas.

   • decide what the best approach would be—and why.

4 Each group should now choose one person to present their approach to the class. Listen to each group and decide who has the best solution.

High school students in a robotics class build a robot to enter into a competition.

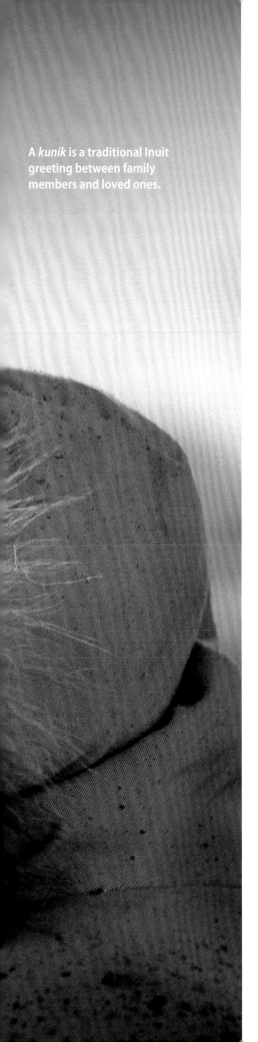

A *kunik* is a traditional Inuit greeting between family members and loved ones.

8A Cultural Crossings

VOCABULARY Identity and communication

1 Work in groups. Look at the photo and discuss the questions.

1 Could this be a typical scene where you are from? Why?
2 How do you normally greet the people in the box? Does it vary at all? Does everyone in the group greet each other in the same way? Why?

friends	friends' parents	sales associates
teachers	visitors from another country	your parents

2 MY PERSPECTIVE

In addition to greetings, are there any rules you think it would be important for a foreign visitor to your country to know? Do you *always* follow these rules?

3 Complete the sentences with these pairs of words.

awkward + compliment	be offended + implied
conscious + discrimination	discourage + reaction
misunderstanding + work it out	response + negative comments

1 If my friends have a(n) _____ or a big argument, I'm good at helping them _____ .
2 I usually feel a bit _____ if someone pays me a(n) _____ or praises what I've done.
3 I would _____ if someone _____ that I looked older than I really am.
4 I think the best _____ to things like _____ is to challenge them.
5 If someone tries to _____ me from doing something, my initial _____ is to want to do it more!
6 I think I'm pretty _____ of how to avoid _____

4 Work in pairs. Read the sentences in Activity 3 aloud. Are they are true or false for you? Why?

5 Complete the collocations with the correct forms, based on the word families.

1 pay me a big **compliment** / _____ me on my work / be very **complimentary** about it
2 _____ against young people / fight **discrimination** / **discriminatory** rules
3 avoid _____ people / a negative _____ / a **stereotypical** person
4 took _____ at what he said / didn't mean to **offend** anyone / use _____ language
5 respond _____ to questions / an **awkward** silence / a sense of **awkwardness** in social settings
6 _____ the instructions / a silly **misunderstanding**

6 Choose five of the collocations from Activity 5. Write example sentences that are true for you.

LISTENING

7 Work as a class. Discuss the questions.

1 How might you define *intercultural communication*?
2 In what situations is it necessary to be considerate of other cultures?

8 Work in pairs. What can cause communication to break down in these situations? What might you do if this

9 Listen to an interview about travel and intercultural communication. What is normal for people from these countries that may be different elsewhere? 🎧 **37**

China	Germany	Russia	US

10 According to the conversation, are the sentences *true*, *false*, or *not stated*? Listen again and check your answers. 🎧 **37**

1 Stacey's parents are diplomats.
2 The German girl who Stacey spoke to was deliberately rude to her.
3 If a Russian person smiles at another Russian they don't know, they may be seen as untrustworthy.
4 Stacey's Korean friend was confused by people in the United States asking "How're you doing?"
5 In Chinese, a common greeting can be translated as *Have you eaten?*
6 Intercultural communication courses are effective.

GRAMMAR Reported speech

11 Look at the Grammar box. Try to complete the sentences. Listen again and check your ideas. 🎧 **37**

> **Reported speech**
>
> **a** *I asked a German girl from my class if she _____ the train station.*
> **b** *And I thought, "That _____ rude."*
>
> _____ *them from smiling at strangers.*
> *There _____ a Russian proverb that says, "Laughter for no reason is a sign of stupidity."*

Check the Grammar Reference for more information and practice.

12 Match the sentences in the grammar box to these points.

1 The sentence includes the actual words that were spoken or thought.
2 The sentence includes advice or instruction the speaker was given.
3 The sentence includes a question (or plan) about an action in progress at the time.
4 The sentence includes a statement about a previous action and consequence.
5 The sentence includes a statement about something which is still generally true.

13 Look at sentences a–c in the Grammar box. What happens to the tenses when we report speech? Why?

14 Complete the responses to the statements that are correcting misunderstandings.

   1 **A** We're meeting on Tuesday.
      B Really? I thought you said we _____ on Thursday!

   2 **A** I got a B on my science essay.
      B Oh, that's pretty good! I thought you said you _____ a D!

   3 **A** I'm interested in seeing the new *Star Wars* movie.
      B Really? I thought you told me you _____ interested!

   4 **A** I'll bring you all the stuff you need next week.
      B You don't have it? I thought you _____ it today.

   5 **A** I'm going to my dance class later.
      B I didn't know you _____ dancing. How long have you been doing that?

   6 **A** We have to leave at 11 o'clock.
      B I thought we _____ leave at 12 o'clock.

15 **PRONUNCIATION** Stress for clarification

   a Work in pairs. Listen to the exchanges from Activity 14. Notice how we stress the corrections. Then practice the exchanges. 🎧 **38**

   b Work in pairs. Take turns saying the sentences. Your partner should respond with something they had misunderstood.
      1 Are you coming to my birthday party on Saturday?
      2 We went to Mexico on vacation last summer.
      3 My mom works at a hospital near here.
      4 I can't stand that band.
      5 Sorry, I can't come out tonight. I have to study.

16 Think of two situations when you might hear these expressions. How might they possibly have different meanings or interpretations?

   1 I've been waiting here forever.
   Someone in a line advising someone not to wait.
   Someone you had arranged to meet being very annoyed because you were late.

   2 Don't be silly!
   3 Are you going to eat that?
   4 What did you do that for?
   5 You'll be sorry.

17 Use your ideas from Activity 16 to tell a short story. Report what was said, how you replied, and what you did next.

   I went to buy tickets for a concert, but when I got to the theater there was a huge line. Someone there said they'd been waiting forever, so I decided to forget it and just went home.

18 **MY PERSPECTIVE**

Choose one of these situations. Spend a few minutes planning how to explain what happened. Include some reporting. Then work in pairs. Tell your partner your story.

- A compliment someone paid you or you paid someone else
- A misunderstanding or argument you once had or saw
- A conversation you wish you hadn't overheard

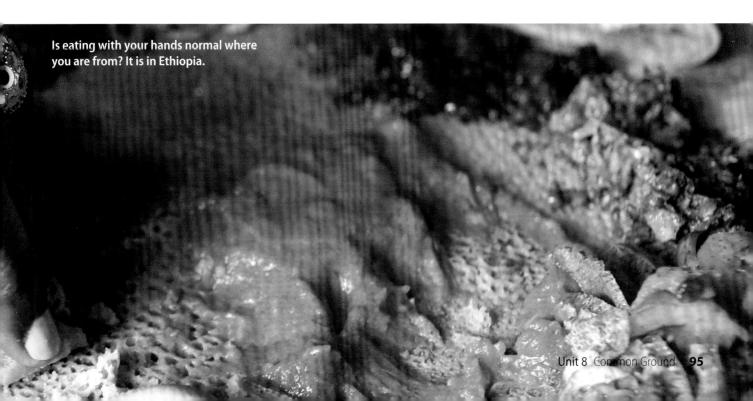

Is eating with your hands normal where you are from? It is in Ethiopia.

8B I Am Who I Am

VOCABULARY BUILDING

Compound adjectives

Compound adjectives are made up of more than one word. As with single-word adjectives, it is important to learn not only the meanings, but also the nouns that they most commonly describe.

1 Match these compound adjectives with their meanings.

cost-effective	deep-rooted
heartbroken	highly respected
like-minded	long-lasting
open-minded	two-faced
well-mannered	worldwide

1 sharing tastes, interests, and opinions
2 dishonest and not to be trusted
3 admired by lots of people because of qualities or achievements
4 willing to consider new ideas and ways of thinking
5 existing or happening everywhere
6 behaving in a polite way
7 firmly fixed; strong and hard to change
8 providing good value for the amount of money paid
9 continuing for a long period of time
10 extremely sad and upset

2 Complete the sentences with compound adjectives from Activity 1.

1 She achieved _____ fame when a video she posted online went viral.
2 Everybody around here knows she does good work. She's a _____ figure.
3 My little brother was absolutely _____ when his team lost the championship game!
4 The problems are too _____ for there to be any real hope of a quick fix.
5 If you only ever spend time talking to _____ people, you don't get to hear different points of view.

3 Work in groups. Use five of the adjectives in Activity 1 to describe people or things from your own experience.

My dog died last year, which left me heartbroken.

I bike almost everywhere. It's the most cost-effective way of getting around.

READING

4 Work in pairs. Look at the photo showing a subculture.* Predict:

1 where the subculture originated.
2 what members of the subculture have in common.
3 what kind of music—if any—is associated with this subculture.

subculture *a group of people within a larger cultural group who share the same interests*

5 Read the article and find the answers to the questions in Activity 4 for all of the subcultures mentioned.

6 What reasons for joining subcultures are mentioned in the article? What downside is mentioned?

7 Which of the four subcultures:

1 is more of a virtual than real-world phenomenon?
2 became known worldwide thanks to a music video?
3 is a combination of the ultra-modern and the old?
4 includes members who identify with animals?
5 can trace its origins back the furthest?
6 involves a form of recycling?
7 rejects a common belief about their characteristics?
8 involves regional rivalries?

CRITICAL THINKING Understanding other perspectives

Learning to think more critically sometimes requires us to suspend our own judgment and instead to try to see things from other points of view.

8 Work in groups. For each of the four subcultures mentioned in the article, decide:

1 what the appeal might be for those who get involved.
2 what common ground might exist with other groups.
3 what concerns parents might have.
4 which are common—or have some kind of local equivalents—where you live.

9 MY PERSPECTIVE

The article is written from the point of view of someone who is not involved in any of the subcultures mentioned. Do you think people who are part of the subcultures might want to change any of the details? Why?

A PLACE TO BE

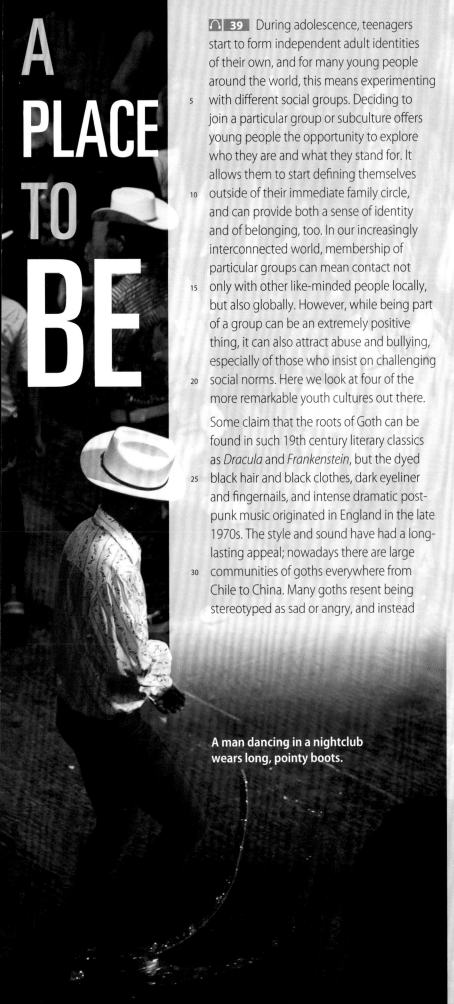

A man dancing in a nightclub wears long, pointy boots.

🎧 39 During adolescence, teenagers start to form independent adult identities of their own, and for many young people around the world, this means experimenting with different social groups. Deciding to join a particular group or subculture offers young people the opportunity to explore who they are and what they stand for. It allows them to start defining themselves outside of their immediate family circle, and can provide both a sense of identity and of belonging, too. In our increasingly interconnected world, membership of particular groups can mean contact not only with other like-minded people locally, but also globally. However, while being part of a group can be an extremely positive thing, it can also attract abuse and bullying, especially of those who insist on challenging social norms. Here we look at four of the more remarkable youth cultures out there.

Some claim that the roots of Goth can be found in such 19th century literary classics as *Dracula* and *Frankenstein*, but the dyed black hair and black clothes, dark eyeliner and fingernails, and intense dramatic post-punk music originated in England in the late 1970s. The style and sound have had a long-lasting appeal; nowadays there are large communities of goths everywhere from Chile to China. Many goths resent being stereotyped as sad or angry, and instead see themselves as romantic, creative, open-minded, and able to find beauty in what others may see as dark or ugly.

Over recent years, a far more localized subculture has been developing in Mexico, where a style of music known as *Tribal Guarachero* has evolved, complete with its own remarkable fashions. More commonly known just as *Trival*, the hugely popular sound mixes traditional regional folk music with electronic dance. Young fans often identify themselves by combining futuristic elements with a basic farmworker look… and wearing extremely long, pointy boots when dancing, often competitively against groups from other local towns. Believe it or not, some items of footwear have apparently reached five feet in length!

Of course, subcultures that develop in a particular area can spread like wildfire in a matter of moments these days, thanks to the internet. This is what's happened with the Scraper Biker subculture. Originally the obsession of a small group of young people in the San Francisco Bay area, scraper bikes are simply ordinary bicycles that have been modified by their owners, typically with decorated wheels and bright body colors. Much of the decoration is done very cheaply, using tinfoil, reused cardboard, candy wrappers, and paint! The craze went global after a hip-hop video featuring these creations went viral. Scraper bikes can now be seen in cities all over the world.

If the internet helps some subcultures grow, for others it's their main home. Otherkin—people who identify to some degree as non-human—have a massive online presence that's growing all the time. While some otherkin believe themselves to actually be, say, dragons or lions or witches or foxes, others simply feel special connections to certain creatures—and have found a space within which to explore these feelings.

It seems that, whatever you're going through and whatever your own personal enthusiasms, there's a worldwide community out there just waiting for you to find it—and to assure you that you belong!

Iceland was the first European country to elect a female president. Vigdis Finnbogadottir was elected in 1980.

8C Fight for Your Rights

GRAMMAR Patterns after reporting verbs

1 Look at the Grammar box. Match the patterns and sentences (1–6) with the examples (a–f) that have the same pattern.

1 verb + infinitive (with *to*)
The government **intends to introduce** new laws to tackle the problem.

2 verb + someone + infinitive (with *to*)
I **reminded you all to bring** in your permission slips.

3 verb + preposition + *-ing*
They **apologized for doing** what they did.

4 verb + (*that*) clause
She **argued (that)** things really need to change.

5 verb + *-ing*
He **denied answering** the question.

6 verb + someone + (*that*) clause
He **promised me (that)** he'd never do anything like that again.

Patterns after reporting verbs

a *Deciding to join a particular group offers young people the opportunity to explore who they are.*

b *Many goths resent being stereotyped as sad or angry.*

c *Some claim that the roots of Goth can be found in 19th century literary classics.*

d *There's a worldwide community out there just waiting to assure you that you belong!*

e *It allows them to start defining themselves outside of their immediate family circle.*

f *It can also attract abuse and bullying of those who insist on challenging social norms.*

Check the Grammar Reference for more information and practice.

2 Work in pairs. Decide which patterns in Activity 1 these verbs use. Some verbs use more than one pattern.

acknowledge	advise	agree	be accused
be blamed	convince	imagine	invite
persuade	pretend	state	suggest

3 Choose the correct options.

Many governments have been criticized (1) *of / in / for* turning a blind eye to racism. Some have even been accused (2) *of / for / from* encouraging it when it suits them. However, the Bolivian government recently announced (3) *to launch / launching / that it's launching* an app designed to encourage citizens (4) *that they should report / to report / reporting* any incidents of racism or discrimination that they encounter. The app is called No Racism. Reports can be submitted 24 hours a day. The government has promised (5) *responding / for responding / to respond* to all complaints and take legal action, where appropriate.

4 Complete the report with the correct forms of the verbs. Add prepositions where necessary.

It was recently announced that Iceland (1) _____ (be) now the best place in the world to be female. However, young Icelandic women have previous generations to thank (2) _____ (fight) for their rights. On October 24th, 1975, fed up with their status as second-class citizens, 90 percent of all women in the country refused (3) _____ (work). Their goal was to remind men that the success of the nation (4) _____ (depend) women and to urge them (5) _____ (accept) greater equality. They threatened (6) _____ (continue) their general strike until changes were made. Men listened, and within five years the country had become the first to elect a female president, Vigdis Finnbogadottir. Iceland can now claim (7) _____ (have) one of the highest proportions of female politicians—over 40 percent—in Europe. In the spring of 2017, a law was passed (8) _____ (require) employers to prove that their companies are free from gender-based salary discrimination.

5 Work in pairs. Look at the ideas for tackling gender inequality. Discuss:

- how they might change things.
- which you think are good ideas. Why?
- other ways in which things could be improved.

a Encourage stores to stop selling toys aimed at either boys or girls.
b Demand that companies employ an equal number of female and male bosses.
c Insist on mothers and fathers getting equal amounts of parental leave when they have children.
d Advise schools to ensure that both boys and girls do school subjects such as cooking and woodwork.
e Force schools to have equal numbers of men and women in photos on the walls.
f Persuade parents to discuss images of men and women in the media with their children.

6 Complete the short news article with the correct forms of these pairs of linked verbs.

accuse + discriminate	agree + examine	decide + make
deny + be	force + change	insist on + have

A 13-year-old girl in South Africa has been (1) _____ schools three times because of her hair. Zulaikha Patel has (2) _____ her current school, Pretoria High School for Girls, of _____ against black students through its uniform policies that (3) _____ students _____ a "neat, conservative appearance." Angry that this was being interpreted as meaning that she couldn't wear her hair in her natural afro style, she launched a silent protest, which attracted the attention of the national media. The school (4) _____ discriminatory in any way, but (5) _____ its policies before (6) _____ whether or not _____ any significant changes.

7 CHOOSE

Choose one of the following activities.

- Think of conversations you have had—or heard—recently. Use some of the reporting verbs from pages 98 and 99 to describe what they were about.

- Work in pairs. Write a news report about one of these topics. Use at least four reporting verbs.
  - an incident of discrimination
  - a protest
  - a new project that's trying to change things

- Work in groups. Tell each other about a time that:
  - you intended to do something, but then didn't. Explain why you didn't do it.
  - you refused to do something. Why?
  - someone famous was accused of doing something bad.
  - you had to apologize for doing something.
  - someone powerful acknowledged they'd done something wrong.

Zulaikha Patel and her classmates are fighting for rights that go beyond the style of their hair. They are standing up against racism.

SAFWAT SALEEM

Read about Safwat Saleem and get ready to watch his TED Talk. ▶ **8.0**

AUTHENTIC LISTENING SKILLS

Just

Just has several meanings—*only, simply, exactly, soon, recently*—and is also used to emphasize a statement or soften a request, to make it sound smaller or more polite.

1 Look at the Authentic Listening Skills box. Listen to these extracts from the TED Talk and add *just* in the correct place. 🎧 **40**

1 I had to grunt a lot for that one.
2 I sat there on the computer, hitting "refresh."
3 This was the first of a two-part video.
4 I could not do it.
5 If I stutter along the way, I go back in and fix it.
6 And the year before, that number was about eight percent.
7 Like the color blue for Ancient Greeks, minorities are not a part of what we consider "normal."

2 Work in pairs. Discuss each meaning of *just* in Activity 1. Then practice saying the sentences.

WATCH

3 Work in pairs. Discuss the questions.

1 In what ways do people make fun of others?
2 In what ways might people react to being made fun of?
3 Why do you think people make fun of others?

4 Watch Part 1 of the talk. Are the sentences *true* or *false*? ▶ **8.1**

1 People have sometimes joked, "Have you forgotten your name?" because of Safwat's stutter.
2 Safwat is interested in video games.
3 The video Safwat posted only got negative feedback.
4 The negative comments were mainly about Safwat's stutter.
5 The incident led Safwat to do more voice-overs in order to prove his critics wrong.
6 In the past, Safwat used video and voice-overs to become more confident in speaking.
7 Safwat practiced to improve his voice and accent to sound more normal.

5 Work as a class. Read the conclusion of Safwat's talk. Discuss the questions.

The Ancient Greeks didn't just wake up one day and realize that the sky was blue. It took centuries, even, for humans to realize what we had been ignoring for so long. And so we must continuously challenge our notion of normal, because doing so is going to allow us as a society to finally see the sky for what it is.

1 How do you think the Ancient Greeks and the color of the sky might be related to what you have talked about and seen so far?
2 What do you think Safwat means by "the sky," with regard to society today?

6 Put the sentences in order. The first one is given. Then watch Part 2 of the talk and check your answers. ▶ 8.2

1 Few colors are mentioned in ancient literature. Why?

a In the same way, narrators with strong accents are not part of people's "normal."

b People discriminate because they don't "see" or relate to people who are different from themselves.

c Should Safwat accept or challenge ideas of normality?

d Blue was "invisible" and not part of ancient people's "normal," unlike red.

e Minorities are not part of society's "normal," like the color blue wasn't for the Greeks.

f One theory is that colors weren't named or "seen" until people could make them.

g This is why Safwat has gone back to using his voice in his work.

h People learn not to relate to minorities because there are few images of minorities in books.

i People's ideas of "normal" can lead to discrimination, such as offering fewer interviews to people with black-sounding names.

7 MY PERSPECTIVE

How do you feel about your own accent in English? Would you like to change it at all? What would be a "normal" accent for you?

8 VOCABULARY IN CONTEXT

a Watch the clips from the TED Talk. Choose the correct meanings of the words and phrases. ▶ 8.3

b Work in pairs. Tell each other about:
- something *humorous* you have seen or read recently.
- a time you felt a bit *self-conscious*.
- a time you took *a big step*.

CHALLENGE

Work in groups. You are going to discuss a video you could make about ONE of these topics. Choose a topic and follow the steps (1–5).

- Challenge the idea of what is "normal."
- Raise awareness of discrimination.
- Discourage bullying.
- Show how different groups share experiences, likes, and dreams.
- Encourage people to do activities with different groups of people.

1 Decide on one aspect of the topic to focus on.

2 Think of two or three different messages for the campaign.

3 Brainstorm some ideas to illustrate these messages.

4 Choose the best idea and develop it further.

5 Share your idea with the rest of the class.

8E Teenage Kicks

Useful language

Identify yourself

As a… / someone who…

Speaking as…

If you look at it from… point of view…

Agree or disagree

I totally support it.

I'm in favor.

I'm (totally) for / against the idea.

It's crazy.

I don't get it.

Challenge ideas and assumptions

Just because…, (it) doesn't mean…

…are we supposed to…?

Give examples

I mean, …

SPEAKING

1 Work in pairs. Look at the photo and discuss the questions.

  1 Where was the photo taken?

  2 What are the people doing? What else might they do?

  3 How do you think others might react to these people? Why?

2 Listen to five people giving opinions about a policy. What do you think the policy is about? 🎧 **41**

3 Listen to the five people again. 🎧 **41**

  1 Who is speaking in each case?

  2 Are they for or against the policy? Why?

4 Complete the sentences by adding two words in each blank—contractions count as one word. Then listen again and check your answers. 🎧 **41**

  1 We've lost some stock recently, which I think might be _____ .

  2 I mean, where else are we _____ go? Or are we just _____ to hang out at all?

  3 As _____ goes there pretty often, I _____ the idea.

  4 _____ one or two misbehave _____ they all do. _____ , adults shoplift and cause problems, too.

  5 If I look _____ from my grandpa's _____ view, I can kind of understand it.

5 Work in pairs. Look at the statements. Which ones are normal in your country? Which ones do you agree or disagree with? Why? Use some of the expressions in the Useful language box to discuss them.

  1 Teenagers shouldn't hang out without a responsible adult around.

  2 Everyone should wear a school uniform.

  3 Boys and girls should be educated separately.

  4 Men are better at certain subjects or in certain jobs than women.

  5 You can only get a good job if you go to college.

  6 Students need to do lots of homework to succeed.

6 Work in groups. Choose a role. Discuss the statements in Activity 5 in your role. Then think about the statements from a different perspective.

| businessperson | parent | politician | teacher |

Just hanging out?

WRITING A complaint

7 One of the speakers in Activity 2 mentioned negative stereotypes about teenagers in the media. What stereotypes do you think you fit? How does that make you feel? Why?

8 Do you think there are any stereotypes in the media about these groups of people? Are they positive, negative, or neither?

boys	businesspeople	girls
old people	people from your country	students

9 Read the complaint on page 152 and answer the questions.

1 Who is the person writing to and why?
2 How does she feel? Why?
3 What does she want to happen? Why?

10 **WRITING SKILL** Using appropriate tone

Work in pairs. Read the complaint on page 152 again. Discuss the questions.

1 Does the writer follow the advice in the Writing strategy box?
2 What other details could the writer give, if any?
3 Do you think complaints are worth writing? Why?

11 Work in groups. Think of reports, policies, rules, TV programs, or movies you know about. Discuss the questions.

1 Have you read or seen anything that you thought was untrue, unfair, or stereotyped people?
2 What was the problem?
3 Who was responsible?
4 How could it have been changed?

12 Write a complaint about one of the ideas you discussed in Activity 11. Follow the structure of the writing model on page 152. Try to use some of the language from this unit.

Writing strategy

When we write to complain about something, we:

- say what the general problem is in the first sentence.
- give details of the problem (including times and examples).
- explain more about how the problem has affected us.
- ask for some kind of action.
- sometimes say what we will do next if we are unsatisfied with the response.

The writing is more effective if it:

- is polite.
- is fairly formal.
- uses linking words such as *however* and *while*.

9 Lend a Helping Hand

IN THIS UNIT, YOU...

- talk about natural disasters and technology that helps to deal with them.

- read about how the United Nations gives a voice to young people.

- learn about local community action and dealing with crime.

- watch a TED Talk about helping people recover after a disaster.

- write a letter of application for a volunteer position.

9A In Times of Crisis

VOCABULARY Dealing with disaster

1 Work in pairs. Look at the photo and discuss the questions.

1 What do you think has happened?
2 What do you think the three main challenges in this area would be at this time?
3 What would be needed to help people overcome these challenges?

2 Check that you understand these pairs of words. Use a dictionary, if necessary. Then complete the series of events following an earthquake.

appealed + aid	blocked + supplies
debris + task	earthquake + devastation
infrastructure + flee	launched + evacuate
rise + crisis	shortages + limited

1 The _____ struck coastal areas just after midnight and caused widespread _____ .
2 Much of the _____ was damaged or destroyed, and thousands of people started to _____ the worst-affected areas.
3 As the number of injuries continued to _____ , it became clear that a humanitarian _____ was starting to unfold.
4 There were food _____ and a _____ amount of clean drinking water.
5 The government _____ to the international community for _____ .
6 The roads were _____ , so they had to use helicopters to drop _____ to people.
7 They _____ a relief effort and started to _____ people from the disaster zones.
8 They finally managed to clear the _____ and started the huge _____ of rebuilding.

3 Work in pairs. Discuss the questions.

1 In addition to earthquakes, what else can cause **widespread devastation**?
2 What kind of systems form the **infrastructure** of a town or city?
3 What else might there be **shortages of** after a disaster?
4 What else might **rise** after a natural disaster?
5 What kind of **aid** can the international community provide in crises?
6 How is **debris** usually cleared?
7 How are people usually **evacuated from disaster zones**?
8 What other reasons are there that roads may be **blocked**?

4 Think about a natural disaster you know about and prepare to discuss it. Write notes on:

- what happened, where, and when.
- the immediate impact of the disaster.
- the relief effort involved—and how effective it was.
- the biggest challenges.

5 Work in groups. Discuss your notes from Activity 4. Try to use some of the language from Activity 2.

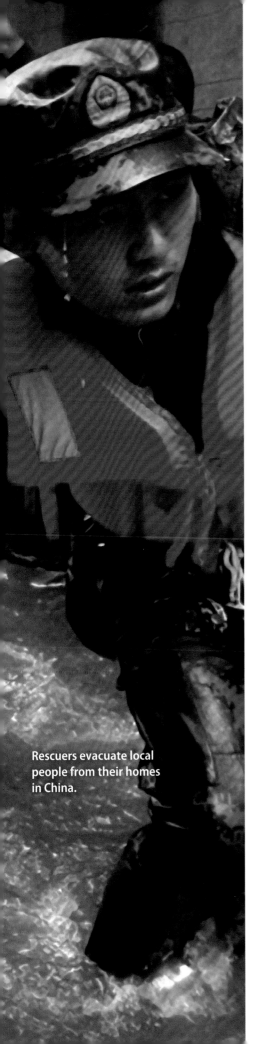

Rescuers evacuate local people from their homes in China.

When a powerful earthquake struck Nepal in 2015, Patrick Maier's team used drones to take photos of the affected areas.

LISTENING

6 Listen to the first part of a radio program. Find out:
🎧 **42**

1 what the disaster was, where it happened, and when.
2 what the impact of the disaster was.

7 Work in groups. Discuss the questions.

- Had you heard about the disaster described in Exercise 6 before? Do you know anything more about it and how the country is now?
- How do you think social media, maps, and photographs, such as the one above, could help in this situation?

8 Listen to the second part of the radio program about how Patrick Maier first used an online mapping technology called Ushahidi in Haiti. Answer the questions. 🎧 **43**

1 How did he get information to update the online maps on Ushahidi?
2 How did this information help the people affected by the disaster?
3 How else has Ushahidi helped people elsewhere in the world?

9 Work in pairs. Try to remember what was said about the following. Then listen again and check your ideas.
🎧 **43**

1 Christine Martin
2 Kenya
3 Haitian roots
4 one million
5 helicopters
6 world attention
7 Russia
8 a smartphone

10 Patrick Maier calls the work he does *crisis mapping*. In recent years, crisis mappers have started using more technological tools in their work. How might these tools be useful to them? Can you think of anything else that might help?

3D modeling technology	artificial intelligence
drones	GPS
hashtags	satellites

Hashtags might be useful for crisis mappers because they can use social media to see where the most requests for aid are coming from.

GRAMMAR Relative clauses

11 Look at the Grammar box. Answer the questions.

1 What are the relative pronouns in each sentence?
2 When do you think each one is used?
3 Defining relative clauses qualify nouns and tell us exactly which thing, person, or place is being referred to. Which sentences include them?
4 What is the difference between the defining relative clauses in the sentences you just identified and the others?
5 In which sentence can the relative pronoun be left out? Why?
6 Look at sentence *d*. Where does the preposition go in relation to the verb? How else could you write this clause?

Relative clauses

a *The earthquake that struck Haiti measured seven on the Richter scale.**

b *The devastation which it caused was simply staggering!*

c *The country, which has long been one of the poorest in the world, struggled to cope.*

d *The seaport, which supplies would normally have been delivered to, was also unusable.*

e *Watching all of this in his Boston home was Patrick Maier, who decided that he had to do something to help.*

f *Maier, whose girlfriend was doing research in Haiti at the time, came up with the idea of using technology to create an interactive online map.*

g *He had to reach out for volunteers, many of whom had Haitian roots and were very happy to help.*

h *Helicopters were able to drop tents and food to desperate people whose homes had been destroyed and evacuate people who were trapped or injured.*

Richter scale *a scale for measuring the size of an earthquake*

Check the Grammar Reference for more information and practice.

12 Complete the summary with a relative pronoun in each blank. Can any of the blanks contain a different word or be left blank? If so, which ones? Explain your choices.

The year 1945 was an important one for Europe. Some people see it as the year (1) _____ the modern world started. Europe was in a mess, the kind of mess (2) _____ is almost impossible for people today to imagine. Six years of war had devastated the continent. Tens of millions had died; millions more had been forced to move from the places (3) _____ they had previously lived—and life was unbelievably hard for those (4) _____ had survived. The majority of the survivors were women and children (5) _____ husbands and fathers had been killed or imprisoned. Nobody had anything (6) _____ they could sell, and men with weapons wandered the land, taking whatever they wanted. How was the task of rebuilding achieved?

Well, most importantly, Harry Truman, (7) _____ was then President of the United States, put into place systems (8) _____ were intended to help all states regarded as allies. In 1947, the US Secretary of State, General George Marshall, (9) _____ name was given to the plan, announced massive amounts of aid for war-torn countries, much of which was to be used for reconstruction. The Marshall Plan ran for over ten years and paid for the rebuilding of infrastructure, (10) _____ provided employment and sped up the return of normal life.

13 Work in pairs. Add relative clauses to the sentences.

1 Crisis mapping has been used in many countries.
2 At 4:35 AM local time, the hurricane hit the coastal town.
3 The International Red Cross and Red Crescent have over 50 million volunteers.
4 Donations have now topped ten million dollars.
5 People are taking shelter in the local school.

14 MY PERSPECTIVE

Work in groups. Discuss the questions.

1 Have any disasters affected your country? In what way?
2 Did there need to be any rebuilding after the disaster(s)? How was this done?

Shouting Out for the Young

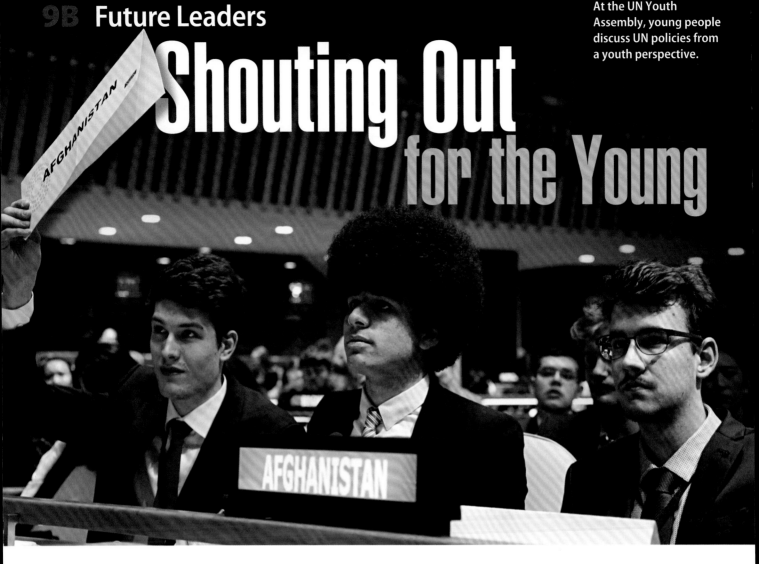

At the UN Youth Assembly, young people discuss UN policies from a youth perspective.

VOCABULARY BUILDING

the + adjective

We sometimes talk generally about groups of people using *the* + adjective.

*These days, **the young** face many challenges that didn't exist in the past.*

1 Work in pairs. Discuss whether you agree or disagree with the sentences.

1 The old need to listen to the young more.
2 There is one set of rules for the rich and another for the poor.
3 The loud and outgoing get too much attention.
4 Only the brave or the stupid would believe they could change the world.
5 Only the best get to the top.

2 Write your own sentence starting *Only the*. Then share your idea with the class and discuss what it means.

READING

3 Look at the photo and discuss the questions.

1 Who do you think the people are?
2 Would you like to take part in something like this?
3 Do you think young people can change policies in these areas? Why?

the world	your country	your school	your town

4 Read the article quickly. Write a one-sentence summary. Then work in pairs and discuss your summaries.

5 Read the article again. Find:

1 someone who started a trend.
2 an organization that provides aid.
3 someone who created a record.
4 someone who showed determination.
5 someone who founded an organization.
6 a country that has changed a law to benefit children.

44 Almost half of the world's seven billion citizens are under the age of 25, and they have huge potential to shape the countries they live in. A few countries, such as Argentina, have tried to empower their youth by giving
5 them the right to vote at the age of 16, but it still seems that in many places young people's opinions are often overlooked or simply not heard. However, one organization that has a long history of giving a voice to young people is the United Nations (UN).

10 In 1946, the UN created a fund called UNICEF to support the millions of children affected by World War II, thanks to the leadership of the Polish medical scientist Ludwik Rajchman. The fund distributed aid without discrimination because, as its director Maurice Pate said, "There are no enemy
15 children." One of those helped by the fund was seven-year-old Dzitka Samkova from Czechoslovakia, as it was known then. She painted a picture of five dancing girls as a thank you and it was turned into a greeting card, the first of many such cards sold to raise money for millions more children.

20 Having campaigned on behalf of young people, UNICEF also had a key part in the creation of the UN's Convention on the Rights of the Child (CRC) in 1989, now signed by more countries than any other convention. The 54 articles of the CRC declare different rights connected to housing, health,
25 the economy, culture, and politics, including such things as the right to a safe home, the right to play and rest, and a child's right to choose their own friends.

In recent years, the UN has opened up new ways to address Article 12 of the CRC, which states that children
30 have the right to give their views, and for adults to listen and take them seriously. UNICEF's Voices of Youth website brings together young bloggers and activists working on development issues to share their ideas and successful projects for change in a huge range of countries, from Sierra
35 Leone to the Philippines. Using online discussion boards as a "meeting place," the initiative provides a space for youngsters who care.

The UN also established the Youth Assembly in 2002 and a network of Youth Observers. Since starting, the assembly
40 has brought around 20,000 people between the ages of 16 and 28 from over 100 countries to its headquarters in New York. Through workshops, panel discussions, and networking events, these young people discuss UN policies from a youth perspective. The assembly also helps to build
45 friendships across different cultures and give political experience to those who can bring change for children. One of its graduates, Ahmad Alhendawi of Jordan, became the UN Secretary General's first ever representative for youth and the youngest ever senior official in the UN.

50 Of course, the Youth Assembly and its delegates are only a tiny number of those three and a half billion young people, but they are important role models. It can be easy to find reasons not to act, but as Nicol Perez, a youth observer to the UN General Assembly says, "I have a voice, and I'm going to
55 use it. I'm going to shout it out till somebody hears me."

---

7 an online initiative that brings together politically active people.
8 a place where young people help to decide how things are done in the world.
9 a document that states the rights of children.

6 In your opinion, how influential were these people from the article? Put them in order from most influential to least influential. Then work in small groups. Compare your answers and discuss your choices.

Ahmad Alhendawi	Dzitka Samkova
Ludwik Rajchman	Maurice Pate
Nicol Perez	Voices of Youth bloggers

CRITICAL THINKING Detecting bias

> Even though articles give a lot of factual details, the way that the arguments are organized and the vocabulary that is used can show if the writer has an underlying opinion.

7 What do you think the author's general opinion is about the UN and young people? Why?

8 Identify the words and phrases in the opening paragraph which reveal the author's opinion. How does the structure of the paragraph reinforce these opinions?

9 Rewrite the first paragraph so that it is neutral. Change words and the structure of the paragraph. Remove words or phrases as necessary.

10 Work in groups. Discuss ideas you have to achieve these UN 2030 goals. Then share your ideas as a class.

- End poverty in all its forms everywhere.
- Ensure inclusivity and equality for all and promote lifelong learning.
- Achieve gender equality.
- Make cities inclusive, safe, resilient, and sustainable.

Malala Yousafzai is a young activist for female education. She spoke at the United Nations on her 16th birthday.

9C Community Service

GRAMMAR Participle clauses

❶ Identify all the relative clauses that are correct and could have the same meaning as the corresponding reduced clause in the Grammar box.

1 The UN created a fund
  a who is called UNICEF.
  b which was called UNICEF.
  c that is called UNICEF.

2 The fund supported millions of children
  a who were affected by World War II.
  b which affected World War II.
  c that had been affected by World War II.

3 The CRC declares different rights
  a where connected to housing, health, the economy and politics.
  b which the UN connected to housing, health, the economy and politics.
  c which are connected to housing, health, the economy and politics.

4 The Voices of Youth website brings together young bloggers and activists
  a who work on development issues.
  b who have been working on development issues.
  c that are working on development issues.

Reduced relative clauses

  a *In 1946, the UN created a fund (1) called UNICEF to support the millions of children (2) affected by World War II.*
  b *The 54 articles of the CRC declare different rights (3) connected to housing, health, the economy, culture, and politics, (4) including such things as the right to a safe home and the right to play.*
  c *The Voices of Youth website brings together young bloggers and activists (5) working on development issues to share their ideas.*

Check the Grammar Reference for more information and practice.

❷ When do we use an *-ing* participle and when do we use an *-ed* participle to shorten a relative clause?

❸ Read about some research findings and projects available to young people. Fill in the blanks with the correct participle of each verb.

Research has found that the number of young people (1) _____ (involve) in dangerous behavior has fallen greatly over recent years. In fact, youths are actually far more likely to be victims of crime rather than criminals. Yet most people think that the amount of youth crime and antisocial behavior is getting worse. The suggestion is that this may be because media reports still focus on youngsters (2) _____ (misbehave), (3) _____ (ignore) the many community projects (4) _____ (reduce) crime. These community projects involve such things as cafes (5) _____ (set up) for teenagers to meet after school, community gardens (6) _____ (teach) teens about sustainability, and a "time bank" (7) _____ (design) by young people (8) _____ (allow) them to earn rewards for doing volunteer work.

4 Work in pairs. Discuss the questions.

1 Do you think the research explained in Activity 3 would produce similar results in your country? Why?
2 How are community projects successful in reducing crime and antisocial behavior?

5 PRONUNCIATION *-ing* forms

a Listen to the statements. Note the pronunciation of the /ŋ/ sound. 🎧 45
b Practice repeating the statements. 🎧 45

Adverbial participle clauses

a *Having campaigned* on behalf of young people, UNICEF also had a key part in the creation of the UN's Convention on the Rights of the Child (CRC) in 1989.

b *Using* online discussion boards as a "meeting place," the initiative provides a space for youngsters who care.

Check the Grammar Reference for more information and practice.

6 Look at the sentences in the Grammar box. Choose the correct options.

1 The subject of the participle clause is *the same as / different from* the subject of the verb in the main clause.
2 The present participle (*Using*) shows the action happened *at the same time as / before* the action in the main clause.
3 A perfect participle (*Having campaigned*) shows the action happened *at the same time as / before* the action in the main clause.

7 Complete this story about a foolish criminal by choosing the correct options.

(1) *Having walking / Walking* home from school one day with a friend, we came across a man on his bike. He started asking us where we were going and what phones we had. We just ignored him, but then he blocked us, (2) *shouted / shouting* at us to give him our phones. (3) *Not wanting / Wanting* to

get into a fight, we handed them over and he biked off. (4) *Returned / Having returned* home, I told my mom what had happened and we reported the incident to the police.

A week or so later, (5) *arresting / having arrested* someone, the police asked us to go and see if we could identify him. Unfortunately, it wasn't the man who had robbed us. We left kind of frustrated. But then, two days later, my friend's mom got a WhatsApp message from my friend's stolen phone! The robber had actually sent her a message, (6) *thinking / thought* it was his own mom—and he had his picture on the account he was using!

Even after (7) *having seen / seeing* the evidence against him, the robber still tried to tell the police he was innocent! I think he was hoping we wouldn't go to court, but (8) *faced / facing* with us actually giving evidence, he changed his mind and pleaded guilty.

8 Do the participle clauses in Activity 7 add information about time, reason, or method? Can you rewrite them with words like *because, after, while,* etc.?

9 MY PERSPECTIVE

What other stories about failed crimes or foolish criminals have you heard?

10 CHOOSE

Choose one of the following activities.

• On your own, write a story about a failed crime or a foolish criminal.

• Work in pairs. Think of six different ways you could promote young people and their issues.

• Work in pairs. Using participle clauses, describe four other trends using similar patterns to the examples in Activity 5. Then, in groups, discuss why these trends are happening.

The number of young people playing sports has fallen a lot.

Young people volunteer to serve food to less fortunate people in their community.

" We take photos constantly. A photo is a reminder of someone or something, a place, a relationship, a loved one. "

BECCI MANSON

Read about Becci Manson and get ready to watch her TED Talk. ▶ **9.0**

AUTHENTIC LISTENING SKILLS

Intonation and completing a point

We often use a rising intonation to show we are going to add an idea and a falling intonation to show that our point is complete. This pattern is common in lists and contrasts.

1 Look at the Authentic Listening Skills box. Then listen to Becci. Practice saying the extract yourself. 🎧 **46**

A photo is a reminder of someone or something, a place, a relationship, a loved one . They're our memory-keepers and our histories, the last thing we would grab and the first thing you'd go back to look for.

2 Decide where you might use a rising intonation and where you might use a falling intonation in these extracts from the TED Talk. Practice saying them.

1 We make skinny models skinnier, perfect skin more perfect, and the impossible possible.

2 We pulled debris from canals and ditches. We cleaned schools. We de-mudded and gutted homes.

WATCH

3 Work in groups. Tell each other about—and show each other, if you can—photos that remind you of special people, places, or times in your life.

4 Watch Part 1 of the talk. Find an example of where Becci: ▶ **9.1**

1 makes a joke about her profession.
2 defends her profession.
3 gives an example of an unpleasant job she did.
4 had an initial moment of realization.
5 felt a sense of pride.
6 had a positive reaction from her contacts.

5 Work in pairs. Tell each other about:

- things you've lost or broken and wish you still had.
- things you're good at repairing.

6 Watch Part 2 of the talk. Are these statements *true, false,* or *not stated*? ▶ **9.2**

1 The little girl in the first photo didn't survive the tsunami.
2 Before long, Becci and her team were scanning photos every other day.
3 Some of the people who brought photos were unfamiliar with the technology Becci was using.
4 The kimono in the photo took months to retouch.
5 Photos would only get retouched once their owners had come forward.
6 The lady who brought the family portraits already had extra copies.
7 Both of the lady's children were caught in the waves when the tsunami reached land.
8 All of the photos Becci and her team retouched were returned to their owners.
9 Becci and her team needed new printers.

TEDTALKS

7 MY PERSPECTIVE

Work in pairs. Discuss the questions.

1 Why do you think the response to Becci's request for help on social media was so high?

2 What other causes do you think might receive a high response on social media? Why?

8 Watch Part 3 of the talk. Which sentence is the best summary of the main point Becci makes? ▶ 9.3

a Everyone loves taking photos.

b Photographs are the most important things most people own.

c Both survivors and volunteers involved in the project benefited in a major way.

d Without photos, we wouldn't be able to remember our past that well.

9 Work in pairs. Which of these statements do you think are lessons from the talk? Do you agree with them?

1 Our differences matter, but our common humanity matters more.

2 In times of crisis, individuals can make a difference in ways that governments cannot.

3 We don't think enough about the psychological and emotional side of recovery after disasters.

4 It's important to feel that the work you do has a positive impact on society.

5 Some people volunteer because they feel guilty about how lucky they've been.

6 Countries shouldn't be expected to deal with large-scale disasters on their own.

10 VOCABULARY IN CONTEXT

a Watch the clips from the TED Talk. Choose the correct meanings of the words and phrases. ▶ 9.4

b Work in pairs. Tell each other about:
- a film, book, photo, or piece of art that *struck a chord* with you.
- three places around *the globe* you'd love to visit.
- a time you remember watching a major news story *unfold*.

CHALLENGE

Work in groups. Look at the situations (1–3). Thinking about both the immediate and the longer-term future, list what you think are the most important things that could be done in each situation by:

- the local government.
- other governments around the world.
- NGOs (Non-Governmental Organizations).
- volunteers on the ground.
- individuals in other places around the world.
- you.

1 A remote Pacific island has been hit very badly by flooding caused by global warming. Whole villages have been washed away and land has been lost to the sea.

2 A humanitarian crisis is developing in a country that has been devastated. There's a shortage of food and medicine, with children and old people being particularly at risk.

3 A big fire has destroyed dozens of homes in a town near you, leaving over a hundred people homeless and causing serious environmental damage.

9E Give It a Try

Useful language

Countering possible opposition

Now, I know what you might be thinking.

I realize there's a perception that…

I'm obviously not denying that…

Listing

To begin with, consider the fact that…

On top of that,…

Let's not forget that…

And finally, it's important to note that…

SPEAKING

1 Work in pairs. Look at these jobs. Discuss how they might be useful in a crisis or disaster. How might they generally be good for society?

actor	banker	chemistry teacher
computer programmer	photo retoucher	plastic surgeon
politician	street cleaner	

2 Work in pairs. Which job in Activity 1 do you think each sentence describes? Do you agree?

1 They are often criticized for creating fake images, but they can also help restore things that are very precious to people.
2 Some people say they're only motivated by greed and self-interest, but they generate jobs, and businesses couldn't work without them.
3 Without them, we'd be surrounded by piles of trash and dirt.
4 They can bring a huge amount of joy to millions of people.
5 They can transform the lives of people who have been injured.
6 They are fundamental to the technological world.
7 Yes, they can be corrupt and lie, but they can also be a huge force for good.
8 They don't just have knowledge, they have the ability to pass it on.

3 Listen to a student explain a job she thinks is important for society. Answer the questions. 🎧 47

1 What job is she talking about?
2 What reasons does she give?

4 Work in pairs. Answer the questions.

1 What did the student mention before listing positive aspects of the job? Why?
2 Which aspects of her argument do you agree and disagree with? Explain why.

5 Work in groups. Discuss which person or job in Activity 1 is best suited to help in a crisis. Follow these steps.

1 Give each person in the group a job to defend.
2 Spend some time preparing what you'll say. Use the Useful language box.
3 Take turns presenting your arguments.
4 Discuss who is the best person to help in the crisis.
5 Vote to choose the best person for the job.

After an oil spill, people volunteer to help with the clean-up operation which can involve helping wildlife.

WRITING A letter of application

6 Read the advertisement. Discuss the questions.

> Spend your winter vacation this year doing something different. We're looking for volunteers between the ages of 16 and 21 to rebuild a school in Belize that was destroyed in a hurricane last year. You will learn traditional building methods to provide a great space where learning can take place. For more details, write and tell us who you are and what you would bring to the project.

1 What do you think daily life for volunteers on this project would involve?
2 What problems might they face?
3 What kind of skills do you think would be required to do this work?
4 How do you think any volunteers who take part might benefit?
5 Would you be interested in doing something like this? Why?

7 WRITING Structuring an application

If you were writing in response to an advertisement, decide how you would order each of these features. Compare your ideas with a partner.

a Refer to the ad that you saw
b List the skills and abilities you have
c Describe who you are and where you are from
d Outline your plans for the future
e Explain why you are writing

8 Work in pairs. Read the letter of application on page 153. Which order did the writer choose? Do you think this person would be a suitable volunteer? Why?

9 Complete the sentences by adding the correct prepositions from the letter.

1 I'm writing _____ response to your recent letter.
2 Please send me more information _____ the post.
3 Please send details _____ how to apply.
4 I'm currently _____ my last year of high school.
5 _____ terms of my experience, I have a part-time job.
6 _____ _____ addition, I have experience working with animals.
7 I feel that I would be suitable _____ the post.
8 I look forward _____ hearing from you soon.

10 Look at the advertisement. List the skills and abilities you have that might make you a suitable volunteer.

> Spend your summer in Mexico helping to preserve some of the world's most endangered species by participating in wildlife volunteer projects. Depending on where you're placed, you may care for animals, conduct research, or help with community programs. You may also be asked to teach basic English to local guides. You may find yourself working with dolphins or even jaguars. Contact us for details and to let us know why you'd be a great fit for our team.

11 Write letter of application in response to the advertisement in Activity 10. Use the Useful language box to help you.

Useful language

Introducing subjects that you want to discuss

In terms of my experience, I have…
With regard to my degree, I have…
As far as language skills go, I can…

Explaining your suitability

I feel I would be suitable because…
I'm prepared to…
I feel confident that I'd be able to…

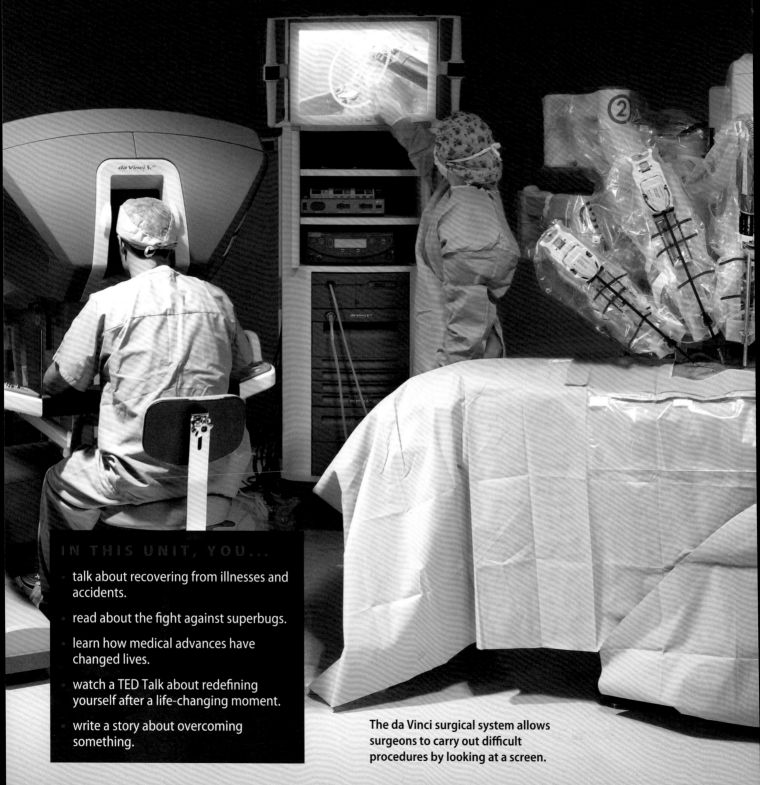

IN THIS UNIT, YOU...

- talk about recovering from illnesses and accidents.

- read about the fight against superbugs.

- learn how medical advances have changed lives.

- watch a TED Talk about redefining yourself after a life-changing moment.

- write a story about overcoming something.

The da Vinci surgical system allows surgeons to carry out difficult procedures by looking at a screen.

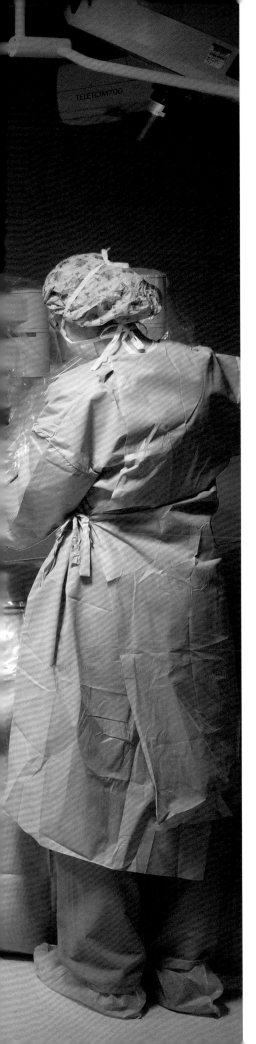

10A Road to Recovery

VOCABULARY Illness and injury

1 Look at the photo. Discuss the questions.

  1 What do you think is happening?
  2 What do you think has happened to the patient?
  3 How might an operation like this have been carried out in the past?

2 Complete the sentences with the words in bold.

  1 action / health / leg
    I slipped on the stairs and broke my *leg*, so I was out of *action* for a while, but I'm back to full *health* now.

  2 cure / drugs / symptoms
    There's no for it, but she takes to control the, and she leads a fairly normal life.

  3 injury / operation / physical therapy
    It was quite a serious wrist, but thanks to the and all the I had, it's almost as good as new.

  4 detected / made / spread
    Luckily, they the cancer early before it to his lungs, and he a full recovery.

  5 bleeding / damage / intensive care
    They managed to stop the, but he was in for days. Thankfully, it didn't leave any permanent brain.

  6 normal / therapy / stroke
    He couldn't really speak after the, but he had a lot of speech, and he's more or less back to now.

  7 lost / think / slammed
    I the tip of my finger after I it in a car door. To be honest, I hardly about it now.

  8 car accident / waist / wheelchair
    He started playing basketball after he was left paralyzed from the down in a.

  9 antibiotics / chest / prescribed
    She said I just had a infection and nothing life-threatening! She me some, and it cleared up after a week.

  10 feel / had / keep down
    I an upset stomach, and I could hardly any food. It was horrible, but I a lot better now.

3 Work in groups. Look at your completed sentences in Activity 2. Find:

  1 eight parts of the body.
  2 at least five nouns that are medical problems.
  3 four adjectives describing illnesses or injuries.
  4 at least five phrases which show that someone has recovered from something.

4 Work in pairs. Discuss the questions.

  1 Have you ever broken any bones? What happened?
  2 When was the last time you had a day off of school due to illness? Why?
  3 What do you do to recover from an illness? Are you a good patient?
  4 What stories have you heard of people recovering from illnesses or injuries? What happened?

LISTENING

5 Listen to Jaime and Clara talking about movies. Answer the questions. 🎧 48

1 What four movies do they talk about?
2 What is the connection between the movies?
3 What doubts do they have about recommending the first three movies?

6 Work in pairs. Complete the sentences with three words in each blank. Listen again and check your answers. 🎧 48

1 He was in the _____ and no one could help because he hadn't told anyone where he was going.
2 It is horrible, but they managed to film it in a way which isn't _____ .
3 It's the same with that film about the guy who had a stroke and was left completely paralyzed and _____ .
4 It's based on his book which he actually _____ by only moving his eye.
5 Yeah, it is incredible, but, sorry the movie didn't _____ me.
6 This is about Frida Kahlo, the Mexican artist who _____ all her life after a terrible bus accident.

7 Work in pairs. Discuss the questions.

1 Have you seen any of the movies Jaime and Clara talked about? If yes, what did you think of them? If not, would you like to see them? Why?
2 Can you think of any other movies that could fit the same category as those discussed? Are they based on true stories? What happened?

8 MY PERSPECTIVE

Think again about what you do when you are recovering from something. Answer the questions.

1 Would these stories inspire you to act differently? Why?
2 What things might you do to overcome challenges you face?

GRAMMAR Expressing past ability

9 Look at the Grammar box and answer the questions.

1 What forms of the verb follow *could*, *manage*, *able*, and *succeed in*?
2 How do you make negatives in the past with *could*, *able*, and *manage*?
3 Which sentences describe a general ability / inability?
4 Which sentences describe success in a task in the past?

Expressing past ability
a *He couldn't move his arm.*
b *No one could help.*
c *She managed to deal with that pain in the end and was able to turn it into incredible art.*
d *She succeeded in becoming a world-renowned artist.*
e *He was unable to speak.*
f *They weren't able to do anything about it.*
g *I didn't manage to see it when it was playing in theaters.*

Check the Grammar Reference for more information and practice.

Frida Khalo managed to deal with her pain and turn it into art that is admired by people all around the world.

10 Work in pairs. Are all the sentence endings in 1–3 correct? Explain those that are incorrect.

1 After I recovered from the illness,
   a I could see perfectly well in front of me, but I couldn't see anything to the side.
   b I was able to see perfectly well in front of me, but I wasn't able to see anything to the side.
   c I managed to see things perfectly well in front of me, but I didn't succeed to see anything to the side.

2 Following the accident,
   a she couldn't walk to begin with, but she could learn again since then.
   b she was unable to walk to begin with, but she's been able to learn again since then.
   c she wasn't able to walk, but she's managed to learn again since then.

3 He wrote a book about his experiences
   a and managed to get it published.
   b and succeeded in getting it published.
   c and could get it published.

11 Discuss how you think the paralyzed man Clara and Jaime talk about managed to dictate his book. Then read the summary and find out what happened.

Although his mind was working perfectly, his thoughts were locked inside him. He (1) *couldn't move* a muscle in his body. He (2) *couldn't make* a sound or even see clearly. So how did the ex-actor and magazine editor Jean-Dominique Bauby write a whole book? Well, first the nurses started communicating with him by asking a question and saying "yes" or "no." Bauby (3) *was able to indicate* his answer by blinking the only part of his body he (4) *could move*—his left eye. Then his speech therapist invented a way of arranging the alphabet in the order of the most frequent letters in French. She pointed to each letter, and Bauby blinked at

the correct one so (5) *she was able to spell* the word. Claude Mendible, an editor, then took up the job of writing with Bauby. Together, they (6) *managed to complete* a 120-page book about Jean-Dominique's life and his experience of "locked in" syndrome. After its publication, Bauby's memoir became a bestseller.

12 Rewrite the italicized words in Activity 11 using these words at least once.

able	could	managed	succeeded	unable

13 PRONUNCIATION Stress on auxiliaries

> Stress is sometimes added to the verbs *be* or *have* to emphasize that something is true—especially when clarifying or contrasting with another viewpoint.

a Listen and repeat the sentences. 🎧 **49**

b Complete these sentences with your own ideas. Then work in pairs. Practice saying the sentences.
   1 It is an amazing story, but _____ .
   2 I have heard of the story, but _____ .
   3 I am happy to be here. It's just _____ .
   4 It was a difficult situation, but _____ .

14 Work in pairs. Think of an inspiring story about someone who survived an accident or managed to deal with an illness. Think about:

- who it happened to and how old they were.
- how the accident happened or the person got sick.
- what the consequences were.
- how they survived and recovered.
- what the lessons from the story are.

15 Tell your stories to each other in groups or as a class.

10B The Battle against Bacteria

VOCABULARY BUILDING

Dependent prepositions

Certain verbs, adjectives, and nouns are often followed by specific prepositions, which we call *dependent*, because their choice depends on the particular word and its meaning. There are no fixed rules about which dependent prepositions go with which words, so it is important to pay attention to them as you learn them.

*She was **diagnosed with** a rare eye disease.*

*I'm **allergic to** nuts.*

*The drug offers at least some **protection from** disease.*

1 Complete the sentences with the correct prepositions. Use a dictionary, if necessary.

1 I would love it if more time was **devoted** _____ physical education at school.

2 I would be very **capable** _____ living on my own on a desert island.

3 Most fast food advertising is **aimed** _____ children.

4 We're all **exposed** _____ far too much air pollution.

5 A lot is done to raise **awareness** _____ health issues—especially among young people.

6 Any **investment** _____ health care has to be a good thing.

7 I think I have a good **chance** _____ living until I am 100.

8 It's natural for people to be **resistant** _____ change.

9 I can't remember the last time I needed a **prescription** _____ anything.

2 Work in pairs. Do you agree or disagree with the sentences in Activity 1? Why?

READING

3 Work in groups. Look at the title of the article you are going to read. Then discuss:

- how you think some of the words in bold in Activity 1 might be connected to the story.
- what, if anything, you know about the discovery of antibiotics.
- why antibiotics are important and how you think they may have changed medicine.
- what you think antibiotics are generally used for.
- what the "apocalypse" in the title might refer to—and how it might be avoided.

4 Read the article. Find out what the "antibiotic apocalypse" is and how it can be avoided.

5 Read the article again. Which of the points below are not made?

a Airplane cabins provide perfect conditions for bacteria to multiply.

b New forms of old diseases are now proving fatal.

c The WHO doubts that the worst-case scenario will happen.

d The possibility of resistant bacteria has been known since the early days of antibiotics.

e Technology is contributing to the overuse of antibiotics.

f Agricultural uses of antibiotics increase the likelihood that deadly superbugs will develop.

g Hosam Zowawi is developing a way of treating bacterial infections faster.

h The slower the recognition of resistant bacteria, the greater the risk of superbugs spreading.

6 MY PERSPECTIVE

Work in pairs. Discuss the questions.

1 Had you heard about the battle against bacteria before? If yes, did you learn anything new?

2 How does the article make you feel? Scared? Optimistic? Determined to change things? Or something else? Why?

CRITICAL THINKING Thinking through the consequences

The consequences of an action are the results or effects that the action produces. One element of reading critically is being able to see possible consequences of actions mentioned in a text.

7 Work in groups. How many possible consequences of these actions can you think of?

1 Drug-resistant diseases spread as a result of international air travel.

2 Antibiotics can no longer be used in hospitals.

3 Online sites selling antibiotics are closed down.

4 The use of antibiotics in farming is banned.

5 The government decides to greatly increase investment in medical research.

Avoiding the Antibiotic Apocalypse

🔊 50 This may sound like the stuff of nightmares or of terrifying science-fiction movies, but according to the World Health Organization (WHO) the threat of an "antibiotic apocalypse" is very real, and many experts
5 fear that it's only a matter of time before we see the emergence of a superbug—a very powerful type of bacteria that normal drugs cannot kill—capable of wiping out huge numbers of people.

Perhaps most disturbing of all is the fact that this
10 potential disaster has been predicted for many decades. In fact, the earliest warnings came from Sir Alexander Fleming, the Scottish doctor and bacteriologist who in 1928 discovered the world's first antibiotic substance— penicillin.

15 Like many groundbreaking scientific finds, the discovery of penicillin was largely accidental. Its importance wasn't realized for at least another ten years, and mass production didn't start until the 1940s. However, there's no doubting the fact that it changed
20 medical practices beyond all recognition. Infections that had previously been fatal were now treatable.

In the speech he made when accepting the Nobel Prize for his work, Fleming warned that bacteria could easily become resistant to antibiotics if regularly exposed to
25 concentrations insufficient to kill them. He went on to express his fears that penicillin would end up being so widely used that such changes were inevitable. Worryingly, this is precisely what happened!

Antibiotics are now regularly prescribed for such
30 non-life-threatening illnesses as sore throats, colds, and ear infections, and if doctors refuse their requests, many patients turn to the internet for their desired medication. On top of this, a large percentage of all antibiotics sold are now being used in farming. They
35 are, for instance, often given to healthy animals to ensure rapid weight gain. Given all of this, it's no surprise that more and more bacteria are evolving a resistance.

One man determined to overcome this challenge is
40 the Saudi microbiologist Hosam Zowawi, who has devoted a considerable portion of his time to developing a test that's able to identify bacteria in hours rather than days, allowing doctors to act more quickly and efficiently, and slowing the potential
45 spread of any deadly infections. Zowawi is also very actively involved in campaigns designed to raise public awareness of the risks of antibiotic overuse.

In addition to reducing the use of antibiotics, there are many other ways that the situation is now being
50 addressed. For instance, in the Netherlands, the government has started putting pressure on farmers to reduce the amount of antibiotics given to animals. Elsewhere, there's a growing understanding of the need to address the underlying conditions that allow
55 new diseases to spread, which, in turn, leads to better trash collection, better drainage, and better housing. Finally, we're starting to see increased investment in research aimed at finding the new antibiotics that could be the penicillin of tomorrow.

E. coli **infections make up a large percentage of antibiotic-resistant infections.**

New technology is helping people to recover their sight and see for the first time.

10C Medical Advances

1 Work in groups. The photos show different ways that technology is helping to improve vision. Discuss what you think each picture shows and how it might work.

2 Listen to an extract from a radio program. Find out: 🎧 **51**

   1 which of the photos is being discussed.
   2 if the technology is expensive.

3 Work in pairs. Can you explain how the technology works using these words? Listen again and check your answers. 🎧 **51**

camera	cells	chip	electrical signals

4 MY PERSPECTIVE

Work in pairs. Think of as many different ways to fund medical research and treatments as you can. Then discuss these questions with another pair of students.

   1 What is the best way to fund medical research and treatment?
   2 How might a health service decide when a treatment is too expensive?
   3 How might a health service decide between two very expensive treatments?

GRAMMAR Emphatic structures

5 As well as pronunciation grammar can also be used to add emphasis. Look at the Grammar box and answer the questions.

   1 How is emphasis added in sentences *a* and *b*?
   2 What adverbs are used in sentences *c* and *d* to introduce the point being emphasized?
   3 What happens to the order of the words that follow these adverbs?

Emphatic structures

   a *While surgical options did exist before, none were nearly as effective.*
   b *While each bionic eye does cost a lot, reports from users have been incredibly positive.*
   c *We're all used to hearing news about terrible things, but rarely do we hear much about exciting new developments.*
   d *When Second Sight started experimenting, little did they know that they were on their way to revolutionizing the treatment of blindness!*

Check the Grammar Reference for more information and practice.

6 Rewrite the sentences in a more emphatic style, using the words in parentheses.

   1 Some doctors read research about new medicine, but too many just accept what big drug companies tell them. (do)
   2 While caffeine increases energy levels, in large doses it can actually prove fatal. (does)

3 In the old days, doctors sometimes removed arms or legs without using any painkillers! (did)

4 When the patient started having terrible headaches, she didn't know it was because a spider was living in her ear. (little)

5 No research suggests that there is anything unhealthy about a vegetarian diet. (in no way)

6 Doctors didn't often cut people open in the days before penicillin. (rarely)

7 You don't fully become an adult until the age of 24. (only after)

8 In the Middle Ages, doctors were never in doubt that releasing blood from the body kept people healthy. (at no time)

9 Plastic surgery didn't become very popular until the 1980s, despite having been around for over 200 years before then. (not until)

10 People in the United States do less exercise than anyone else in the world. (nowhere)

7 PRONUNCIATION Adding emphasis

> *Do / Does / Did* is usually stressed in sentences where it has been added for emphasis. Negative adverbs are also usually stressed when they introduce a point to be emphasized.

a Listen and check your answers in Activity 6. Then listen again and note the way stress is used to add emphasis. 🎧 52

b Practice saying each sentence in an emphatic way. Which of the ideas most and least surprised you? Why?

8 Complete the short article by adding one word in each blank.

There are 39 million blind people in the world. But (1) _____ do people realize that perhaps half of those affected by blindness could be cured, simply by removing the cataract* which causes it. Many people (2) _____ already have surgery to remove cataracts. In fact, it is a very common operation in many countries, and only very (3) _____ does the patient fail to recover good sight. However, until recently the procedure (4) _____ cost quite a lot and was too expensive for sufferers in developing countries. That was until Dr. Sanduk Ruit, a doctor from Nepal, created a new system for conducting cataract surgery. (5) _____ only did he manage to reduce the cost of the operation to around 25 dollars per patient, he reduced the time it took and developed a production-line approach. In fact, (6) _____ in the world do they conduct the operation more efficiently and successfully than in Nepal. The result makes a huge difference to thousands of lives. Not only (7) _____ the operation bring sight back, it (8) _____ brings back the ability to farm and do similar work, which in turn helps to reduce poverty.

cataract *a medical condition which causes the lens of the eye to become cloudy, resulting in blurred vision*

9 CHOOSE Choose one of the following activities.

- On your own, find out about an amazing development in medical history. Write a summary of your findings, explaining what happened, when, and why it was important.

- Work in pairs. Decide what you think the biggest health risk facing your country is. Think of five ways it could be tackled.

Eye exams can now be carried out using common forms of technology.

AUTHENTIC LISTENING SKILLS

Collaborative listening

Fast speech can be difficult to understand. Focus on what you did hear. Think about the context and what you know about the subject or situation to guess what might have been said. If you are with someone, compare what you heard; you may have heard different things.

1 Look at the Authentic Listening Skills box. Then work in groups. Listen to the extract from the beginning of Janine's talk. 🎧 **53**

- Student A: Listen and note the nouns and things you hear.
- Student B: Listen and note the verbs and actions you hear.
- Student C: Listen and note whatever you want.
- Student D: Listen carefully without taking notes.

2 Work in your groups. Write a complete text based on your combined notes. Your text does not have to be exactly the same as the extract you heard in Activity 1.

3 Listen to the extract again and compare it with what you wrote in Activity 2. In what ways is your text different from the extract? 🎧 **53**

WATCH

4 Watch Part 1 of the talk. Are the sentences *true* or *false*? ▶ **10.1**

1 The accident took place at the time of the Olympics.
2 The vehicle that hit Janine was going fast.
3 Janine's bike helmet protected her head from any damage.
4 Janine had an out-of-body experience as she was fighting for her life.
5 Janine had no movement below her waist after the operation.
6 The doctor said the result of the operation meant that Janine would eventually be as good as new.

5 Work in pairs. Watch Part 2 of the talk. Take notes on what you hear and compare. ▶ **10.2**

6 Work in pairs. Complete the sentences together. Then watch Part 2 of the talk again and check your answers. ▶ **10.2**

1 Janine did not know what the other people in the spinal ward _____ .
2 Janine felt the friendships she made there were unusual because they were _____ .
3 The other people in the ward shared their hopes and _____ rather than have _____ .
4 When Janine left the ward and first saw the sun again, she felt _____ for her life.
5 The head nurse had told Janine she would _____ , but she did not believe her.
6 Janine wanted to give up because she was in _____ .

7 Look at these phrases. How do you think they are connected? What new activity and job do you think Janine took up?

buttons and dials	get a license
learn to navigate	pass a medical
sense of freedom	slide up on the wing
take the controls	teach other people

8 Watch Part 3 of the talk. Was your answer to Activity 7 correct? ▶ 10.3

9 Work in pairs. Explain what happened to Janine using the phrases in Activity 7.

10 Watch Part 4 of the talk. What do you think Janine's message is? Discuss your idea with a partner. ▶ 10.4

11 VOCABULARY IN CONTEXT

a Watch the clips from the TED Talk. Choose the correct meaning of the words and phrases. ▶ 10.5

b Work in pairs. Discuss the questions.
   1 What might be something that is difficult to *grasp*? Have you ever experienced this?
   2 Do you think it is good to get *out of your comfort zone*? Why? Have you ever been in that situation? What happened?
   3 Do any of your friends or family have a *nickname* you like? Why do they have it?

12 Work in pairs. Discuss the questions.
   1 Did you enjoy Janine's talk? Why?
   2 Do you think you could have overcome something like Janine's experience? Why?
   3 What judgments do people make when they meet people for the first time?
   4 Have your friends ever helped you overcome a problem or difficulty? How?
   5 Is there something you would like to do but have not? What's stopping you?

CHALLENGE

Work in pairs. Discuss what challenges these situations might create for a person and what opportunities might be created. Then work with another pair of students and put your challenges in order from the most difficult to the easiest. Discuss your reasons.
   • Having a serious accident like Janine's.
   • Moving to a new country because of a parent's job.
   • Failing your final exams at school.
   • Going to college in a new city.

10E Getting Better

Speaking strategy

Developing the conversation

When we respond to news, we don't just show sympathy or surprise. We often add a follow-up comment or a question to keep the conversation going.

You're joking! When did he do that?

Poor guy. So is he OK?

Useful language

Reporting stories / news
Apparently,…
I heard (that)…

Expressing surprise
You're kidding!
Oh no!

Responding to good news
Wow! That's great!
Awesome!

Showing sympathy
Poor guy
He must be fed up!

Passing on a message
Say "hi" from me.
Tell him to get well soon.
Tell her I'm thinking of her.

SPEAKING

1 Work in pairs. What would you say or ask if you heard that someone you knew:

- got good grades on their exams?
- was moving from where they live?
- had been kicked out of school?
- was sick or had an accident?

2 Listen to two conversations between friends. Answer the questions. 🎧 54

1 Who are they talking about? Why?
2 What happened to the person they are talking about?

3 Which of the phrases in the Useful language box did you hear in each conversation? Listen again and check. 🎧 54

4 Work in pairs. Take turns saying the sentences below. Your partner should respond and add a follow-up question or comment.

1 Apparently, he'll have to have an operation.
2 Her mom said she was grounded.*
3 I saw him yesterday and he said he was feeling a lot better.
4 Apparently, it's a really bad cold. He's going to be out all week.
5 Did I tell you? My older sister's going to have a baby!

grounded *not allowed to go out as a punishment for doing something wrong*

5 Practice having conversations based on your ideas in Activity 1. Use the Useful language box to help you.

WRITING A success story

6 Work in groups. Can you think of a time you overcame one of the following? Tell each other your success stories.

a difficulty	disgust	a fear
an illness	an inability	an opponent

7 Work in pairs. Student A: read the story on this page. Student B: read the story on page 153. Then tell each other:

1 which of the things mentioned in Activity 6 each writer overcame.
2 what the writer finally managed to do.

I looked down at the water and the waves crashing against the rocks. My legs immediately started to shake. Someone shouted "Come on Yasine, you can do it!" I was on an adventure vacation. This is what I had wanted to do—walking, climbing, camping—and now here I was doing these things and I couldn't move. I wanted to be anywhere else but here. We were doing a walk along a narrow coastal path, but it had become less and less like a path and more like a cliff we had to climb along. We finally came to a point where we had to hold on to a rock and jump over a small gap to get to the rest of the path. Everyone else had done it and I was the last one. It wasn't far—not much more than a few feet. But I just couldn't do it. I was sure I was going to fall. I was stuck. The rest of the group then started to shout together, "You can do it! You can do it!" I grabbed the rock and leapt to the other side. I made it! Everyone cheered. I had finally managed to do it and it felt like I was champion of the world.

8 Read the story that you did not read in Activity 7. Can you find these features in either text? Compare your findings.

1 An interesting opening sentence that grabs the reader's attention
2 Inversion to make part of the story more emphatic
3 Examples of direct speech
4 Descriptive verbs that make the story more exciting

9 WRITING SKILL Using descriptive verbs

Complete each sentence with the correct form of these descriptive verbs.

creep	grab	leap	peer
rush	scream	slam	stare

1 They _____ me to the hospital and we got there just in time!
2 I _____ the top of the table and pulled myself up.
3 "Watch out!" she _____ as the motorcycle came speeding towards me.
4 I could hear a strange noise, but as I _____ into the darkness, I couldn't see anything!
5 When I heard the scream, I _____ out of my chair and ran into the kitchen to see what the problem was.
6 I _____ at the letter in complete amazement! I just couldn't believe my eyes!

10 Write a story of between 200 and 250 words about overcoming something. Use the phrase *I finally managed to…* somewhere in the story.

Explaining how you felt before you succeeded

I was absolutely terrified.

I was sure I was going to fall / fail / lose!

I'd tried absolutely everything.

I was ready to just give up.

Explaining how you felt in the end

It was the best day / one of the best days of my life.

It was a moment I'll never forget.

It was a truly memorable experience.

It was a day that changed my life.

Have you ever overcome a fear?

PRESENT AND PAST FORMS

Simple present

The simple present describes things that are generally true, habits, or permanent states.

*I **miss** my host family.*

The simple present also describes things scheduled to happen at a particular time in the future.

*We **arrive** at seven in the morning and then **leave** the following evening.*

Present continuous

The present continuous describes actions seen as temporary, in progress, or unfinished.

*We**'re talking** about study-abroad programs.*

The present continuous is also used to talk about things in the future that one has arranged to do with other people.

*I**'m meeting** some friends on Sunday.*

Simple past

The simple past is used to describe finished actions in the past, especially when there is one finished action after another.

*I **spent** six months in Berlin in 2015. Then I **came** home.*

Past continuous

The past continuous is used to emphasize an action in progress around a time in the past.

*I **was** actually **thinking** about canceling my trip before I left.*

Past perfect

The past perfect emphasizes that one thing happened before a particular point in the past.

*I**'d** never **left** Argentina.*

Past perfect continuous

The past perfect continuous (*had been* + *-ing*) is the preferred form for talking about something in progress over a period of time *up to* or *before* a particular point in the past. However, the past perfect can also be used in most of these cases.

*I**'d been wanting** to go there for ages.*

Remember that some "state" verbs that do not express action are not used in continuous forms.

USED TO AND WOULD

To talk about habits, regular actions, or events in the past, use *used to* and *would*. The simple past can also be used. Often, these habits or events no longer happen.

Would is more common than *used to*. *Used to* is often used to start a topic, and then *would* or the simple past is used to give extra details.

*I **used to do** it all the time when I was a student going home to visit friends… Often, when you **went** to some hitching spots, **you'd have to line up** behind several others already waiting for a ride… I often argued with my parents about the dangers of hitchhiking and **I would tell them** about all the amazing experiences I'd had.*

Used to or the simple past (not *would*) are used to describe past states existing over a period of time.

*Hitchhiking **used to be** / **was** / ~~would be~~ so common when I **was** / **used to be** / ~~would be~~ a student.*

Describe individual past events and situations with the simple past only. Do not use *used to* or *would*.

*I also **spent** / ~~used to spend~~ / ~~would spend~~ one summer hitching around South America.*

To form negatives, use *didn't* to show the past tense. Notice that *use to* is used in negatives.

*People **didn't use to worry** about sharing their space.*

It is common to form negatives using *never* instead of *didn't*. Notice that *used to* is used to indicate the past tense in this case.

*People **never used to worry** about sharing their space.*

When asking questions, use the auxiliary *did* to show the question is in the past tense. Notice that *use to* is used in questions.

***Did** you **use to go** there?*

There is no present form of *used to*. The adverb *usually* or the verb *tend to* is used.

*People **don't** ~~used to~~ **usually** hitchhike now.*

1 Choose the correct option.

I (1) *was going / went* on a student exchange to France recently. I (2) *was staying / stayed* with a French boy named Olivier and his family for three weeks over Easter. I (3) *had / was having* an amazing time there. They (4) *were taking / took* me skiing for ten days, which was incredible! I (5) *didn't go / hadn't been* before, but (6) *I'd been taking / I was taking* lessons to get myself ready, so I wasn't completely clueless when I got there. Over the next few weeks, both my skiing and my French (7) *had improved / improved*. The only bad thing about the trip was that while we (8) *had been staying / were staying* in the mountains, I got really sick. I don't know if it was food poisoning or what, but I (9) *felt / had felt* really bad. Olivier (10) *has been coming / is coming* here in July. I'm a little worried because I can't take him to do exciting things like skiing! Most of the time here, (11) *I just hang out / I'm just hanging out* with my friends. (12) *I still look / I'm still looking* forward to seeing him, though.

2 Complete the sentences. Use the past perfect continuous form of the verb if appropriate. If not, use the past perfect.

1 My sister _____ (talk) about doing a student exchange for years, so it's great that she finally went.

2 We _____ (know) each other for years before we decided to travel together.

3 I got really badly sunburned. I _____ (lie) around on the beach all day and just forgot to put sunscreen on!

4 I _____ (see) a lot of the country during my time there, but that was my first time in the capital.

5 This was my third time in the city. I _____ (enjoy) it the other two times but didn't have much of a feel for it yet.

6 They were so nice. We _____ (stay) in a B&B, but they said we could sleep at their place.

3 Complete the text about HitchBot with *would*, *used to*, or the simple past.

HitchBot was a special robot designed by scientists at two Canadian universities as an experiment to see how humans react to robots. They (1) _____ send the robot on hitchhiking trips with instructions to try to visit certain places along the way. They (2) _____ leave the robot at the side of the road, and when someone pulled up to see what it (3) _____ (be), the robot (4) _____ read a message explaining what it wanted to do. The driver then had to pick up the robot, put it in their car, and then leave it by the side of another road to be picked up by someone else. The vast majority of people (5) _____ (treat) the robot well and it (6) _____ (complete) four trips in Canada, Holland, Germany, and the United States.

4 Rewrite each sentence using *used to* or *would* and the word in bold.

1 My grandparents usually came on vacation with us when I was younger. **come**
My grandparents _____ on vacation with us when I was younger

2 In the past, most workers only had one day a week off. **work**
In the past, most workers _____ six days a week.

3 In the 19th century, women usually traveled with someone. **travel**
Women _____ on their own in the 19th century.

4 My hair's a lot longer now. **have**
I _____ shorter hair.

5 My dad gave up playing soccer professionally because he got injured. **to be**
My dad _____ a professional soccer player until he got injured.

5 Complete each pair of sentences with the correct form of the verb in bold, and a pronoun. Use the adverb in parentheses, if given. Put one sentence in a past form and the other in a present form.

leave

1a When I went to Mexico in 2016, it was the first time _____ my country. (ever)

1b _____ ? You've hardly seen the city. (already)

get used to

2a I was in the UK for almost nine months, but I can't say I _____ the food. (ever)

2b It's taken a while, but _____ speaking in Spanish. Hopefully, I'll be fluent by the time we leave. (slowly)

stay

3a I was a little worried because _____ with a host family before, but it was fine. (never)

3b Where _____ on your study-abroad trip next year?

get

4a We took a wrong turn back there. _____ way off the beaten path.

4b We went to seven cities in four days, so _____ a feel for the places. (hardly)

PRESENT PERFECT FORMS AND SIMPLE PAST

Present perfect

The present perfect is used:

- to introduce or list experiences connected to a present situation / discussion.
- to refer to a completed event within a period of time including now.
- to talk about the duration of something that is still true now.

Most successful entrepreneurs **have failed** *at least once.*

Entrepreneurs **have always needed** *the confidence to recover from failure.*

The present perfect continuous is used:

- to talk about duration of activities that are still true now.
- to emphasize the process (not the completed action).

The number of entrepreneurs **has been growing** *over the last few years.*

Kickstarter **has been running** *for several years now.*

The continuous form is preferred when talking about duration, but the simple form can also be used with no difference in meaning.

The number of entrepreneurs **has been growing** *over the last few years.*

The number of entrepreneurs **has grown** *over the last few years.*

The simple form is usually used when talking about a completed action, while the continuous form is usually used to emphasize the process. This is why the simple form is preferred with specific amounts.

Since it started, Kickstarter **has** ~~been raising~~ **raised** *two billion dollars.*

He's ~~been starting~~ **started** *ten different companies over the last fifteen years.*

Simple past

The simple past is used:

- to tell a story of completed events.
- with time phrases that show completed time.
- to talk about the duration of completed events.

D'Aloisio's first investor **contacted** *him via email from Hong Kong.*

She **wrote** *for ten years without success.*

VERB PATTERNS (-*ING* OR INFINITIVE WITH *TO*)

The -*ing* form is commonly used with the following verbs.

admit	avoid	can't stand	consider
delay	enjoy	finish	keep
mind	miss	practice	recommend

The infinitive with *to* is commonly used with the following verbs.

agree	arrange	decide	expect
fail	hope	intend	need
offer	plan	promise	refuse

Objects before -*ing* and *to*

Some verbs can have an object before an -*ing* form or an infinitive with *to*.

catch sb/sth -*ing*	discover sb/sth -*ing*	feel sb/sth -*ing*
find sb/sth -*ing*	got sb/sth -*ing*	hear sb/sth -*ing*
imagine sb/sth -*ing*	leave sb/sth -*ing*	mind sb/sth -*ing*
notice sb/sth -*ing*	remember sb/sth -*ing*	see sb/sth -*ing*

advise sb/sth *to*	allow sb/sth *to*	ask sb/sth *to*
beg sb/sth *to*	cause sb/sth *to*	challenge sb/sth *to*
convince sb/sth *to*	dare sb/sth *to*	expect sb/sth *to*
force sb/sth *to*	get sb/sth *to*	hire sb/sth *to*
invite sb/sth *to*	order sb/sth *to*	pay sb/sth *to*
permit sb/sth *to*	prepare sb/sth *to*	remind sb/sth *to*

Negatives can be made using *not*.

I hate **not having** *a cell phone with me.*

Verbs with two objects

These verbs are commonly followed by two objects.

ask	book	bring	build
buy	cook	find	get
give	lend	make	owe
pass	save	show	tell

With most verbs that can be followed by two objects, the order of the objects can be reversed if *for* or *to* is put in front of the person / group of people. The preposition used depends on the initial verb.

Can you **email me the report** *sometime today, please?*

Can you **email the report to me** *sometime today, please?*

1 Do the time phrases show a completed time (a), a time period that includes now (b), or both (ab)?

a The company's profits rose _____ .
b The company's profits have been rising _____ .

1 over the last five years
2 last year
3 in 2015
4 in the past few months
5 since they found a different distributor
6 when we did the marketing campaign
7 for a long time
8 over the last year

2 Complete the summary with one word in each space.

Madison Forbes has (1) _____ loved drawing and design, and (2) _____ 2010, she's been turning her designs into a successful business called Fishflops, which produces flip flops with Madison's cute sea characters on them. She came up with the name in 2006—(3) _____ she was just eight years old—and, with the help of her father, (4) _____ up the business, which now sells to clothing stores like Nordstrom as well as to the Association of Zoos and Aquariums (AZA). Over the (5) _____ few years, they have also started producing shoes and T-shirts, and the company has (6) _____ several million dollars in sales—not that Madison has been (7) _____ a life of luxury with the profits; instead, she (8) _____ saved most of the money to pay for college. The company also gives to several charities, and a portion of the AZA sales goes to protect endangered animals.

3 Explain the use of these verb forms from Activity 2.

1 Madison Forbes has always loved drawing…
2 She's been turning her designs into a successful business…
3 She came up with the name…
4 They have also started producing shoes…
5 The company has made several million dollars in sales…
6 Not that Madison has been living a life of luxury…

4 Are the sentences correct (C) or incorrect (I)? Correct the incorrect sentences.

1 I need to practice giving this presentation before class.
2 We've almost finished to raise the money we need.
3 Have you considered to pay someone who can do it?
4 I'm going to keep to write to them until I get an answer!
5 He admitted sending thousands of spam emails.
6 I'd recommend to report it. It doesn't look right.

7 I tried to get a better deal, but they basically just refused negotiating.
8 That report needs checking before you send it.

5 Complete the sentences with the correct form of the verbs.

1 I can't imagine him _____ (post) something like that! It's so out of character.
2 I accidentally downloaded a virus and it caused the whole system _____ (crash).
3 Our teacher always forces us _____ (speak) in English in class.
4 I got some bad feedback on my project. It left me _____ (feel) very upset.
5 We'd like to remind you _____ (change) your password within the next two weeks.
6 Websites _____ (play) music while they load is so annoying!
7 I can still remember begging my parents _____ (buy) me my first Xbox!
8 They caught him _____ (try) to access the school's online records.
9 If I could, I'd hire someone _____ (take) my science exam so I didn't have to study for it.
10 I just can't see them _____ (win). They have too many players injured.

6 Look at each first sentence. Add three words to complete each second sentence so that it has a similar meaning to the first.

1 My parents didn't let me use social media until I was 16.
My parents never allowed _____ social media when I was younger.
2 That video really made me think. Online companies have so much power over us!
That video really got _____ how much power online companies have!
3 I warned her about sending her details, but she didn't listen!
I begged _____ send her personal details, but she didn't listen.
4 Every time you enter the site, they make you change your password.
Every time you enter the site, they _____ change your password.
5 That video is amazing. How could anyone not like it?
I can't imagine _____ that video! It's so amazing!
6 Don't let me forget how terrible that site is!
_____ to use that site again! It's awful!

DETERMINERS

Determiners are words used before nouns. They have two main functions:

- to show which noun is being referred to.
- to show how much / how many of something.

Articles

The indefinite article is used:

- before nouns when they are one of several, when it is not important which one is meant, or when something is mentioned for the first time.
- to say what people or things are / were.

The definite article is used:

- before nouns when it is thought to be clear which thing or things is / are meant.
- before superlative adjectives.
- as part of some fixed expressions.

No article is used:

- before uncountable nouns.
- with plural nouns to talk about things in general.
- after prepositions in many expressions with places.
- before the names of most cities, countries, continents, street names, airports, or stations.

Quantifiers

Quantifiers are determiners that show *how much* or *how many* of something. Some can only be used with uncountable nouns or plural countable nouns.

Both is used to talk about two people and / or things.

Either and *neither* are followed by singular countable nouns. They are used before a noun to talk about two choices or possibilities. *Neither* is a negative, so it is not used with *no* or *not*.

Every and *each* are used only with singular countable nouns. Sometimes it is not important which word is used, but generally:

- *each* is used to focus on individual things in a group, or to list two or more things.
- *every* is used to talk about a group or to list three or more things.
- *all* is used to talk about the whole of something. *All* is followed by uncountable or plural nouns.
- *any* is used in positive sentences when it is not important to specify the exact person or thing, because what is being said applies to everyone or everything.
- when quantifiers are used with pronouns, *of* is added after the quantifier.

COMPARATIVES AND SUPERLATIVES

Comparatives and superlatives can be made with adjectives, adverbs, or nouns.

To emphasize that something is "less than," the comparative form *…not as X as…* is often used.

*Their training was **not as hard as** it is now.*

Size differences can be shown by modifying the comparative with a number or measurement, or a modifier.

*On average, shot putters are now **two and a half inches taller** and **130 pounds heavier** than they were in the past.*

***Over a thousand more people** have run sub-four-minute miles since Bannister did it.*

Big difference	much / a lot / a great deal / far	better more efficient
Small difference	a little / slightly	

We can also add modifiers to "not as" comparatives.

not nearly as fast	*not nearly as many*
not quite as good	*not quite as much*

Remember, *many* and *few* go with countable nouns, and *much* and *little* go with uncountable nouns.

The pattern *the more… , the more…* can be used to show how two or more changes happen together or affect each other.

Comparative	Clause remainder	Comparative	Clause remainder
The longer and thinner	*your legs are,*	*the more energy-efficient*	*they are to swing.*

Look at the box to see how situations now are compared with the past.

Athletes are training harder and more intelligently than	*they used to do.* *before.* *in the past.* *they did before.*
Elite shot-putters now are two and a half inches taller than	*they were in the past.* *they used to be.* *40 years ago.*

1 Choose the correct option.

1 Mia Hamm started playing soccer when she was living in *the Italy / Italy*. Later, when she was in *the junior high school / junior high school*, she played on *the boys' team / boys' team*.

2 Hamm has done a lot to promote *a women's / the women's / women's* soccer.

3 To tell you *the truth / truth / a truth*, I'm not really interested in *motorcycles / the motorcycles*, but I admire Valentino Rossi. He has *charm / a charm / the charm* and *a lovely personality / lovely personality / the lovely personality*.

4 Jesse Owens was born in *the Alabama / Alabama* in 1913. He was *the youngest / youngest / a youngest* of ten children, and his father was *farmer / the farmer / a farmer*.

5 As *the teenager / teenager / a teenager*, Owens helped his family by delivering *the groceries / groceries* and working in *a shoe repair shop / shoe repair shop / the shoe repair shop*.

6 Susi Susanti now runs *company / the company / a company* selling *the badminton rackets / badminton rackets*. She imports *a material / the material* for *rackets / the rackets* from Japan, and they're then produced in China.

2 Choose the correct option. In some cases, both may be correct.

1 There's *not much / only a few* difference between the two teams.

2 I have *almost no / hardly* interest in sports, to be honest.

3 *Very few / Not many* talented young athletes actually become successful.

4 I've never really had *no / any* talent for sports.

5 I don't have *very much / very little* respect for most soccer players.

6 *A lot of / Most* medals we win at the Olympics are in long-distance running.

7 When the World Cup is on, I usually try to watch *all / every* game.

8 I couldn't see much because there were *a lot of / so many* people in front of me.

3 Complete the sentences with these determiners.

all	any	both	each
either	every	neither	no

1 I like the fact that you can play the game anywhere. _____ special equipment is needed.

2 Mia Hamm was named FIFA's World Player of the Year in _____ 2001 and 2002.

3 _____ his school nor his family had the money to send Jesse Owens to the 1932 Olympics.

4 My brother can name _____ player who's played for the team in the last ten years!

5 I admire _____ athlete who works hard and has a good attitude.

6 It's a very close game. _____ team could win, but I still think Brazil looks stronger.

7 _____ my friends are really into boxing, but I can't stand it!

8 There's a website that shows you how much _____ player earns.

4 Complete each second sentence so that it has a similar meaning to the first sentence, using the word in bold and two or three extra words.

1 This season they have scored 65 goals and we've only scored 30.
This season they've scored _____ we have. **far**

2 Usain Bolt actually ran only slightly faster than Jesse Owens.
Jesse Owens _____ as Usain Bolt. **fast**

3 I used to play basketball a lot, but I hardly ever play now.
I don't play basketball _____ I used to. **much**

4 No one has ever won as many gold medals in swimming for her country as she has.
She is our _____ ever. **successful**

5 If you continue to play, your injury will only get worse.
The _____ worse your injury will get. **longer**

6 The number of professional athletes has increased dramatically.
There _____ athletes in the past. **far**

5 Complete the comparatives using your own ideas.

1 I'm slightly _____ than _____ .

2 I'm nowhere near _____ .

3 Young people these days are far more _____ .

4 There _____ as _____ as there _____ in the past.

5 I _____ than I used to.

6 _____ , the more successful you will be.

FUTURE FORMS 1

Be going to + verb is usually used to talk about what has already been planned. Unless an adverb like *probably* is used, it means it is a definite plan.

They're going to build a new museum in our town.
I'm going to stay in tonight and study.

The present continuous is also often used, particularly with plans and arrangements involving other people.

I'm meeting a friend of mine later.

Sometimes *will* is used to talk about scheduled plans.

The coach will arrive at nine and will take everyone to the museum, where the tour will start at ten.

Will + infinitive is usually used at the moment of making a decision.

A: What's your flight number?
B: I don't know. I'll check later and I'll send you a text with it.

Will is usually used to make promises, threats, refusals, etc. (see Unit 6).

Will or *be going to* can be used to talk about predictions. Unless an adverb like *probably* or *possibly*, or an introductory verb such as *think* or *guess* is used, they both mean the speaker is certain about their prediction. *May / might* can also be used to show less certainty.

Certain	Less certain
It's going to create jobs.	It's possibly going to create jobs.
It's going to be a disaster.	It's probably going to be a disaster.
They'll go over budget.	They'll probably go over budget. / I think they'll go over budget.
They won't get many visitors.	They might not get many visitors.

The future continuous is used to emphasize that an action is ongoing / unfinished in relation to a particular point in time or a second future action. The future continuous is *will be* + *-ing*. (*Be going to be* + *-ing* is also used.)

It's going to create jobs, and they'll be employing local artists.

When a future time clause is used, the verb is in the simple present or present perfect.

But what about once it's been completed?

Be about to is sometimes used to talk about a plan, arrangement, or prediction concerning what is going to happen in the immediate future. *Just* is sometimes added to emphasize it is the next thing planned.

We're about to hold a community festival.
He's just about to leave, but if you rush you might catch him before he does.

FUTURE FORMS 2

The future in the past

When the future is talked about as seen from a time in the past, *was / were going to*, *would* as the past tense of *will*, and the past continuous can all be used.

My son was struggling, and I was worried he was going to drop out of school and maybe end up hanging out with the wrong kids.

He went several steps further and promised those 11 students that he would turn the orchestra into a world leader!

Abreu had managed to get 50 music stands for the 100 children he was expecting to come and rehearse.

Future perfect

The future perfect is formed using *will / won't* + *have* + past participle.

Soon, over 10 million people will have seen it.

The future perfect emphasizes actions completed by a certain time.

I'll call you after six. I'll have finished work by then. (= already finished before six)

The future perfect continuous is formed using *will / won't* + *have been* + *-ing*.

It'll soon have been running for 70 years.

The future perfect continuous emphasizes an ongoing action that is taking place in the present and will continue up until a point in the future.

By the end of this course, I will have been studying English for ten whole years!

The future perfect is usually accompanied by a time reference such as *before the weekend*, *by Thursday*, etc.

❶ Complete the sentences using the two future forms in bold and the verbs in parentheses. Decide which form is the best for each space.

present continuous / be going to

The festival _____ (be) great because some of my favorite bands _____ (play).

The festival *is going to be* great because some of my favorite bands *are playing*.

1 simple present / *will*

What do you think you _____ (do) after you _____ (leave) school?

2 simple present / future continuous

Let's hope that when we _____ (have) the concert outside, it _____ (not / rain).

3 present perfect / *going to*

They _____ (start) the project once they _____ (raise) enough money.

4 present continuous / present perfect

We _____ (go) on a school trip to Hong Kong after we _____ (finish) all our exams.

5 *will* / future continuous

I _____ (not do) much this weekend, so I _____ (show) you around the city, if you want.

6 present perfect / *be about to* / *will*

I'm sorry, the movie _____ (start). I _____ (call) you when it _____ (finish).

❷ Complete the second sentences using 3–5 words—including the words in bold—so that they have the same meaning as the first sentences.

I'll come over to your house after I have finished my homework. **am**

I'll come over to your house, but *I am going to finish* my homework first.

1 The tickets are going to sell out immediately. **soon**

The tickets will sell out almost _____ gone on sale.

2 First they're going to repair the houses, and then they'll paint them. **before**

They're going to repair the houses _____ them.

3 They need to raise a lot of money so they can complete the project. **to**

If _____ the project, they have to raise a lot of money.

4 I don't think that the project will be a failure. **should**

The project _____ .

5 I could meet you when I go shopping in town on Saturday. **be**

I _____ in town on Saturday, so I could meet you then.

❸ Complete the summary with these words.

expected	going	than	wasn't	were	would

In many ways, Sheffield and Bilbao are similar. By the 1990s, both were post-industrial cities wondering how they were (1) _____ to cope in the coming years. Like the Guggenheim, the National Centre for Popular Music was (2) _____ to be a landmark building that (3) _____ boost tourism in the city. Bosses at the Centre (4) _____ hoping for 400,000 visitors a year, but numbers were far lower (5) _____ expected, with only around 140,000 showing up in the first 12 months. People soon realized that the center on its own (6) _____ going to be enough to transform the city, and it closed down before even reaching its second birthday.

❹ Complete the second sentences using the words in parentheses and 1–3 additional words.

1 I had high hopes for it, but it was actually sort of a letdown.

It wasn't as good as _____ (thought) be.

2 I had high expectations, but it totally exceeded them.

It was even better than _____ (expecting) to be.

3 They ended up with three million visitors—far more than initially expected.

They _____ (hoping) to get around a million visitors, but ended up with three times that!

4 I'd planned to go out and meet some friends, but in the end I was too tired.

I _____ (going) to go out and meet some friends, but in the end I was too tired.

5 I hadn't planned to return yet, but I ran out of money.

I _____ (stay) longer, but I ran out of money.

❺ Choose the correct option.

1 Hurry up! The movie will *start / have started* by the time we get there, if we don't get moving!

2 *I'm going / I will have gone* to a concert tomorrow night, so can we meet on Friday instead?

3 *I'm helping / I'll have helped* a friend with something tomorrow, but *I'll have finished / I'm finishing* by five, so I'll call you then.

4 *I'll have been living / I'm going to live* here for the last five years in July.

5 I read somewhere that by the time you're 60, you will have *been sleeping / slept* for twenty years!

PASSIVES 1

The passive is used to focus on who or what an action affects. The passive is also used when it is unclear or unimportant who performs an action. The passive is formed using *be* + a past participle.

Simple present

*The cup **is** then **left** far away from your bed.*
*The machines **are exported** all over the world.*

Present continuous

*If your phone **is being** charged…*
*The wrong questions **are being** asked.*

Present perfect

*I **have** just **been sent** an email by Maxine.*
*It **has been designed** to track your sleep patterns.*

Simple past

*I **was** recently **given** this lovely new smartphone.*
*We **were** only **told** about it at the last minute.*

Past continuous

*There was a power outage while the experiment **was being carried out**.*
*They **weren't being produced** in Mexico, so I saw an opportunity.*

Past perfect

*I wanted to produce them, but a patent **had** already **been taken out**.*

After modals

*You**'ll be forced** to get up.*
*It **would be thrown** around all over the place.*

After prepositions

*I'm scared of **being asked** questions I can't answer.*

Some verbs have two objects: the <u>direct object</u> and an **indirect object**.

*My parents gave **me** <u>a great new smartphone</u>.*
*Maxine sent **me** <u>an email</u>.*

A passive sentence can be made in two ways when there are two objects.

I was recently given <u>this great new smartphone</u>.

*<u>A new smartphone</u> was given **to me**.*

I have just been sent <u>an email</u> by Maxine.

*<u>An email</u> has just been sent **to me** by Maxine.*

PASSIVES 2

Passive reporting verbs

A passive structure is often used to report general knowledge, beliefs, and assumptions. There are two common patterns after the passive.

The brain	is thought	to have over 12,000 miles of blood vessels.
	was believed	to be controlled by four different elements or "humors."
	is estimated	to weigh six and a half pounds.
	is known	to recover from serious damage.
It	is thought	(that) the brain works like a watch.
	is claimed	(that) the brain is like a computer.
	is assumed	(that) people know what they are doing.
	is well known	(that) smoking causes cancer.

In the second pattern, *it* is impersonal. It is there because in English sentences with a verb need a subject.

Causative *have* and *get*

Have / get + something + past participle is a passive construction, similar in meaning to the sentences in **b**. However, with this structure the person or thing that causes the action or is affected by the action can be brought in (*I* and *My brother* in the sentences in **c**). This structure is used to show that someone else does something for or to the subject.

a *Someone stole my bag.*   *The hairstylist dyed my brother's hair.*
b *My bag was stolen.*   *My brother's hair was dyed.*
c *I **had** my bag stolen.*   *My brother **got** his hair dyed.*

Causative *get* is usually:

- less formal and uncommon in writing.
- used when the subject is the cause of the action. (*My brother paid the hairdresser to dye his hair.*)

1 Complete the sentences with the correct active or passive form of the verbs in parentheses.

1 Language (1) _____ obviously _____ (exist) for many thousands of years before writing (2) _____ (invent), but the existence of written records really (3) _____ (mark) the beginning of history as we know it. The earliest writing (4) _____ (find) in part of what (5) _____ now _____ (call) Iraq.

2 The printing press (1) _____ often _____ (call) one of the most important inventions of all time. Of course, books (2) _____ (produce) before Johannes Gutenberg (3) _____ (present) his first creation to the world, but always by hand! Before too long, thousands of books (4) _____ (print) and (5) _____ (distribute) all over Europe.

3 If you're worried about your phone (1) _____ (steal), here's a helpful hack. A special app can (2) _____ (install) so that you can (3) _____ (track) the phone if it's lost or stolen. You'll also be able to see if the phone (4) _____ (use). It can even (5) _____ (wipe) clean remotely, to stop criminals from (6) _____ (get) hold of your data.

4 The first self-driving car only (1) _____ (hit) the road very recently, but it's quite possible that cars as we know them will soon (2) _____ (replace) by this new model. Over recent years, much of the research into these cars (3) _____ (fund) by Elon Musk, a TED speaker who (4) _____ (start) lots of different companies. Thousands of self-driving cars (5) _____ already _____ (build)—and they (6) _____ (get) more sophisticated.

2 Complete each sentence by making these verbs with two objects into the passive.

award Ahmed Zewail the Nobel prize in Chemistry
give me it
give us some tricky questions
~~show the queen one of the first telephones~~
teach us how to do it

1 In January 1878, one of the first telephones *was shown to the queen* by its inventor, Alexander Graham Bell.
2 In 1999, the Nobel prize in Chemistry _____ , who was the first Egyptian to receive the prize.
3 The science test was sort of a nightmare because we _____ !

4 I can type very fast because we _____ in elementary school.
5 I had my watch stolen, and I was really upset because it _____ by my grandparents.

3 Complete each pair of sentences using the word in bold. One sentence should be in the active form and the other should be in the passive form.

1 accept
  a It _____ now that increases in global temperatures are due to human activity.
  b Most scientists _____ that we need to take action to reduce global warming.

2 not know
  a We _____ exactly how many stars there are in the solar system.
  b It _____ exactly how stars were first formed.

3 think
  a Some researchers _____ that it could be possible to live on Mars.
  b Mars _____ to have water under its surface.

4 believe
  a In the past, many diseases _____ to be caused by having too much blood in the body.
  b Doctors in the past _____ that they could cure diseases by removing blood from the body.

4 Complete the short report with one word in each space.

The government is (1) _____ air quality tested because high levels of pollution (2) _____ thought to (3) _____ increasing. The government is also having research (4) _____ in schools to try to find out whether air pollution is having any effect on students' performance. Air pollution is known (5) _____ affect health and is estimated to (6) _____ thousands of deaths each year. (7) _____ is also claimed (8) _____ it affects the development of the brain and young people's intelligence, but more research is needed to determine if there is a clear link.

MODALS AND MEANING

Modals never change their form. They go with normal verbs and are followed by the infinitive without *to* form of those verbs. Modals add meaning to verbs. A phrase or normal verb can sometimes be used instead of a modal.

Will/would

Will is used to express that something is certain or sure to happen, and to express promises, offers, habits, and refusals.

*The first thing that **will** strike people…*

Would is used to express that something is theoretically certain to happen, to report as the past form of *will*, and to express a habit in the past.

*If the habitat disappeared, they**'d** die out.*

Should/shall

Should is used to express a good or better idea, or if something is expected to happen in the future.

***Should** we be trying to conserve these species?*

Shall is used to ask for and give suggestions, or to make offers about a current or future situation.

*What **shall** we do about it?*

Can/could

Can expresses ability and permission. It is also used if something is only possible sometimes and factually possible (or not, in the negative).

*They **can** be difficult to see in the wild.*

Could is used to express past ability / inability, if something happened sometimes, or is theoretically possible. *Could* is also used in polite requests.

*I **couldn't** swim until I was in my twenties.*

may/might/must

Might is used if something is uncertain but possible.

*You **might** stop weak species from going extinct.*

May is also used if something is uncertain but possible, and for permission.

*These changes **may** bring benefits.*

Must is used if something is necessary and if the speaker is sure of something based on experience.

*These changes **must** bring benefits.*

Have can sometimes behave as a modal.

*You **have** to go to school.*

MODALS AND INFINITIVE FORMS

Modals can be followed by different kinds of infinitive forms.

To talk about actions generally, use a modal + the infinitive without *to* form.

*As you **can see**, it does look quite professional.*

To talk about actions in progress or extended over time, use a modal + *be* + *-ing* (the continuous infinitive without *to*).

*We **should be doing** more to protect them.*

To talk about the past in general, use a modal + *have* + past participle (the perfect infinitive without *to*).

*You **could have (could've) told** me how cruel it was and I honestly **wouldn't have cared**.*

To emphasize that an action was in progress when another thing happened, use a modal + *have been* + *-ing* (the perfect continuous infinitive without *to*).

*I **can't have been paying** attention when I read about it.*

Modals can also be used with passive forms.

*More **should be done** to reduce the suffering of animals.*
(= generally)

*I got really sick after eating that meat. It **can't have been** cooked properly.* (= in the past)

① Choose the correct option.

Juliana Machado Ferreira is a conservation biologist who is trying to stop illegal wildlife trade in Brazil. People in Brazil (1) *will / shall* often keep wild birds as pets, but Machado says they (2) *shouldn't / couldn't*. Taking animals from nature (3) *can / should* have a terrible impact on the habitat and other animals there. For example, if a large proportion of the wild birds that are captured are female, this (4) *might / will* inevitably reduce future populations. The birds (5) *may / would* also be predators for other animals or consume particular plants, so a reduction in the bird numbers (6) *can / can't* have an impact on the rest of the ecosytem. She believes the public (7) *must / might* be educated about these effects. In the past, she has worked with the police to help return birds to their original habitat. The problem is that they (8) *could / shall* be from any number of different places, so Machado used a genetic test to determine where the birds (9) *might / will* be from. She developed her ideas at the US Fish and Wildlife Service Forensics Laboratory. She got an internship there because she (10) *would / could* write regularly to them asking if she (11) *would / could* become a volunteer until eventually they said yes! And now Juliana shows the same determination in her work. She has a very varied work life but, in the next few years, she (12) *may / can* spend more time in her home office. She also says that if she (13) *can / could* talk to her younger self, she (14) *would / should* tell herself to learn something about finance and marketing. This is because she is now in a management position, and students aren't taught how to deal with money in biology classes.

② Choose the best self-follow-up comment to each question.

1 Would I ever do it?
  a Only if I had no other option.
  b Of course I can.

2 Shall I do it for you?
  a I still haven't decided.
  b It's no trouble.

3 Must I do it?
  a It'll be fun.
  b Can't someone else?

4 Should I really do it?
  a There's no other option.
  b I'm not sure it'll improve things.

5 Will I do it at some point?
  a I still haven't decided.
  b I don't mind if you don't want to.

6 Can I do it?
  a I'd really like to try.
  b I might not.

③ Choose the correct option.

1 New research has shown that there *can't / might* once have been a creature similar to a unicorn.

2 I can't believe how little he ate. He *can't be feeling / can't have been feeling* very hungry.

3 I can't believe you thought that story was true. You *should / must* have checked it on some other sites!

4 I'm not surprised his parents were angry. He *shouldn't have had / shouldn't have been having* snakes without telling them!

5 Surely there *would / will* have been more in the papers about the tree octopus if it were true.

6 I'm guessing that you *might / should* have heard about the tree octopus, right?

7 We promise that any cat you buy from us *will have been being / will have been* thoroughly checked by a vet.

8 You *shouldn't have scared / shouldn't scare* the dog. He *wouldn't / couldn't* have barked at you otherwise.

④ Complete the rewrite for each sentence. Use the best modal and two or three other words in each space.

1 It's just not possible for the Loch Ness monster to have survived that long without being found.
The Loch Ness monster _____ that long without being found. It's impossible.

2 It's possible that Loch Ness was once connected to the ocean.
Loch Ness _____ connected to the ocean.

3 I can't believe I didn't realize the movie was a fake. I'm so stupid. I really _____ the movie was a fake.

4 If there really was a monster, why aren't there more photos of it?
People _____ more photos of the monster if it really existed!

5 It's impossible to get near the loch now without being filmed by security cameras.
By the time you get to the edge of the loch, you _____ by security cameras.

6 There's no way he was telling the truth about what he saw.
If you ask me, he _____ about what he saw.

7 Loch Ness is only 10,000 years old. Plesiosaurs died out 60 million years ago.
Loch Ness _____ around when plesiosaurs still existed.

8 I swear I saw something. Honestly, if only I'd had my camera with me!
I _____ my camera with me. I _____ what I saw if I'd had it.

FIRST, SECOND, THIRD, AND MIXED CONDITIONALS

First conditional

First conditionals describe possible results of real situations now or in the future.

If you're in school today, *you'll* probably start working sometime in the 2020s.

I'm going to take the test again *if I fail.*

Second conditional

Second conditionals describe imaginary situations and results now or in the future.

If these drawings **were painted** more realistically, they **would look** amazing.

I wouldn't joke about it *if I were you.*

Third conditional

Third conditionals describe imaginary situations and results in the past.

If she'd wanted pictures, **she'd have told** us.

If he hadn't spent that day with his niece, the Monster Engine **would never have happened**.

Mixed conditional

Mixed conditionals describe imaginary past situations and imaginary present results.

If their schools had encouraged unusual ways of seeing the world, lots of adults **would be** more creative.

I wouldn't be here now **if she hadn't helped** me.

Other modals can also be used in the result clauses of conditional sentences.

If I do OK on my exams, I **might / may try** to study fine art in college. = Maybe I will study fine art.

If I get really good grades, I **can go** and study abroad. = It will be possible for me to study abroad.

If he had been a little taller, he **could have become** a really great basketball player. = It would have been possible for him to become a great player.

WISH, IF ONLY, WOULD RATHER

Wish, if only, and *would rather* all introduce hypothetical ideas—things that a speaker wants to be true, but sees as impossible. As with conditional sentences, past forms of verbs are used to talk about hypothetical events.

The simple past, the past continuous, *could,* and *would* are used to hypothesize about present situations.

The simple past is used when hypothesizing about general situations or states.

I wish I **was** better with words.

I wish I **was** as creative as her / him.

I wish I **didn't have** to take art classes.

If only I **had** an extra eye in the back of my head!

I'd rather the teacher **didn't give** homework.

The past continuous is used to hypothesize about an action or specific situation happening now.

If only I **wasn't sitting** here now!

I wish I **was doing** something else. This is boring.

Could is used to hypothesize about an ability we want.

I wish I **could draw** better.

I wish I **could help** you, but I just can't.

Would is used to hypothesize about a habit or behavior we want to stop (or start).

I sometimes wish my classmates **wouldn't make** so much noise.

I wish she **would speak** slower. I can't understand anything she says.

The past perfect is used to hypothesize about the past and express regrets.

I wish my parents **hadn't forced** me to learn an instrument.

I often say to myself, "If only I'd spent more time thinking about this before I started."

Note that, where the subject of *would rather* is the same as the verb that follows it, an infinitive without *to* is used.

I'd rather **you did** it.

I'd rather **do it** myself.

1 Choose the correct option.

1 If you *will want* / *want* to study abroad, you'll need to save some money first.

2 I wouldn't play this instrument well if my dad *hadn't helped* / *doesn't help* me when I first started.

3 If I *would have* / *had* more time, I'd love to learn how to paint with watercolors.

4 It's your fault! If you hadn't been late, everything *would've been* / *was* fine.

5 The test's next week and you *don't* / *are not going to* do well if you don't work more!

6 If we hadn't changed things when we did, the situation *would* / *will* be worse now.

7 It might not have worked if we *tried* / *had tried* it that way.

8 If I spoke to my mother like that, she really *won't* / *wouldn't* be happy!

2 Complete the sentences with the correct form of the verbs in parentheses.

1 If I _____ (not ask) lots of questions when I was at school, I wouldn't be a scientist now.

2 If you _____ (create) a culture that encourages creativity, people will be happier.

3 I don't think I _____ (start) painting if my parents hadn't encouraged me.

4 If I _____ (be) fluent in English, life would be so much easier!

5 Just think! Things _____ (be) very different today if ways of writing hadn't developed.

6 If you don't practice, you _____ (never get) better at it.

7 I _____ (not do) that if I was you.

8 If it _____ (not be) so noisy in the exam room, I would've done better.

3 Make conditional sentences based on the information below.

1 They only realized how talented she was after giving all the children tests to assess creativity levels.

They wouldn't have realized how talented she was if they hadn't given all the children tests to assess creativity levels.

2 Follow the rules or fail the course. It's your choice!

3 I can't really play this. I haven't practiced recently.

4 Some colleges don't value creativity. That's why they don't really help students develop it.

5 She didn't obey the rules when she started her business. That's why she's successful today.

6 Creativity in children is like anything else: encourage it or be prepared for it not to grow.

4 Choose the correct options.

1 A This is taking too long to do.
  B Yeah, sorry. I thought it was a good idea at the time, but I wish I *hadn't suggested* / *didn't suggest* it now.

2 A Shall I ask my mom or dad if they can take us there?
  B I'd rather we *go* / *went* on our own.

3 A I'd like to study abroad somewhere.
  B Me too. If only I *can* / *could* speak Chinese! I'd love to go to Shanghai.

4 A I wish the teacher *would* / *wouldn't* make us copy everything from the book.
  B I know. It's a little boring, isn't it?

5 A Did you go to the gig yesterday?
  B No, but I wish I *had* / *did*. I heard it was great.

6 A If only I *didn't have to* / *wouldn't have to* leave. I'd love to talk more.
  B Don't worry. I need to be home before 12, anyway.

5 Complete each second sentence so that it has a similar meaning to the first sentence, using the word given and three extra words.

1 I'm afraid we can't do anything more to help. **only**
  If _____ more to help.

2 My brother is so negative. It's really annoying. **would**
  I wish my brother _____ about things.

3 I wanted to walk here, but we took the car. **rather**
  I _____ the car at home.

4 We should have done a better analysis of the problem. **wish**
  I _____ the problem better.

6 Complete each sentence with one word. Contractions count as one word.

1 A Is it OK if I put some music on?
  B I'd rather you _____ . I'm trying to study.

2 A Do you want to go to the mall?
  B I'd rather _____ somewhere else. I don't like the stores there.

3 A I wish we _____ asked someone to help us.
  B Really? I'd rather _____ to do it myself first, even if I make a mistake.

4 A I'd rather you _____ this a secret between us. It's a bit embarrassing.
  B Don't worry. I'd rather _____ knew what happened! If _____ I could forget it myself!

REPORTED SPEECH

When an anecdote or story is told, what people said is often reported. This can be done with:

- direct speech.

*She said, "I **love** you," and then he said, "**Will** you marry me?"*

- indirect speech.

*She said she **loved** him, and he then asked (her) if she'**d** marry him.*

- a mixture of the two.

*She said, "I **love** you," and then he asked if she'**d** marry him.*

When reporting with indirect speech, follow the normal rules of tenses within a story. This often involves a tense backshift from direct speech. Look at the direct and indirect speech used to report statements about:

- a situation or action at the time it was said / thought.

I said, "I need to go back to school."
*I said I **needed** to go back to school.*

- an action in progress at the time it was said.

She said, "I'm going to the station."
*She said she **was going** to the station.*

- an action further back in time before it was said.

He said, "I've forgotten my money."
*He told me he'**d forgotten** his money.*

- a plan or prediction for the future at the time it was said.

I asked and they said, "We'll try!"
*They said they **would** try.*

When the statement being reported is still true, present and other tenses can be used, as they apply to now.

*Miriam told me to tell you she'**ll be** late.*
= She's not here yet, so she still will be late.
*He told me he'**s never had** tea.*
= As far as I know, he still hasn't had tea.

When correcting a misunderstanding, the backshift is preferred because the misunderstanding is no longer true, but it is not essential.

A: We are meeting at 10.
*B: I thought we **were** meeting at 11.*

In indirect reporting of questions the normal word order of a statement is used.

*I said, "**What are you doing** here?"*
*I asked her **what she was doing** there.*

*I thought, "**Why did you ask** that?"*
*I wondered **why she'd asked** me that.*

*She said, "**Do you need** any help?"*
*She asked **if I needed** any help.*

Remember that when what was said is reported, different words must be used for times or places if what is being reported has finished, is no longer true, and / or was in a different place.

*They said, "Can we wait until **tomorrow**?"*
*They asked if they could wait until **the next day**.*

*He said, "I talked to her **yesterday**."*
*He said he'd talked to you **the day before**.*

*I told them, "I was here **last Tuesday**!"*
*I told them I'd been there **the previous Tuesday**.*

Other useful time phrases for reporting:

today	*that day*
now / immediately	*at that moment / right away*
tomorrow	*the next day*
next week	*the next week / the following week*
last week	*the week before / the previous week*

PATTERNS AFTER REPORTING VERBS

Notice the patterns that often go with particular verbs.

verb + infinitive (with *to*): agree; arrange; claim; decide; intend; offer; pretend; promise; refuse; threaten

verb + *-ing*: admit; avoid; consider; continue; deny; imagine; resent; recommend; suggest

verb + (*that*) clause: acknowledge; announce; argue; claim; confess; declare; deny; insist; recommend; state

verb + someone + (*that*) clause: assure; convince; notify; persuade; promise; remind; tell; warn

verb + someone + infinitive (with *to*): advise; ask; encourage; force; invite; persuade; remind; tell; urge; warn

verb + preposition + *-ing*: accuse somebody of; admit / confess to; apologize for; blame somebody for; criticize somebody for; forgive somebody for; insist on; thank somebody for

1 Choose the correct option.

A few years ago, a Chinese friend of my parents asked if I (1) *want / wanted* to visit (2) *the following summer / this summer* to spend time with their daughter, who was my age. It was a great opportunity, so I agreed to go. I had to fill out a long visa application. My father and I took it to the Chinese embassy, and they told us to come back (3) *next week / the next week* to pick up the visa. When we went back, there was a long line for some reason. My dad explained to the security people that we had been (4) *here / there* (5) *the previous week / last week* and we were just picking up a visa, but he was told that we (6) *have to / had to* line up like everyone else. So we stood there and started chatting with the man in front of us. He asked my dad where (7) *I was / was I* going, and it turned out it was the same place where he lived. "What (8) *were / are* you doing there?" he asked. My dad told him I (9) *was going to / will* stay with a friend of his from college. Then the man asked, "What college?" When my dad told him, the man said one of his best friends (10) *had been / be* at the same college a few years before. He said his friend's name, and it was actually my dad's friend, too! It was an amazing coincidence!

2 Complete the story with the verbs in parentheses and the correct modals, verb forms, or tenses.

Yesterday, I was trying to get to sleep when I heard my dog barking. I got up and my dog was there with some paper in his mouth. I told him (1) _____ (let) it go. I pulled, and the piece of paper tore. I suddenly realized it was my math homework and asked my mom (2) _____ (come) and take a look. When she saw what had happened, she just laughed. I said it (3) _____ (be not) funny and I (4) _____ (have to) do it all over again, but my mom said it (5) _____ (be) too late. She promised she (6) _____ (write) a note to the teacher in the morning and said I (7) _____ (not worry). However, the next morning my mom got a call from work before I got up. They told her someone (8) _____ (call) in sick and asked her if she (9) _____ (go) in early. She completely forgot about the note. So of course, in my math class, when the teacher asked why I (10) _____ (not do) my homework and I explained, he didn't believe me! His exact words were, "Do you (11) _____ (think) I was born yesterday?" But I swear that (12) _____ (be) exactly what happened!

3 Complete the second sentences so they have a similar meaning to the first. Use two to five words, including the correct form of the verb in bold.

1 My mom said I should write to the TV company and complain about it.
My mom *suggested writing* to the TV company to tell them how I felt. **suggest**

2 They said that they'd meet me to explain their decision.
After I complained, they _____ me and explain their decision. **agree**

3 I felt terrible for what I said, so I wrote to say sorry.
I wrote them a letter _____ for such awful things. **apologize**

4 Of course, they reject all accusations and claim that they're in the right.
Naturally, they _____ anything wrong. **deny**

5 The goal of the rule was prevention of discrimination.
The rule _____ discrimination. **intend**

6 There has been a lot of pressure on the school to change its dress code.
The school _____ its dress code. **urge**

7 He knew what the rules were, but he decided to ignore them!
He basically just _____ the rules! **refuse**

8 They have an employment policy that prioritizes total gender equality.
The school _____ an equal number of male and female teachers. **insist**

4 Which two options are possible in each sentence?

1 My parents *advised / recommended / urged* my sister to complain to her boss about it.

2 He's been *blamed / accused / criticized* for not employing enough staff from minority backgrounds.

3 We've been trying to *tell / warn / state* them that there will be problems if things don't change!

4 I read online that she'd *admitted / apologized / denied* sending racist emails.

5 They've *avoided / promised / refused* to tackle the problem.

6 He was *arguing / telling / insisting* that nothing will change unless people take direct action.

5 Rewrite each sentence in Activity 4 using one of the verbs with a different verb pattern.

1 *My parents **recommended** that my sister complain to her boss about it.*

RELATIVE CLAUSES

Relative clauses add information after nouns. Different relative pronouns are used depending on the nouns being qualified or on the information that follows.

Defining and non-defining clauses

Some relative clauses explain exactly what the thing or person is (defining), and some just add extra information that may be of interest (non-defining).

With defining relative clauses:

- commas are not used.
- the relative pronoun can be left out when it is the object of the relative clause.

*The devastation **(which) it caused** was simply staggering!*

With non-defining relative clauses:

- the clause is separated from the rest of the sentence by commas.
- *that* isn't used as a relative pronoun.
- the relative pronoun is never left out.

*The country, **which has long been one of the poorest in the world,** descended into chaos.*

A relative clause can start with a preposition + *which / whom*. However, this is rather formal in English and the preposition is usually placed at the end of the clause.

Where or *when* can also replace a preposition + *which*.

*Crisis mapping brought about change in the place **in which / where** I was born.*

PARTICIPLE CLAUSES

A relative clause is often reduced by using a participle construction.

Past participle clauses reduce relative clauses which use a passive verb, whichever tense is used.

*The UN created a fund **called** UNICEF.*
*= The UN created a fund **which was called** UNICEF.*

Present participle clauses reduce relative clauses which use an active verb, whichever tense is used.

*The CRC declares different rights **including** things such as the right to a safe home.*
*= The CRC declares different rights, **which include** things such as the right to a safe home.*

Adding *not* to the participle can make a negative.

*Students **not wearing** the correct uniform will be punished.*

Adverbial participle clauses

Participle clauses add information about the time or reason / method connected to the main clause. The subject of both clauses must be the same.

***Having campaigned** on behalf of young people, **UNICEF** also had a key part in the creation of the UN's Convention on the Rights of the Child (CRC) in 1989.*
*= **After UNICEF had campaigned** on behalf of young people, **UNICEF** also had a key part in the creation of the UN's Convention on the Rights of the Child (CRC) in 1989.*

***Using** online discussion boards as a "meeting place," **the initiative** provides a space for youngsters who care.*
*= **The initiative uses** online discussion boards as a "meeting place" through which **the initiative** provides a space for youngsters who care.*

***Having seen** the robbery, I had to go to court to give evidence.*
*= **Because I had seen the robbery** I had to go to court to give evidence.*

-ing participles are more common in this kind of clause, but *-ed* participles can also be used with passives.

***Faced** with a robber in the street, I would give them whatever they wanted.*
= If I was faced with a robber in the street, I would give them whatever they wanted.

The present participle shows that an action happens or happened more or less at the same time as the action in the main clause.

***Working** as a policeman, my dad sees a lot of really scary things.*
= My dad is a policeman and while he's at work, he sees a lot of really scary things.

A perfect participle (*having* + *-ed*) shows that the action happened before the action in the main clause.

***Having just closed** the door, I realized I didn't have my keys.*
= I had just closed the door when I realized I didn't have my keys.

1 Complete the sentences with these relative pronouns.

none of whom	most of which	that	where
which	which is when	who	whose

1 One of the first major events to utilize crisis mapping was the 2010 Haiti earthquake, _____ killed and injured hundreds of thousands of people.
2 Technology is particularly relevant in places _____ official government is limited, or no longer fully functions.
3 More than 40 percent of the population now receives some form of international aid, _____ is food assistance.
4 Many local people, _____ lands have been ruined by illegal mining, are now turning to technology to tackle the problem.
5 The plane crashed in thick fog with 87 people on board, _____ is thought to have survived.
6 The volunteers, _____ come from all across the region, quite literally put roads, buildings, and highways onto the map.
7 The amount of data available via social media increased dramatically in October, _____ the flooding reached the capital.
8 Online mapping _____ relies on volunteers with varying skills to interpret satellite images obviously has its limitations.

2 Rewrite the sentences in a more informal manner with the prepositions at the end of the clauses. Leave out the relative pronouns where appropriate.

1 The town in which we were staying narrowly missed being hit by the hurricane.

The town we were staying in narrowly missed being hit by the hurricane.

2 It's an achievement of which we are all very proud.
3 The following day, a second, smaller earthquake hit the town from which the aid was being distributed.
4 As we fled the city, we encountered an elderly man with whom my son insisted we share our food.
5 The roads out of the west of the city, from where many thousands fled, were largely blocked by debris.
6 The experience varies wildly, depending on the charity with which we're working.
7 On her arrival, Ms. Kuti, with whose approach I totally agreed, took control of the situation.
8 The book to which you're referring was the very first on the subject to be published.

3 Rewrite the following sentences using a participle clause.

1 The policeman who dealt with my case was very helpful.
   The policeman _____ my case was very helpful.
2 The man who was arrested after the incident last night has not been charged.
   Police have not charged the man _____ the incident last night.
3 The number of young people who are not working or in school is rising.
   There has been a rise in the number of young people _____ or in school.
4 The number of people who have personally experienced a crime has actually gone down.
   The number of people _____ a crime has actually gone down.
5 I think that children who are exposed to lots of violent movies often become violent themselves.
   I think that children _____ lots of violent movies often become violent themselves.
6 Anyone that the train strike tomorrow will seriously affect can stay home.
   Anyone seriously _____ by the train strike tomorrow can stay at home.

4 Reduce the underlined clauses.

Police are searching for a man (1) who has been accused of attempting to rob a bank in Vienna today. A man wearing a bright red scarf (2) which was wrapped around his face approached a cashier and told her he wanted money. (3) Because she didn't realize that the man was actually demanding money, the clerk simply said that she didn't deal with cash transactions, (4) and at the same time directed him to the next counter. Apparently, (5) because he was put off by the long line at the next counter and the clerk's calm reply, the man dropped the box he was carrying and ran off. (6) After she had seen the man run off, the cashier suddenly realized what had happened. (7) Because they were concerned that the box looked suspicious, the bank called the police and evacuated the building. The package was found to be harmless and the robber pretty useless.

EXPRESSING PAST ABILITY

Could, *be able to*, and *managed to* describe ability or inability to do something when talking about specific situations or telling stories.

Could expresses that something was possible in a specific situation. *Couldn't* shows it wasn't possible to do something in a specific situation.

*He **couldn't move** his arm because it was trapped by a rock.*

Could can also be used with other words related to negatives.

***No one could** send for help.*

***All** he **could** do was wait.*

*I was so nervous I **could hardly** say a word.*

To talk about a specific ability to do something at a particular time in the past, use *was / were able to* rather than *could*.

*She managed to deal with the pain, and in the end, **was able** to turn it into great art.*

Negatives can be made with *not able to*, *unable to*, or *couldn't*.

*I **wasn't able to / was unable to / couldn't** feel or say anything, I was in such shock.*

Be able to is also used with other tenses and modals, where *could* is not possible.

*At least ~~we've could~~ **we've been able to** agree on one movie.*

Could usually describes a general ability in the past while *manage to* emphasizes an ability to do something that was difficult. It isn't usually used to talk about general ideas or senses.

*When it rained, he ~~could catch~~ **managed to catch** some water to drink.*

Manage to often goes with words and phrases such as *finally / in the end / eventually*.

Manage to can be used in a negative sentence in a similar way to *couldn't*.

*I looked for a long time, but I **didn't manage to / couldn't** find it.*

Sometimes *succeed in + -ing* is used instead of *manage to*, but *manage to* is far more common.

*She **succeeded in making** it as a professional.*
*= She **managed to make** it as a professional.*

EMPHATIC STRUCTURES

Stressing an auxiliary verb like *is* or *have* adds emphasis. When there is no auxiliary verb available to stress, as with verbs in the simple present and simple past, emphasis can be added by putting *do / does / did* before an infinitive.

*It **did make** a huge difference to my quality of life, having the implant.*

Emphasis is often added in this way to contradict what someone has said, or to contrast two opposing ideas.

*While **surgical options did exist before**, none were nearly as effective.*

Emphasis can also be added by starting a clause with a negative adverb or phrase (*rarely*, *not only*, etc.) and then using inversion (changing the order of the subject and verb, as in questions).

*We're all used to hearing news about terrible things, but **rarely do we hear** much about exciting new developments.*

*When Second Sight started experimenting, **little did they know** that they were on their way to revolutionizing the treatment of blindness!*

***Only after** the Second World War **were antibiotics** more widely available to the general public.*

Note that inversion is far more common in academic, literary, or journalistic writing, though it is also used in more formal speech or to make stories more dramatic.

1 Complete the article about Aron Ralston with one word in each space.

If the story of Aron Ralston's escape from a canyon was remarkable, what happened next is no less so. Immediately after freeing himself, he still had to return to safety. With only one arm and still bleeding, he (1) _____ to get down a 65-foot cliff and then walk several miles in the burning sun. Luckily, he met a family walking in the valley who (2) _____ able to give him something to eat and drink and then look for help. Then, a helicopter which was out searching for him was (3) _____ to pick him up. This all happened within four hours and saved his life. Following the accident, the park authorities (4) _____ only remove the rock that had trapped Aron's arm by using a machine and several men. While medics were (5) _____ to save Aron's arm, he otherwise made a full recovery and returned to full fitness. Amazingly, since then he's (6) _____ able to do pretty much all the things he did before the accident. He has since rafted down the Grand Canyon, skied down a volcano in Ecuador and, in 2011, (7) _____ in climbing all the mountains in Colorado that are over 14 thousand feet. He also now works as a motivational speaker.

2 Correct the error underlined in each sentence. You may need to change, add, and remove words.

1 I twisted my ankle very badly, but I still <u>manage walk</u> home. It was really painful, though.

I twisted my ankle very badly, but I still *managed to walk* home. It was really painful, though.

2 Following physical therapy, Janine Shepherd <u>were able walk</u> again with the help of a stick.

3 Doctors have been looking for a cure for motor neuron disease, but they <u>couldn't find</u> one yet.

4 After years of research, scientists believe they have finally <u>succeeded the development</u> a treatment for diabetes which avoids the need to inject insulin.

5 I wish I <u>could meet</u> my grandfather before he died. He sounded like an amazing person.

3 Rewrite the second sentences using the word in bold and the correct form of *could*, *be able to*, *manage to*, or *succeed in*.

1 Bethany Hamilton became a world champion surfer despite losing her arm in an accident. **becoming**
Bethany Hamilton lost her arm in an accident but still _____ a world champion surfer.

2 Luckily, we stopped the bleeding and he was fine. **stop**
We _____ the bleeding and he was fine.

3 After the accident, it was only because of the surgery that he didn't lose his eyesight. **save**
He damaged his eye in the accident, but the surgeon _____ his eyesight.

4 She lost most of her hearing after the accident, but she seems to be back to normal now. **hear**
She's recovered really well, considering she _____ a thing after the accident.

4 Make complete sentences by matching the halves.

1 While they **do** remove the immediate pain,
2 I **do** think that medical research is incredibly important,
3 Don't get me wrong. The operation **did** help,
4 Only after several tests **did they**
5 At no time during my stay in the hospital **did I**
6 Nowhere else in the world **do you**
7 Let's be clear about this. In no way **does this development**
8 We read a lot about medical developments, but rarely **do we**

a think I wouldn't make a complete recovery.
b hear about the psychological advances in managing disease.
c but I don't see why it can't all be privately funded.
d diagnose the problem.
e find so many 100-year-olds as in Okinawa, Japan.
f drugs are not the only solution and can create problems of their own.
g mean the disease has been cured, but it's a step in the right direction.
h just not as much as I was hoping it would.

5 Complete the sentences with these words.

at no time	little	not only
not until	only	rarely

1 What made things even worse was the fact that _____ did doctors ever admit they'd made a mistake.

2 In the days before antibiotics, only very _____ did children survive serious lung infections.

3 _____ after the Second World War did penicillin become widely available.

4 When the doctor first suggested it, _____ did I realize that the treatment was actually centuries old.

5 _____ do we need a massive increase in investment, but we also need to rethink the way we educate the young about physical and mental well-being.

6 _____ in this country do people go bankrupt from trying to pay their medical bills!

INFINITIVE	SIMPLE PAST	PAST PARTICIPLE
arise	arose	arisen
beat	beat	beaten
become	became	become
bend	bent	bent
bet	bet	bet
bite	bit	bitten
blow	blew	blown
break	broke	broken
breed	bred	bred
bring	brought	brought
broadcast	broadcast	broadcast
build	built	built
burn	burned	burned
burst	burst	burst
cost	cost	cost
cut	cut	cut
deal	dealt	dealt
dig	dug	dug
dream	dreamed	dreamed
fall	fell	fallen
feed	fed	fed
fight	fought	fought
flee	fled	fled
forget	forgot	forgotten
forgive	forgave	forgiven
freeze	froze	frozen
grow	grew	grown
hang	hanged/hung	hanged/hung
hide	hid	hidden
hit	hit	hit
hold	held	held
hurt	hurt	hurt
keep	kept	kept
kneel	knelt	knelt
lay	laid	laid
lead	led	led
lend	lent	lent
let	let	let
lie	lay	lain
light	lit	lit
lose	lost	lost
mean	meant	meant

INFINITIVE	SIMPLE PAST	PAST PARTICIPLE
misunderstand	misunderstood	misunderstood
must	had to	had to
overcome	overcame	overcome
rethink	rethought	rethought
ring	rang	rung
rise	rose	risen
sell	sold	sold
set	set	set
shake	shook	shaken
shine	shone/shined	shone/shined
shoot	shot	shot
shrink	shrank	shrunk
shut	shut	shut
sink	sank	sunk
slide	slid	slid
smell	smelled	smelled
spell	spelled	spelled
spend	spent	spent
spill	spilled	spilled
split	split	split
spoil	spoiled	spoiled
spread	spread	spread
stand	stood	stood
steal	stole	stolen
stick	stuck	stuck
strike	struck	struck
swear	swore	sworn
tear	tore	torn
throw	threw	thrown
upset	upset	upset
wake	woke	woken
win	won	won

UNIT 1 A review

When writing reviews, it is common to use relative clauses beginning with *which* in order to express personal comments or beliefs.

1 Wu and Ting Ting were incredibly welcoming and did everything that they could to make me feel at home, although during the stay I was often left to my own devices because they were busy working. I had a lovely big room, my own TV, and a desk to study at. I was a little far from my school, though, which wasn't ideal.

2 I can't complain about the place as a whole. There were plenty of rides, which kept the kids satisfied, but given that the price for a family of four for the day was $195, it's just not worth it. Not when you realize that Fantasyland is cheaper. What's more, the lines are longer than at Fantasyland, as it is packed with locals. If it hadn't been as full, and we'd actually been able to go on more than three rides in seven hours—and it was less expensive—it might have been worth it. As it is, though, I'd skip it and go to Fantasyland instead.

3 After I'd checked in and been given my key, I found that my room wasn't much bigger than a shoebox! Feeling that this wouldn't work for a four-night stay, I went back down to the front desk and asked for a larger room. They then tried to charge me €40 per night to upgrade to a suitable room, which was ridiculous. We finally agreed on €9 per night for the upgrade. On top of that, parking was €15 a day! Terrible place with terrible service. They're trying to make as much extra money as they can. I'm scared to ask for another pillow, which is necessary since the bed only has one!

4 If you like to see and be seen, then grab yourself one of the outdoor seats here, order a coffee, sit back, and enjoy! Looking out over the main square, and close to the museum and the market, this is a great people-watching spot—and it does great breakfasts, lunches, and snacks as well, which is perfect if you're feeling hungry. I can't recommend it enough.

UNIT 2 A persuasive article

Grab the reader's attention by asking a *have you ever…* question to stimulate a shared experience.

Present factual information related to the solution.

Young Entrepreneur Trying to Turn a Nightmare into a Dream Business

Have you ever spent hours working on a project and saved it to your flash drive only to then lose your drive and all your work? You know you should have backed it up, but it's easy to forget, isn't it? And then you have to explain it to your teacher or boss. Awful! Well, all that might soon be a thing of the past thanks to the bright idea of a 16-year-old entrepreneur from Northern Ireland.

Mason Robinson has invented a piece of software that automatically backs up your work to the cloud when you save your work to a flash drive. As Mason says, "It has a unique aspect in saving people's work twice!"

He developed the *i-save USB* idea as part of a summer project at a local science park. Now he is trying to raise two thousand dollars through a Kickstarter campaign to improve the product and distribute it.

So why don't you support Mason to make his business dreams a reality and, at the same time, end the nightmare of lost homework and research?

Persuade the reader to continue reading by saying that you will present a solution.

Provide a reason why the reader should take action in the final paragraph.

UNIT 3 A survey

Start reporting findings by referring the reader to the source of results and explaining the aim of the investigation.

Explain the most important statistics related to your aim.

This bar chart shows the results of a survey carried out on 50 people aged between 13 and 55. The aim of the survey was to find out levels of participation in exercise in the four weeks before the interview.

During this time, 68 percent of those interviewed walked for health and recreation, about one in six biked, and over half did some kind of sport. As can be seen from the chart, the most popular sports during this month were swimming and diving, with almost 15 percent of those asked trying it at least once. This was followed closely by various health and fitness activities.

Obviously, these results were determined to at least some degree by the weather. If the survey were to be repeated in the summer rather than the winter, we might, for instance, expect the popularity of soccer and golf to increase.

Among the people who did not take part in any exercise during the month in question, the main reasons given for not participating were lack of time, cost, and general poor health.

Account for the results and explain how one might make the statistics more reliable.

You may choose to give a further description of interesting findings.

UNIT 4 A *for* and *against* essay

In the opening paragraph of a *for* and *against* essay, demonstrate why the subject is relevant now.

State the advantages of the topic first and follow this with the limitations.

Over recent years, tourism has become more important to the local economy. As the area attracts more tourists, it is only natural that local officials should be thinking about ways of promoting the region further. It has been claimed that the creation of a new museum would boost visitor numbers. However, I believe that such a plan would not have as positive an impact as other possible options.

One argument in favor of a big new museum is that it would put the region on the map and draw in visitors, who would then spend money on accommodation, transportation, and food. In addition to this, it would create jobs—initially in construction, and then within the building. Finally, museums are often seen as being good for the wider community as they help educate people.

However, a museum would be expensive. It might be better to spend that money on other areas of the local community. Local schools and hospitals could be improved greatly if a similar sum of money were made available, and this would benefit a wider range of people. In addition, it is worth asking how many local people would actually visit a new museum. There is already a small museum in town and it is almost always empty.

In conclusion, while a new museum might bring limited benefits and lead to the creation of some jobs, other choices are preferable. Investment in vital facilities may not bring more tourists, but would create a more skilled, healthier, and happier society.

Introduce your opposing argument or point of view by using the passive, and signal you disagree by using words or phrases like *however*. Then provide your own opinion.

Finally, take notice of both sides of the argument and state your position.

UNIT 5 A scientific method

When writing a scientific method, start by introducing the process.

The Blackawton Bee Experiment

The experiment aimed to discover if bees could think in the same ways as humans. The experiment was carried out using a large transparent box called the Bee Arena. The arena contained colored circles representing flowers which had small holes in them that could be filled with sugar water to attract the bees. Before the experiment was started, the bees were marked individually to identify them. In order to do this, forager bees (bees that fly around looking for and collecting pollen) were let into the bee arena. Once all the bees were inside the arena, the lights were turned off in order to make them stop flying. The bees were then picked up using tweezers and put into a pot with a lid. The pot was then placed in a fridge so that the bees would fall asleep. Once they had fallen asleep, the bees were removed from the pot one at a time and painted with different colored dots. Finally, the bees were returned to the pot and warmed up before being released back into the bee arena.

Words linking the steps of the process are used.

Use phrases like *in order to* to explain why certain steps were taken in the process.

UNIT 6 A problem-solution essay

Use topic sentences to start each paragraph. These sentences introduce and express the main idea of the paragraph.

How can we help save tigers?

(1) _____ Tigers are hunted and sold for their fur and other parts. They are losing the habitats they live in and they are shot by local people because they kill farm animals. In this essay, I will suggest solutions to these three problems.

(2) _____ In the US, there may be over 9,000 tigers that are kept as pets, for example. They are sold easily, and Mills says that can encourage the trade of wild tigers because people want "the real thing."

(3) _____ Tigers do not recognize borders, so the area they live in can be in more than one country. According to takepart.com, several countries met and agreed to take action together to save tigers. It has had some success, but they could do more

(4) _____ National Geographic Explorer Krithi Karanth says that sometimes farmers cannot earn enough money to survive because of wildlife destroying their crops and animals. We need to compensate them so they do not take revenge on endangered species like tigers.

Refer to sources to strengthen your argument.

UNIT 7 A report

Use the title to show what the report is about.

Explain the purpose of the report in the introduction.

Subheadings are added to each paragraph.

Finish a report by making recommendations, if necessary.

Improving Learning in the Library

Purpose
The purpose of this report is to find out why so much external noise can be heard in the school library. The report will also make recommendations on how to reduce noise and create a better atmosphere to study in.

Background
Students frequently complain about the noise in the school library and many choose not to use the space at all.

Methods of Investigation
In order to better understand the issues, we visited the library twice and read about how sound travels through different materials. We then explored a range of possible solutions before making our own models, which we used to test our ideas.

Findings
The library windows face a public space and, even when closed, let too much noise through. This problem is made worse by the fact that the curtains in the room are made from a thin material that does not stop sound in any way.

Recommendations
To solve this problem, we would recommend installing two panes of glass in each window. Perhaps we could also consider filling the space between the glass with water. This would prevent up to 75 percent of the outside noise from entering the room.

UNIT 8 A complaint

Say what the general problem is in the first sentence and give details about the problem—including examples—in the first paragraph.

Explain how the problem has affected you.

Complete a complaint by asking for some kind of action.

Dear Sir or Madam,

I am writing to complain about the recent reporting on the issue of immigration in your paper. In your reports, you frequently suggest that migrants who come to this country are looking for benefits and are involved in crime. While there are obviously unemployed people or criminals among the migrant population, official statistics show that there is a larger percentage among people who were born here. You have also used language such as "swarm" and "flood," which suggests migrants are not human and are a dangerous problem.

As the granddaughter of an immigrant, I find use of this language very upsetting and I think that if a paper uses it, it often makes other people feel they can say similar things. My grandfather worked hard to make a home here. And for me it *is* my home, but your reporting makes me feel I am not a normal citizen.

I am not saying you should stop campaigning for immigration controls. Everyone has a right to their point of view. However, I would like you to stop using these stereotypes and generalizations to make your point. Migrants are all individuals like us—just born in a different place.

Sincerely,

Maria Asare

UNIT 9 A letter of application

Start a letter of application by referring to the advertisement or posting that you saw.

Dear Sir or Madam,

I am writing in response to your advertisement looking for volunteers to rebuild a school in Belize. I would be very grateful if you could send me more information about this opportunity and details of how to apply.

Explain why you are writing.

Explain who you are, where you are from and your plans for the future.

My name is Melanie Gleich and I am 17 years old. I am from Aachen in Germany. I am currently in my last year of high school and will be taking my final exams next spring. I hope to then go on to study Spanish and Latin American Studies in college.

In terms of what I would bring to the project, I already have a good level of both Spanish and English, and having traveled widely, I am used to being around people from other cultures. I am also prepared to get my hands dirty and help out in any way I can. I do a lot of sports and would say I have a good level of fitness, so I feel confident that I would be able to cope with the manual labor.

Explain any skills and abilities you have which would make you suitable for the job.

In addition, I have some experience in both gardening and farming because my grandparents live on a farm and I usually spend the summers helping out there. I am also an excellent team player and like to think I possess good social skills.

I hope you feel I am suitable for the post and look forward to hearing from you soon.

Yours sincerely,

Melanie Gleich

UNIT 10 A success story

When writing success stories, it is customary to explain how you felt before you succeeded.

"Stop!" my teacher whispered loudly. "Look over there." I had been dreading this moment—almost hoping we wouldn't find one. But there it was—a python lying in the grass. I hated snakes. I'd never even touched one. My usual reaction would have been to run away screaming, but I had no choice this time. It was a field trip for my biology class, and not only did we have to look for them, we had to catch one too!

There was a group of us. I had to put a special stick at the back of its head while my teacher and other students got hold of it. At least this way I wouldn't have to touch it. We had practiced lots of times with a plastic snake at school. We crept nearer. My hands started to sweat; my heart started beating like a drum. The snake didn't move. And then it all happened in a flash! I put the stick behind its neck and the others leapt over and grabbed it.

Use descriptive verbs to make the story more exciting.

Explain how you felt after succeeding.

As the others held the snake down and measured it, I forced myself to touch it. I finally managed to do it! Little did I know how nice they actually felt! That day changed my life. Rather than being disgusted by snakes, I became fascinated by them, and now I plan to do lots of research on them.

UNIT 1

accessible (adj)	/æk'sɛsəbəl/
anxiety (n)	/æŋ'zaɪəti/
B&B (n)	/'bi ən 'bi/
ban (v)	/bæn/
basically (adv)	/'beɪsɪkli/
be up for (phr v)	/bi 'ʌp ˌfɔr/
break down (phr v)	/'breɪk 'daʊn/
budget (n)	/'bʌdʒɪt/
cause (v)	/kɔz/
come across (phr v)	/'kʌm ə'krɔs/
come down to (phr v)	/ˌkʌm 'daʊn tu/
community (n)	/kə'mjunɪti/
culture shock (n)	/'kʌltʃər ˌʃɒk/
date back (phr v)	/'deɪt 'bæk/
deal (n)	/dil/
decline (n)	/dɪ'klaɪn/
established (adj)	/ɪ'stæblɪʃt/
evaluate (v)	/ɪ'vælju̇ˌeɪt/
extensive (adj)	/ɪk'stɛnsɪv/
fluent (adj)	/'fluənt/
food poisoning (n)	/'fud ˌpɔɪzənɪŋ/
genuinely (adv)	/'dʒɛnju̇ɪnli/
get a real feel for (phr v)	/ˌgɛt ə 'riəl 'fil fɔr/
get used to (the food) (phr v)	/ˌgɛt 'juzd tu/
grand (adj)	/grænd/
hang out (phr v)	/'hæŋ 'aʊt/
hiking (n)	/'haɪkɪŋ/
honesty (n)	/'ɒnɪsti/
host family (n)	/'hoʊst 'fæməli/
ideal (adj)	/aɪ'diəl/
incredibly (adv)	/ɪn'krɛdəbli/
independence (n)	/ˌɪndɪ'pɛndəns/
individual (n)	/ˌɪndɪ'vɪdʒuəl/
influence (v)	/'ɪnfluəns/
investment (n)	/ɪn'vɛstmənt/
keep in touch (idiom)	/'kip ɪn 'tʌtʃ/
left to (your) own devices (idiom)	/'lɛft tu (yər) 'oʊn dɪ'vaɪsɪz/
legal (adj)	/'ligəl/
lie around (phr v)	/'laɪ ə'raʊnd/
look after (phr v)	/'lʊk 'æftər/
look back (phr v)	/'lʊk 'bæk/
major (adj)	/'meɪdʒər/
media (n)	/'midiə/
move on (phr v)	/'muv 'ɒn/
necessarily (adv)	/ˌnɛsə'sɛrəli/
negotiate (v)	/nɪ'goʊʃiˌeɪt/
opt (v)	/ɒpt/
overseas (adv)	/'oʊvər'siz/
participant (n)	/pɑr'tɪsəpənt/
perspective (n)	/pər'spɛktɪv/
pick up (phr v)	/'pɪk 'ʌp/
reinforce (v)	/ˌriɪn'fɔrs/
reliability (n)	/rɪˌlaɪə'bɪlɪti/
reputation (n)	/ˌrɛpjə'teɪʃən/
resource (n)	/'risɔrs/
restriction (n)	/rɪ'strɪkʃən/
revolution (n)	/ˌrɛvə'luʃən/
ridiculous (adj)	/rɪ'dɪkjələs/
robbery (n)	/'rɒbəri/
roots (n)	/ruts/
rush (v)	/rʌʃ/
servant (n)	/'sɜrvənt/
sights (n)	/saɪts/
simply (adv)	/'sɪmpli/
spread (v)	/sprɛd/
standard (n)	/'stændərd/
stare (v)	/stɛər/
step out (phr v)	/'stɛp 'aʊt/
strongly (adv)	/'strɒŋli/
trip up (phr v)	/'trɪp 'ʌp/
turn out (phr v)	/'tɜrn 'aʊt/
tutor (n)	/'tutər/
upgrade (n)	/'ʌpˌgreɪd/
upgrade (v)	/ʌp'greɪd/
vice versa (adv)	/'vaɪsə 'vɜrsə/
wealth (n)	/wɛlθ/
welcoming (adj)	/'wɛlkəmɪŋ/
worry (n)	/'wɜri/

UNIT 2

(a) matter (of) (idiom)	/(ə)'mætər (əv)/
adapt (v)	/ə'dæpt/
aspect (n)	/'æspɛkt/
assume (v)	/ə'sum/
attach (v)	/ə'tætʃ/
automatically (adv)	/ˌɔtə'mætɪkli/
backup (n)	/'bæk,ʌp/
banking (n)	/'bæŋkɪŋ/
bargain (n)	/'bɑrgɪn/
barrier (n)	/'bæriər/
be based (phr v)	/bi 'beɪst/
beg (v)	/bɛg/
businessperson (n)	/'bɪznɪsˌpɜrsən/
campaign (n)	/kæm'peɪn/
capable (adj)	/'keɪpəbəl/
climate change (n)	/'klaɪmɪt ˌtʃeɪndʒ/
code (n)	/koʊd/
confirm (v)	/kən'fɜrm/
corporate (adj)	/'kɔrpərɪt/
cut down (phr v)	/'kʌt 'daʊn/
data (n)	/'deɪtə/
demonstrate (v)	/'dɛmənˌstreɪt/
detect (v)	/dɪ'tɛkt/
discourage (v)	/dɪs'kɜrɪdʒ/
distant (adj)	/'dɪstənt/
distribute (v)	/dɪ'strɪbjut/
distribution (n)	/ˌdɪstrə'bjuʃən/
diverse (adj)	/dɪ'vɜrs/
edit (v)	/'ɛdɪt/
email (n)	/'iˌmeɪl/
entrepreneur (n)	/ˌɒntrəprə'nʊər/

executive (adj)	/ɪg'zɛkjətɪv/
expand (v)	/ɪk'spænd/
export (v)	/'ɛksport/
failure (n)	/'feɪljər/
filter (n)	/'fɪltər/
fund (n)	/fʌnd/
fund (v)	/fʌnd/
gender (n)	/'dʒɛndər/
go too far (idiom)	/'goʊ ˌtu 'fɑr/
guarantee (n)	/ˌgærən'ti/
handle (v)	/'hændl/
harvest (v)	/'hɑrvɪst/
illegal (adj)	/ɪ'ligəl/
impressive (adj)	/ɪm'prɛsɪv/
inbox (n)	/'ɪnˌbɒks/
infect (v)	/ɪn'fɛkt/
intrigue (v)	/ɪn'trig/
invent (v)	/ɪn'vɛnt/
investor (n)	/ɪn'vɛstər/
knock on the head (idiom)	/'nɒk ɒn ðə 'hɛd/
leadership (n)	/'lidərˌʃɪp/
market (v)	/'mɑrkɪt/
network (v)	/'nɛtˌwɜrk/
origin (n)	/'ɔrɪdʒɪn/
out of hand (idiom)	/'aʊt əv 'hænd/
post (v)	/poʊst/
potential (n)	/pə'tɛnʃəl/
pressure (n)	/'prɛʃər/
profile (n)	/'proʊfaɪl/
profit (n)	/'prɒfɪt/
publisher (n)	/'pʌblɪʃər/
put together (phr v)	/'pʊt tə'gɛðər/
raise money (phr v)	/'reɪz 'mʌni/
reality (n)	/ri'ælɪti/
recover (v)	/rɪ'kʌvər/
risk (n)	/rɪsk/
scam (n)	/skæm/
social media (n)	/'soʊʃəl 'midiə/
solar (adj)	/'soʊlər/
source (n)	/sɔrs/
spam (n)	/spæm/
statement (n)	/'steɪtmənt/
store (v)	/stɔr/
strategy (n)	/'strætɪdʒi/
summarize (v)	/'sʌməˌraɪz/
supplier (n)	/sə'plaɪər/
tribe (n)	/traɪb/
turn up (phr v)	/'tɜrn 'ʌp/
victim (n)	/'vɪktɪm/
wealthy (adj)	/'wɛlθi/

UNIT 3

accelerate (v)	/æk'sɛləˌreɪt/
advance (n)	/æd'væns/
agree with (phr v)	/ə'gri ˌwɪð/
amount (n)	/ə'maʊnt/

anticipate (v) /æn'tɪsə,peɪt/
athletic (adj) /æθ'lɛtɪk/
attitude (n) /'ætɪ,tud/
awareness (n) /ə'wɛərnɪs/
billion (n) /'bɪljən/
brand (n) /brænd/
bronze (adj) /brɒnz/
captain (v) /'kæptən/
championship (n) /'tʃæmpiən,ʃɪp/
change the face of (idiom) /'tʃeɪndʒ ðə 'feɪs əv/
closely (adv) /'klousli/
compete (v) /kəm'pit/
conquer (v) /'kɒŋkər/
debt (n) /dɛt/
determine (v) /dɪ'tɜrmɪn/
elite (adj) /ɪ'lit/
energetic (adj) /,ɛnər'dʒɛtɪk/
entire (adj) /ɛn'taɪər/
essentially (adv) /ɪ'sɛnʃəli/
establish (v) /ɪ'stæblɪʃ/
evolution (n) /,ɛvə'luʃən/
evolve (v) /ɪ'vɒlv/
expense (n) /ɪk'spɛns/
fade away (v) /'feɪd ə'weɪ/
fame (n) /feɪm/
formal (adj) /'fɔrməl/
forward (n) /'fɔrwərd/
funding (n) /'fʌndɪŋ/
gardening (adj) /'gɑrdnɪŋ/
glory (n) /'glɔri/
goal (n) /goul/
greatly (adv) /'greɪtli/
hold (a record) (v) /hould/
host (v) /houst/
injury (n) /'ɪndʒəri/
instantly (adv) /'ɪnstəntli/
intensively (adv) /ɪn'tɛnsɪvli/
junk food (n) /'dʒʌŋk ,fud/
largely (adv) /'lɑrdʒli/
long-term (adj) /'lɔŋ,tɜrm/
marathon (n) /'mærə,θɒn/
medal (n) /'mɛdl/
muscle (n) /'mʌsəl/
nation (n) /'neɪʃən/
participate (v) /pɑr'tɪsə,peɪt/
pay off (phr v) /'peɪ 'ɔf/
percentage (n) /pər'sɛntɪdʒ/
personality (n) /,pɜrsə'næliti/
popularity (n) /,pɒpjə'lærɪti/
positive role model (phrase) /'pɒzɪtɪv 'roul ,mɒdl/
preferably (adv) /'prɛfərəbli/
principle (n) /'prɪnsəpəl/
psychological (adj) /,saɪkə'lɒdʒɪkəl/
quote (n) /kwout/
ranking (n) /'ræŋkɪŋ/
real passion (phrase) /'rɪəl 'pæʃən/
recreation (n) /,rɛkri'eɪʃən/
represent (v) /,rɛprɪ'zɛnt/

role model (n) /'roul ,mɒdl/
roughly (adv) /'rʌfli/
schedule (n) /'skɛdjul/
season (n) /'sizən/
select (v) /sɪ'lɛkt/
set (a new record) (v) /sɛt/
set up (v) /'sɛt 'ʌp/
shrink (v) /ʃrɪŋk/
slightly (adv) /'slaɪtli/
slow down (phr v) /'slou 'daun/
smash (v) /smæʃ/
specialize (v) /'spɛʃə,laɪz/
specific (adj) /spə'sɪfɪk/
spirit (n) /'spɪrɪt/
stamina (n) /'stæmɪnə/
status (n) /'steɪtəs/
subsequently (adv) /'sʌbsɪkwəntli/
subway (n) /'sʌb,weɪ/
suit (v) /sut/
sum (n) /sʌm/
surface (n) /'sɜrfɪs/
tackle (v) /'tækəl/
target (n) /'tɑrgɪt/
technique (n) /tɛk'nik/
technological (adj) /,tɛknə'lɒdʒɪkəl/
tend to (phr v) /'tɛnd tu/
terminal (n) /'tɜrmɪnl/
throughout (prep) /θru'aut/
top (adj) /tɒp/
vast (adj) /væst/

UNIT 4

actual (adj) /'æktʃuəl/
authority (n) /ə'θɔrɪti/
behind (prep) /bɪ'haɪnd/
boost (v) /bust/
carnival (n) /'kɑrnɪvəl/
choir (n) /kwaɪər/
claim (v) /kleɪm/
comedy club (n) /'kɒmɪdi ,klʌb/
commitment (n) /kə'mɪtmənt/
confidence (n) /'kɒnfɪdəns/
construction (n) /kən'strʌkʃən/
costume (n) /'kɒstum/
creation (n) /kri'eɪʃən/
creativity (n) /,kriˌeɪ'tɪvɪti/
demolish (v) /dɪ'mɒlɪʃ/
desperate (adj) /'dɛspərɪt/
discipline (n) /'dɪsəplɪn/
diverse social background (col) /dɪ'vɜrs 'souʃəl 'bæk,graund/
dramatic (adj) /drə'mætɪk/
duration (n) /du'reɪʃən/
economist (n) /ɪ'kɒnəmɪst/
economy (n) /ɪ'kɒnəmi/
emphasize (v) /'ɛmfə,saɪz/
engagement (n) /ɛn'geɪdʒmənt/

expression (n) /ɪk'sprɛʃən/
factor (n) /'fæktər/
fatal (adj) /'feɪtəl/
festival (n) /'fɛstɪvəl/
figure out (phr v) /'fɪgjər 'aut/
found (v) /faund/
foundation (n) /faun'deɪʃən/
fulfill (v) /fʊl'fɪl/
gallery (n) /'gæləri/
gang (n) /gæŋ/
generate (v) /'dʒɛnə,reɪt/
hard work (col) /'hɑrd 'wɜrk/
impact (n) /'ɪmpækt/
income (n) /'ɪnkʌm/
industrial (adj) /ɪn'dʌstriəl/
initially (adv) /ɪ'nɪʃəli/
innovative (adj) /ɪnə'veɪtɪv/
inspiration (n) /,ɪnspə'reɪʃən/
lead to (phr v) /'lid tu/
leading orchestra (col) /'lidɪŋ 'ɔrkɪstrə/
literally (adv) /'lɪtərəli/
low income (adj) /'lou 'ɪnkʌm/
mayor (n) /meɪər/
minister (n) /'mɪnɪstər/
minority (n) /mɪ'nɔrɪti/
mixed results (phrase) /'mɪkst rɪ'zʌlts/
museum (n) /mju'ziəm/
official (adj) /ə'fɪʃəl/
organizer (n) /'ɔrgə,naɪzər/
parade (n) /pə'reɪd/
physical (adj) /'fɪzɪkəl/
poverty (n) /'pɒvərti/
pride (n) /praɪd/
private company (col) /'praɪvɪt 'kʌmpəni/
process (n) /'prɒsɛs/
professional (n) /prə'fɛʃənl/
public art (col) /'pʌblɪk 'ɑrt/
redevelopment (n) /,ridɪ'vɛləpmənt/
rehearse (v) /rɪ'hɜrs/
reject (v) /rɪ'dʒɛkt/
relic (n) /'rɛlɪk/
remarkable (adj) /rɪ'mɑrkəbəl/
rhythm (n) /'rɪðəm/
run over (phr v) /'rʌn 'ouvər/
sell out (phr v) /'sɛl 'aut/
signal (v) /'sɪgnl/
skilled (adj) /skɪld/
stand for (phr v) /'stænd fɔr/
straightforward process (col) /,streɪt'fɔrwərd 'prɒsɛs/
strict set (col) /'strɪkt 'sɛt/
struggling (adj) /'strʌgəlɪŋ/
supposedly (adv) /sə'pouzɪdli/
take charge (phr v) /'teɪk 'tʃɑrdʒ/
theater (n) /'θiətər/
venue (n) /'vɛnju/
violence (n) /'vaɪələns/
vital (adj) /'vaɪtl/
volunteer (n) /,vɒlən'tɪər/
widely (adv) /'waɪdli/

UNIT 5

alter (v)	/ˈɔltər/
arm (v)	/ɑrm/
assignment (n)	/əˈsaɪnmənt/
beautiful (adj)	/ˈbjutəfəl/
belief (n)	/bɪˈlif/
bother (v)	/ˈbɒðər/
browser (n) /	/ˈbraʊzər/
bubble (n)	/ˈbʌbəl/
bulb (n)	/bʌlb/
capacity (n)	/kəˈpæsɪti/
chemical (n)	/ˈkɛmɪkəl/
circumstance (n)	/ˈsɜrkəmˌstæns/
conduct (v)	/kənˈdʌkt/
consume (v)	/kənˈsum/
cooperation (n)	/koʊˌɒpəˈreɪʃən/
cooperative (adj)	/koʊˈɒpərətɪv/
curiosity (n)	/ˌkjʊəriˈɒsɪti/
deadline (n)	/ˈdɛdˌlaɪn/
determining (adv)	/dɪˈtɜrmɪnɪŋ/
discovery (n)	/dɪˈskʌvəri/
dissolve (v)	/dɪˈzɒlv/
dominant (adj)	/ˈdɒmɪnənt/
downwards (adv)	/ˈdaʊnwərdz/
effective (adj)	/ɪˈfɛktɪv/
electrical (adj)	/iˈlɛktrɪkəl/
embrace (v)	/ɛmˈbreɪs/
engage (v)	/ɛnˈgeɪdʒ/
evidence (n)	/ˈɛvɪdəns/
function (n)	/ˈfʌŋkʃən/
genius (n)	/ˈdʒiniəs/
grasp (n)	/græsp/
helpful (adj)	/ˈhɛlpfəl/
hopeful (adj)	/ˈhoʊpfəl/
identify (v)	/aɪˈdɛntəˌfaɪ/
imaginative (adj)	/ɪˈmædʒənətɪv/
increasingly (adv)	/ɪnˈkrisɪŋli/
innovation (n)	/ˌɪnəˈveɪʃən/
innovative (adj)	/ˈɪnəˌveɪtɪv/
intelligence (n)	/ɪnˈtɛlɪdʒəns/
journal (n)	/ˈdʒɜrnl/
labor (n)	/ˈleɪbər/
lid (n)	/lɪd/
link (n)	/lɪŋk/
listener (n)	/ˈlɪsənər/
make matters worse (phrase)	/ˈmeɪk ˈmætərz ˈwɜrs/
mark (v)	/mɑrk/
mature (v)	/məˈtʃʊər/
mechanical (adj)	/mɪˈkænɪkəl/
medical (adj)	/ˈmɛdɪkəl/
mode (n)	/moʊd/
movement (n)	/ˈmuvmənt/
myth (n)	/mɪθ/
network (n)	/ˈnɛtˌwɜrk/
place (v)	/pleɪs/
pleasurable (adj)	/ˈplɛʒərəbəl/
pleasure (n)	/ˈplɛʒər/
practical (adj)	/ˈpræktɪkəl/
previously (adv)	/ˈpriviəsli/
ray (n)	/reɪ/
reaction (n)	/riˈækʃən/
reference (n)	/ˈrɛfərəns/
release (v)	/rɪˈlis/
researcher (n)	/rɪˈsɜrtʃər/
return (v)	/rɪˈtɜrn/
reward (n)	/rɪˈwɔrd/
sample (n)	/ˈsæmpəl/
scan (n)	/skæn/
social (adj)	/ˈsoʊʃəl/
society (n)	/səˈsaɪəti/
sophisticated (adj)	/səˈfɪstɪˌkeɪtɪd/
submit (v)	/səbˈmɪt/
substance (n)	/ˈsʌbstəns/
surgeon (n)	/ˈsɜrdʒən/
surgery (n)	/ˈsɜrdʒəri/
surround (v)	/səˈraʊnd/
survey (n)	/ˈsɜrveɪ/
theory (n)	/ˈθɪəri/
threat (n)	/θrɛt/
transform (v)	/trænsˈfɔrm/
transparent (adj)	/trænsˈpærənt/
tremendous (adj)	/trəˈmɛndəs/
ultimate (adj)	/ˈʌltəmɪt/
uncertainty (n)	/ʌnˈsɜrtənti/
use (n)	/jus/
useful (adj)	/ˈjusfəl/
voice (n)	/vɔɪs/

UNIT 6

administration (n)	/ədˌmɪnəˈstreɪʃən/
agriculture (n)	/ˈægrɪˌkʌltʃər/
alarming (adj)	/əˈlɑrmɪŋ/
anger (n)	/ˈæŋgər/
animal product (n)	/ˈænəməl ˌprɒdəkt/
arise (v)	/əˈraɪz/
assess (v)	/əˈsɛs/
breed (v)	/brid/
camp (n)	/kæmp/
capture (v)	/ˈkæptʃər/
catch on (phr v)	/ˈkætʃ ˈɒn/
characteristic (n)	/ˌkærɪktəˈrɪstɪk/
chase (v)	/tʃeɪs/
clue (n)	/klu/
compensate (v)	/ˈkɒmpənˌseɪt/
concern (n)	/kənˈsɜrn/
consequence (n)	/ˈkɒnsɪˌkwɛns/
conservation (n)	/ˌkɒnsərˈveɪʃən/
constantly (adv)	/ˈkɒnstəntli/
cure (n)	/kjʊər/
die out (v)	/ˈdaɪ ˈaʊt/
diversity (n)	/dɪˈvɜrsɪti/
domestic (adj)	/dəˈmɛstɪk/
emotion (n)	/ɪˈmoʊʃən/
endanger (adj)	/ɛnˈdeɪndʒər/

ensure (v)	/ɛnˈʃʊər/
equivalent (adj)	/ɪˈkwɪvələnt/
extinct (adj)	/ɪkˈstɪŋkt/
fake (adj)	/feɪk/
feature (n)	/ˈfitʃər/
fox (n)	/fɒks/
gene (n)	/dʒin/
genetic (adj)	/dʒəˈnɛtɪk/
growth (n)	/groʊθ/
habitat (n)	/ˈhæbɪˌtæt/
historian (n)	/hɪˈstɔriən/
hit a wall (idiom)	/ˈhɪt ə ˈwɔl/
hunt (v)	/hʌnt/
indicate (v)	/ˈɪndɪˌkeɪt/
influential (adj)	/ˌɪnfluˈɛnʃəl/
inspire (v)	/ɪnˈspaɪər/
interfere (v)	/ˌɪntərˈfɪər/
mammal (n)	/ˈmæməl/
mass (adj)	/mæs/
misunderstanding (n)	/ˌmɪsʌndərˈstændɪŋ/
mysterious (adj)	/mɪˈstɪəriəs/
overcome (v)	/ˌoʊvərˈkʌm/
polar bear (n)	/ˈpoʊlər ˌbɛər/
proof (n)	/pruf/
psychologist (n)	/saɪˈkɒlədʒɪst/
purely (adv)	/ˈpjʊərli/
put forward (phr v)	/ˌpʊt ˈfɔrwərd/
rainfall (n)	/ˈreɪnˌfɔl/
rate (n)	/reɪt/
rethink (v)	/riˈθɪŋk/
reveal (v)	/rɪˈvil/
revenge (n)	/rɪˈvɛndʒ/
save (v)	/seɪv/
science teacher (n)	/ˈsaɪəns ˌtitʃər/
sea creature (n)	/ˈsi ˌkritʃər/
short-term (adj)	/ˈʃɔrt ˈtɜrm/
shorten (v)	/ˈʃɔrtn/
significantly (adv)	/sɪgˈnɪfɪkəntli/
social media campaign (n)	/ˈsoʊʃəl ˈmidiə kæmˌpeɪn/
species (n)	/ˈspiʃiz/
sponsor (v)	/ˈspɒnsər/
spot (n)	/spɒt/
strengthen (v)	/ˈstrɛŋkθən/
sudden (adj)	/ˈsʌdn/
surroundings (n)	/səˈraʊndɪŋz/
survival (n)	/sərˈvaɪvəl/
survive (v)	/sərˈvaɪv/
suspect (v)	/səˈspɛkt/
suspicious (adj)	/səˈspɪʃəs/
take to (phr v)	/ˈteɪk tu/
unique (adj)	/juˈnik/
unwilling (adj)	/ʌnˈwɪlɪŋ/
willingness (n)	/ˈwɪlɪŋnɪs/
wipe out (phr v)	/ˈwaɪp ˈaʊt/

UNIT 7

additional (adj)	/əˈdɪʃənl/
alternative (adj)	/ɔlˈtɜrnətɪv/
analysis (n)	/əˈnæləsɪs/
analyze (v)	/ˈænəˌlaɪz/
approach (n)	/əˈproʊtʃ/
assessment (n)	/əˈsesmənt/
bacteria (n)	/bækˈtɪriə/
break (v)	/breɪk/
brick (n)	/brɪk/
combination (n)	/ˌkɒmbɪˈneɪʃən/
come up with (phr v)	/ˈkʌm ʌp ˌwɪð/
commonly (adv)	/ˈkɒmənli/
concerned (adj)	/kənˈsɜrnd/
conclude (v)	/kənˈklud/
conclusion (n)	/kənˈkluʒən/
contribute (v)	/kənˈtrɪbjut/
create (v)	/kriˈeɪt/
creative (adj)	/kriˈeɪtɪv/
creatively (adv)	/kriˈeɪtɪvli/
demonstration (n)	/ˌdemənˈstreɪʃən/
desire (v)	/dɪˈzaɪər/
detailed (adj)	/ˈditeɪld/
displace (v)	/dɪsˈpleɪs/
electrocute (v)	/ɪˈlektrəˌkjut/
external (adj)	/ɪkˈstɜrnəl/
extreme (adj)	/ɪkˈstrim/
flexibility (n)	/ˌfleksəˈbɪliti/
flexible (adj)	/ˈfleksəbəl/
fluency (n)	/ˈfluənsi/
follow (v)	/ˈfɒloʊ/
format (n)	/ˈfɔrmæt/
freedom (n)	/ˈfridəm/
functional (adj)	/ˈfʌŋkʃənl/
genuine (adj)	/ˈdʒenjuɪn/
get (your) meaning across (phrase)	/ˈget (jər) ˈminɪŋ əˌkrɔs/
grab (v)	/græb/
heartbroken (adj)	/ˈhɑrtˌbroʊkən/
imaginary (adj)	/ɪˈmædʒəˌneri/
implication (n)	/ˌɪmplɪˈkeɪʃən/
integrate (v)	/ˈɪntɪˌɡreɪt/
intelligent (adj)	/ɪnˈtelɪdʒənt/
know (v)	/noʊ/
knowledge (n)	/ˈnɒlɪdʒ/
learner (n)	/ˈlɜrnər/
lifestyle (n)	/ˈlaɪfˌstaɪl/
logic (n)	/ˈlɒdʒɪk/
logical (adj)	/ˈlɒdʒɪkəl/
make up (phr v)	/ˈmeɪk ʌp/
manners (n)	/ˈmænərz/
measure (v)	/ˈmeʒər/
needle (n)	/ˈnidl/
obey (v)	/oʊˈbeɪ/
original (n)	/əˈrɪdʒənl/
outcome (n)	/ˈaʊtˌkʌm/
preference (n)	/ˈprefərəns/
publication (n)	/ˌpʌblɪˈkeɪʃən/
publish (v)	/ˈpʌblɪʃ/
realistically (adv)	/ˌriəˈlɪstɪkli/
recommendation (n)	/ˌrekəmenˈdeɪʃən/
rely on (phr v)	/rɪˈlaɪ ɒn/
resolve (v)	/rɪˈzɒlv/
safety (n)	/ˈseɪfti/
score (v)	/skɔr/
sketch (n)	/sketʃ/
solution (n)	/səˈluʃən/
stimulate (v)	/ˈstɪmjʊˌleɪt/
supervise (v)	/ˈsupərˌvaɪz/
task (n)	/tæsk/
treatment (n)	/ˈtritmənt/
truly (adv)	/ˈtruli/
usage (n)	/ˈjusɪdʒ/
usefulness (n)	/ˈjusfəlnɪs/
variety (n)	/vəˈraɪəti/

UNIT 8

abuse (n)	/əˈbjus/
accuse (v)	/əˈkjuz/
acknowledge (v)	/ækˈnɒlɪdʒ/
apparently (adv)	/əˈpærəntli/
appropriate (adj)	/əˈproʊpriit/
associate with (phr v)	/əˈsoʊʃiˌeɪt ˌwɪð/
assumption (n)	/əˈsʌmpʃən/
assure (v)	/əˈʃʊər/
awkward (adj)	/ˈɔkwərd/
awkwardness (n)	/ˈɔkwərdnɪs/
belong (v)	/bɪˈlɒŋ/
breakdown (n)	/ˈbreɪkˌdaʊn/
bully (v)	/ˈbʊli/
campaign (v)	/kæmˈpeɪn/
cardboard (n)	/ˈkɑrdˌbɔrd/
citizen (n)	/ˈsɪtəzən/
classic (n)	/ˈklæsɪk/
combine (v)	/kəmˈbaɪn/
compliment (v)	/ˈkɒmpləˌment/
conscious (adj)	/ˈkɒnʃəs/
conservative (adj)	/kənˈsɜrvətɪv/
cost-effective (adj)	/ˈkɒst ɪˌfektɪv/
criticize (v)	/ˈkrɪtɪˌsaɪz/
decoration (n)	/ˌdekəˈreɪʃən/
deep-rooted (adj)	/ˈdip ˈrutɪd/
define (v)	/dɪˈfaɪn/
deliberately (adv)	/dɪˈlɪbərɪtli/
deny (v)	/dɪˈnaɪ/
diplomat (n)	/ˈdɪpləˌmæt/
discriminate (v)	/dɪˈskrɪməˌneɪt/
dishonest (adj)	/dɪsˈɒnɪst/
elect (v)	/ɪˈlekt/
element (n)	/ˈeləmənt/
elsewhere (adv)	/ˈelsˌwear/
encounter (v)	/enˈkaʊntər/
enthusiasm (n)	/ɪnˈθuziˌæzəm/
equality (n)	/ɪˈkwɒliti/
experiment (v)	/ekˈsperəˌment/

UNIT 9

fed up (phr v)	/ˈfed ˈʌp/
fingernail (n)	/ˈfɪŋɡərˌneɪl/
firmly (adv)	/ˈfɜrmli/
forget (v)	/fərˈget/
generalization (n)	/ˌdʒenərələˈzeɪʃən/
global (adj)	/ˈgloʊbəl/
highly-respected (adj)	/ˈhaɪli rɪsˈpektɪd/
humorous (adj)	/ˈhjumərəs/
identity (n)	/aɪˈdentɪti/
ignore (v)	/ɪgˈnɔr/
immigrant (n)	/ˈɪmɪgrənt/
incident (n)	/ˈɪnsɪdənt/
insist on (v)	/ɪnˈsɪst ˌɒn/
intense (adj)	/ɪnˈtens/
interpret (v)	/ɪnˈtɜrprɪt/
invisible (n)	/ɪnˈvɪzəbəl/
like-minded (adj)	/ˈlaɪkˈmaɪndɪd/
long-lasting (adj)	/ˈlɒŋˈlæstɪŋ/
make fun (phr v)	/ˈmeɪk ˈfʌn/
massive (adj)	/ˈmæsɪv/
misbehave (v)	/ˌmɪsbɪˈheɪv/
misunderstand (v)	/ˌmɪsʌndərˈstænd/
modify (v)	/ˈmɒdɪˌfaɪ/
norm (n)	/nɔrm/
notion (n)	/ˈnoʊʃən/
obsession (n)	/əbˈseʃən/
offended (adj)	/əˈfendɪd/
open-minded (adj)	/ˈoʊpənˈmaɪndɪd/
phenomenon (n)	/fəˈnɒmɪˌnɒn/
policy (n)	/ˈpɒləsi/
praise (v)	/preɪz/
presence (n)	/ˈprezəns/
pretend (v)	/prɪˈtend/
proportion (n)	/prəˈpɔrʃən/
protest (n)	/ˈproʊtest/
racism (n)	/ˈreɪsɪzəm/
react (v)	/riˈækt/
refresh (v)	/rɪˈfreʃ/
regional (adj)	/ˈridʒənl/
response (n)	/rɪˈspɒns/
self-conscious (adj)	/ˈself ˈkɒnʃəs/
shopkeeper (n)	/ˈʃɒpˌkipər/
sort (it) out (phr v)	/ˈsɔrt (ɪt) ˈaʊt/
statistic (n)	/stəˈtɪstɪk/
stereotype (n)	/ˈsteriəˌtaɪp/
stock (n)	/stɒk/
two-faced (adj)	/ˈtuˌfeɪst/
well-mannered (adj)	/ˈwel ˈmænərd/

UNIT 9

absence (n)	/ˈæbsəns/
affect (v)	/əˈfekt/
aid (n)	/eɪd/
ally (n)	/ˈælaɪ/
appeal (v)	/əˈpil/
assistance (n)	/əˈsɪstəns/
block (v)	/blɒk/

care for (phr v) /ˈkɛər ˌfɔr/
coastal (adj) /ˈkoʊstl/
convention (n) /kənˈvɛnʃən/
cope (v) /koʊp/
corrupt (adj) /kəˈrʌpt/
crisis (n) /ˈkraɪsɪs/
debris (n) /dəˈbri/
delegate (n) /ˈdɛlɪgɪt/
devastation (n) /ˌdɛvəˈsteɪʃən/
disaster (n) /dɪˈzæstər/
donation (n) /doʊˈneɪʃən/
earthquake (n) /ˈɜrθˌkweɪk/
edit (n) /ˈɛdɪt/
evacuate (v) /ɪˈvækjuˌeɪt/
flee (v) /fli/
frustrate (v) /ˈfrʌstreɪt/
give (sth) a go (phr v) /ˈgɪv ə ˈgoʊ/
global warming (n) /ˈgloʊbəl ˈwɔrmɪŋ/
globe (n) /gloʊb/
graduate (n) /ˈgrædʒuɪt/
greed (n) /grid/
headquarters (n) /ˈhɛdˌkwɔrtərz/
homeless (adj) /ˈhoʊmlɪs/
housing (n) /ˈhaʊzɪŋ/
humanity (n) /hjuˈmænɪti/
imprison (v) /ɪmˈprɪzən/
inclusive (adj) /ɪnˈklusɪv/
infrastructure (n) /ˈɪnfrəˌstrʌktʃər/
initiative (n) /ɪˈnɪʃətɪv/
interactive (adj) /ˌɪntərˈæktɪv/
joy (n) /dʒɔɪ/
launch (v) /lɔntʃ/
limited (adj) /ˈlɪmɪtɪd/
neutral (adj) /ˈnutrəl/
on behalf of (phr v) /ˌɒn bɪˈhæf əv/
on the ground (phrase) /ˈɒn ðə ˈgraʊnd/
overlook (v) /ˌoʊvərˈlʊk/
panel (n) /ˈpænl/
portrait (n) /ˈpɔrtrɪt/
precious (adj) /ˈprɛʃəs/
programmer (n) /ˈproʊgræmər/
psychological (adj) / /ˌsaɪkəˈlɒdʒɪkəl/
realization (n) /ˌrɪələˈzeɪʃən/
reconstruction (n) /ˌrikənˈstrʌkʃən/
recovery (n) /rɪˈkʌvəri/
relief (n) /rɪˈlif/
reminder (n) /rɪˈmaɪndər/
remote (adj) /rɪˈmoʊt/
representative (n) /ˌrɛprɪˈzɛntətɪv/
restore (v) /rɪˈstɔr/
right (n) /raɪt/
rise (v) /raɪz/
satellite (n) /ˈsætlˌaɪt/
scale (n) /skeɪl/
senior (adj) /ˈsinjər/
shelter (n) /ˈʃɛltər/
shortage (n) /ˈʃɔrtɪdʒ/
skip (v) /skɪp/
staggering (adj) /ˈstægərɪŋ/
strike a chord (phr v) /ˈstraɪk ə ˈkɔrd/

supply (n) /səˈplaɪ/
survivor (n) /sərˈvaɪvər/
sustainable (n) /səˈsteɪnəbəl/
the best (n) /ðə ˈbɛst/
the brave (n) /ðə ˈbreɪv/
the loud (n) /ðə ˈlaʊd/
the old (n) /ði ˈoʊld/
the outgoing (n) /ði ˈaʊtˌgoʊɪŋ/
the poor (n) /ðə ˈpʊər/
the rich (n) /ðə ˈrɪtʃ/
the stupid (n) /ðə ˈstupɪd/
trap (v) /træp/
unfamiliar (adj) /ˌʌnfəˈmɪljər/
unfold (v) /ʌnˈfoʊld/

UNIT 10

actively (adj) /ˈæktɪvli/
address (v) /əˈdrɛs/
aim (v) /eɪm/
allergic (adj) /əˈlɜrdʒɪk/
amazement (n) /əˈmeɪzmənt/
antibiotics (n) /ˌæntibaɪˈɒtɪks/
apocalypse (n) /əˈpɒkəˌlɪps/
award (v) /əˈwɔrd/
bench (n) /bɛntʃ/
bestseller (n) /ˈbɛstˈsɛlər/
blindness (n) /ˈblaɪndnɪs/
blink (v) /blɪŋk/
cast (n) /kæst/
category (n) /ˈkætɪˌgɔri/
cell (n) /sɛl/
chance (n) /tʃæns/
cheer (v) /tʃɪər/
chest (n) /tʃɛst/
clarify (v) /ˈklærəˌfaɪ/
clear up (phr v) /ˈklɪər ˈʌp/
close down (v) /ˈcloʊz ˈdaʊn/
combine (v) /kəmˈbaɪn/
comfort zone (n) /ˈkʌmfərt ˌzoʊn/
concentration (n) /ˌkɒnsənˈtreɪʃən/
consciousness (n) /ˈkɒnʃəsnɪs/
considerable (adj) /kənˈsɪdərəbəl/
contribute (v) /kənˈtrɪbjut/
convert (v) /kənˈvɜrt/
darkness (n) /ˈdɑrknɪs/
deadly (adj) /ˈdɛdli/
dependent (adj) /dɪˈpɛndənt/
design (v) /dɪˈzaɪn/
determined (adj) /dɪˈtɜrmɪnd/
device (n) /dɪˈvaɪs/
devote (v) /dɪˈvoʊt/
diagnose (v) /ˈdaɪəgˌnoʊs/
dictate (v) /ˈdɪkteɪt/
disgust (n) /dɪsˈgʌst/
disturbing (adj) /dɪˈstɜrbɪŋ/
dose (n) /doʊs/
drug (n) /drʌg/

editor (n) /ˈɛdɪtər/
efficiently (adv) /ɪˈfɪʃəntli/
expose (v) /ɪkˈspoʊz/
express (v) /ɪkˈsprɛs/
extract (n) /ɪkˈstrækt/
fascinated (adj) /ˈfæsəˌneɪtɪd/
flash (n) /flæʃ/
force (v) /fɔrs/
get out (phr v) /ˈgɛt ˈaʊt/
gripping (adj) /ˈgrɪpɪŋ/
heath care (n) /ˈhɛlθ ˌkɛər/
helmet (n) /ˈhɛlmɪt/
honor (n) /ˈɒnər/
house (v) /haʊz/
inability (n) /ˌɪnəˈbɪlɪti/
inevitable (adj) /ɪnˈɛvɪtəbəl/
infection (n) /ɪnˈfɛkʃən/
insufficient (adj) /ˌɪnsəˈfɪʃənt/
intensive (adj) /ɪnˈtɛnsɪv/
keep down (phr v) /ˈkip ˈdaʊn/
lead (v) /lid/
lung (n) /lʌŋ/
make the most of /ˈmeɪk ðə ˈmoʊst əv/
 (phrase)
misery (n) /ˈmɪzəri/
nickname (n) /ˈnɪkˌneɪm/
optimistic (adj) /ˌɒptəˈmɪstɪk/
partial (adj) /ˈpɑrʃəl/
peer (v) /pɪər/
portion (n) /ˈpɔrʃən/
precisely (adv) /prɪˈsaɪsli/
prescribe (v) /prɪˈskraɪb/
prescription (n) /prɪˈskrɪpʃən/
procedure (n) /prəˈsidʒər/
punishment (n) /ˈpʌnɪʃmənt/
rapid (adj) /ˈræpɪd/
resistant (adj) /rɪˈzɪstənt/
respond (v) /rɪˈspɒnd/
risk (n) /rɪsk/
run away (v) /ˈrʌn əˈweɪ/
slam (v) /slæm/
slide (v) /slaɪd/
slow (v) /sloʊ/
stroke (n) /stroʊk/
sweat (n) /swɛt/
symptom (n) /ˈsɪmptəm/
thankfully (adv) /ˈθæŋkfəli/
therapist (n) /ˈθɛrəpɪst/
therapy (n) /ˈθɛrəpi/
think through (phr v) /ˈθɪŋk ˈθru/
threatening (adj) /ˈθrɛtnɪŋ/
treat (v) /trit/
turn to (phr v) /ˈtɜrn tu/
vision (n) /ˈvɪʒən/
visual (adj) /ˈvɪʒuəl/
waist (n) /weɪst/
ward (n) /wɔrd/
watch out (phr v) /ˈwɒtʃ ˈaʊt/